221^B

Studies in Sherlock Holmes

221^B

Studies in Sherlock Holmes

By

VARIOUS HANDS

Edited by Vincent Starrett

OTTO
PENZLER
BOOKS

New York

Copyright © 1940 by Macmillan Publishing Company, a division of
Macmillan, Inc.

Otto Penzler Books, 129 W. 56th Street,
New York, NY 10019   (Editorial Offices only)

Macmillan Publishing Company, 866 Third Avenue,
New York, NY 10022

Maxwell Macmillan Canada, Inc., 1200 Eglinton Avenue East,
Suite 200, Don Mills, Ontario M3C 3N1

Macmillan Publishing Company is part of the Maxwell
Communication Group of Companies.

Library of Congress Cataloging-in-Publication Data
221 B : studies in Sherlock Holmes / by various hands ; edited by
Vincent Starrett.
        p.   cm.
    "First published in 1940 by The Macmillan Company"
—T.p. verso.
    ISBN 1-883402-07-7
    1. Doyle, Arthur Conan, Sir, 1859–1930—Characters—
Sherlock Holmes.   2. Detective and mystery stories, English—
History and criticism.   3. Holmes, Sherlock (Fictitious
character)   4. Private investigators in literature.   I. Starrett,
Vincent, 1886–1974.   II. Title: Two twenty-one B.
PR4624.S83   1994   93-4650   CIP
823'.8—dc20

10 9 8 7 6 5 4 3 2 1

Printed in the United States of America

CONTENTS

▼

ILLUSTRATIONS

EXPLANATION

"LET US GET back to reality," cried Balzac, impatiently, to a friend who was boring him with tidings of a sick sister. "Who is going to marry Eugénie Grandet?" And, dying, he murmured: "Bianchon would have saved me!"—referring to the great physician of Paris whom he had himself created.

That is the way one feels about Sherlock Holmes. Let us be done with all this talk of—anything you may happen to dislike in the daily headlines. Let us talk rather of those things that are permanent and secure, of high matters about which there can be no gibbering division of opinion. Let us talk of the realities that do not change, of that higher realism which is the only true romance. Let us talk again of Sherlock Holmes. For the plain fact is, gentlemen, that the imperishable detective is still a more commanding figure in the world than most of the warriors and statesmen in whose present existence we are invited to believe.

In time, no doubt, there will come a day when research students will seek to prove that Adolf Hitler (to take an obvious example) never lived. On that day, I think, a grateful nation will be wearing away the doorstep of a house in Baker Street, London—a house marked by a tablet certifying it to be the indubitable dwelling-place of Sherlock Holmes and Doctor Watson. Already there are indications of this happy development. Did you know that for some years there has been a railway engine wearing the detective's name? It runs in and out of the Baker Street Station, a pleasant reminder of the many railway journeys of Mr. Sherlock Holmes. Already, at the Lyons Prefecture, there is a salon named for the indestructible fathomer; and at Constantinople, during 1920— according to the London *Times*—the Turks were certain that

the great English detective was at work behind the scenes. It
is asserted that, in Switzerland, no year goes by that does not
bring to M. Chapuiset, editor of the *Journal de Genève*, re-
quests for copies of that journal dated May 6, 1891; for it
was in that issue, according to Watson in *The Final Problem*,
that an account appeared—later, happily, proved false—of
the death of Sherlock Holmes at Reichenbach. Best of all, as
more and more the interest of the world centers upon his exploits and every item of association becomes enchanting, the
scholars who toil obscurely in the shadow of his reputation
dig ever more deeply into available records, seeking new clues
and inferences that may help to illustrate this remarkable
personality.

Hence, in part, the Baker Street Irregulars; and hence, perhaps, this book. Or, to put it all a little differently, a reprehensible number of us, nowadays, elect to remain—as far as
possible—in the predicament of Walter de la Mare's Jim Jay.
This lad, it will be remembered, got stuck fast in yesterday.
The difference between Jim Jay and those others of whom I
am speaking is that we glory in it. It is comforting in these
troubled times to recall the old *Strand Magazine* of the nineties
—of the turn of the century—when, as Earle Walbridge puts
it, Sherlock Holmes was adventuring, memoiring, hounding
and returning. Recently we have passed through some of
the most dramatic months, I suppose, of contemporary history.
Stirred by a confusion of emotions, too tangled to untease, we
hung above the radio waiting each fresh installment of the
fantastic serial, and found it difficult to believe that this indeed
was actuality. In one of the intervals of the tragic comedy
there were, as I recall, two letters on my desk. In the
first, Mr. Arthur Machen, writing from Old Amersham, in
Bucks, asked me whether, in my opinion, the house in Baker
Street was double or single, and how the lower rooms were
occupied. Mrs. Hudson, he agreed, might use one as a "best

parlour," though he believed this to be unlikely. In the other, Mr. Cornélis Helling, writing from Amsterdam, sent me the first French printing of *The Dancing Men*, which he thought particularly notable for its half-tone illustration of Sherlock Holmes in his laboratory. With a sigh of relief and pleasure, I knew that I was back in the world of sanity again. There were still men who knew the difference between the false gods and the true, even in that bedeviled phantasmagoria of Europe. Perhaps this personal anecdote will suggest what I mean by the importance of being Jim Jay.

The Baker Street Irregulars (as an organization outside the pages of Dr. Watson) were born in the Bowling Green department of the *Saturday Review of Literature*, conducted by Mr. Christopher Morley, some time (I should imagine) during the year 1933. Its first formal meeting was held in Chris Cella's Restaurant, in New York City, on the evening of June 5, 1934, at which time, a high autumnal wind being out of season, every effort was made to create a favorite alternative atmosphere of thick yellow fog. Simultaneously, the first dinner of the Sherlock Holmes Society of London was going forward in Canuto's Restaurant in Baker Street, and suitable greetings were exchanged between the celebrating groups. Some months later, the Honorable Secretary of the English organization, Mr. A. G. Macdonell, visited New York and was a guest of honor (with the late William Gillette) at the second meeting of the Irregulars, also at Cella's, on December 7th, a happy occasion of both wind and fog. Although the original plan of the Irregulars was to foregather annually on the anniversary of Sherlock's birth—worked out as falling on January 6—no meeting ever has been held upon that date. The dinner of December 7, 1934, indeed, is the last meeting of formal record, at this writing. To quote Mr. Morley, who holds the exalted office of Gasogene, the Baker Street Irregulars are "too wise to hold stated meetings, which would belie

their name and take the fun out of their indoctrinated ama-
teurishness."

The purpose of the society, obviously, is the study of the
Sacred Writings. Like other learned and scientific societies,
its members exchange notes of research and occasionally con-
tribute "papers" to the general knowledge. It is extraordinary
the number of problems that arise—and require elucidation—
out of the confused Watsonian text. There is, for example,
the problem of the brothers Moriarty, referred to in a footnote to Mr. Smith's delightful repertory (*q.v.*). And there
is the curious error in which Professor Lord of Oberlin caught
the devoted Watson, some years ago. As this matter has not
had the publicity it deserves, and the original paper is difficult
to come by, I mention it again here. . . .

The scene is the dangerous adventure called by Watson—
with his flair for titles—*The Red Circle.* Signora Lucca's
husband, old inhabitants will recall, is signaling her by means
of successive light flashes from a darkened window—one flash
for A, two flashes for B, and so on through the alphabet. The
language used is Italian, we are informed, although Holmes
and Watson, who are intercepting the message, do not at first
suspect it. The first letter of the message is a single flash, $A;$
the next is twenty flashes—"T," says Sherlock Holmes. But,
alas, the Italian alphabet has no letter K, Professor Lord points
out, and so its twentieth letter is U. The full message as read
by Holmes is "Attenta, pericolo!" Yet the omission of K
must have misplaced every letter below it, and Holmes should
have read, not "Attenta, pericolo!" but "Assemsa, oeqicnkn!"
Or, if Signor Lucca, sending his warning, had—for the con-
venience of Holmes and Watson—used the English alphabet
for an Italian message, his wife, who knew little English and
who was expecting the message in Italian, would have read
"Auueoua, qesicpmp!"

Well, it is a sufficiently startling message, either way; and it is no slight testimony to the ability of Sherlock Holmes that he brought off the case with honors.

And also, of course, there is the moot subject of the detective's residence in the United States. Somewhere in America there are yet living, one fancies, men who, if they would, could tell a tale or two of Sherlock Holmes. Should this volume reach the eye of any such, let it be said that they will confer a favor on posterity by writing down their memories. It is possible that they do not realize how intimately they have been in touch with personal immortality; and so I shall give them a hint. "Altamont" was the name taken by Sherlock Holmes when he came to the United States; the year was 1912. He was in the service of his government, in those days before the Great War when every nation was overrun with secret agents. To gain the confidence of Germany's master spy, it was necessary for Holmes to provide himself with an unsavory past. So to America he came. The record—it is very brief—is in *His Last Bow*.

"It has cost me two years, Watson," he told the doctor, on that historic second day of August, in 1914; "but they have not been devoid of excitement. When I say that I started my pilgrimage at Chicago, graduated in an Irish secret society at Buffalo, gave serious trouble to the constabulary at Skibbareen, and so eventually caught the eye of a subordinate agent of Von Bork, who recommended me as a likely man, you will realize that the matter was complex."

There is great need of further information concerning those two years of preparation for his war services; and such Buffalo and Chicago thugs, gangsters, hoodlums, and secret societarians as may remember an elderly tallish man named Altamont, much given to tobacco, should at once communicate with some one of the contributors to this volume. It may be added that those who come in person will be asked to leave their weapons outside the door.

These instances perhaps will help to explain the nature of the problems for the solution of which the Baker Street Irregulars occasionally meet together. In this volume, this—if Mr. Morley may be permitted—"Handbook of 221B Culture," a first selection of their memoirs and adventures is given permanence between a single set of covers.

VINCENT STARRETT

221ᴮ

Studies in Sherlock Holmes

THE MEMOIRS OF SHERLOCK HOLMES
THE FIELD BAZAAR *

By A. Conan Doyle

"I should certainly do it," said Sherlock Holmes.

I started at the interruption, for my companion had been eating his breakfast with his attention entirely centred upon the paper which was propped up by the coffee pot. Now I looked across at him to find his eyes fastened upon me with the half-amused, half-questioning expression which he usually assumed when he felt that he had made an intellectual point.

"Do what?" I asked.

He smiled as he took his slipper from the mantelpiece and drew from it enough shag tobacco to fill the old clay pipe with which he invariably rounded off his breakfast.

"A most characteristic question of yours, Watson," said he. "You will not, I am sure, be offended if I say that any reputation for sharpness which I may possess has been entirely gained by the admirable foil which you have made for me. Have I not heard of debutantes who have insisted upon plainness in their chaperones? There is a certain analogy."

Our long companionship in the Baker Street rooms had left us on those easy terms of intimacy when much may be said without offence. And yet I acknowledge that I was nettled at his remark.

"I may be very obtuse," said I, "but I confess that I am unable to see how you have managed to know that I was . . . I was . . ."

* Reprinted from *The Student* November 1896.

"Asked to help in the Edinburgh University Bazaar."

"Precisely. The letter has only just come to hand, and I have not spoken to you since."

"In spite of that," said Holmes, leaning back in his chair and putting his finger tips together, "I would even venture to suggest that the object of the bazaar is to enlarge the University cricket field."

I looked at him in such bewilderment that he vibrated with silent laughter.

"The fact is, my dear Watson, that you are an excellent subject," said he. "You are never *blasé*. You respond instantly to any external stimulus. Your mental processes may be slow but they are never obscure, and I found during breakfast that you were easier reading than the leader in the *Times* in front of me."

"I should be glad to know how you arrived at your conclusions," said I.

"I fear that my good nature in giving explanations has seriously compromised my reputation," said Holmes. "But in this case the train of reasoning is based upon such obvious facts that no credit can be claimed for it. You entered the room with a thoughtful expression, the expression of a man who is debating some point in his mind. In your hand you held a solitary letter. Now last night you retired in the best of spirits, so it was clear that it was this letter in your hand which had caused the change in you."

"This is obvious."

"It is all obvious when it is explained to you. I naturally asked myself what the letter could contain which might have this effect upon you. As you walked you held the flap side of the envelope towards me, and I saw upon it the same shield-shaped device which I have observed upon your old college cricket cap. It was clear, then, that the request came from Edinburgh University—or from some club connected with the University. When you reached the table you laid down the letter beside your plate with the address uppermost, and you walked over to look at the framed photograph upon the left of the mantelpiece."

It amazed me to see the accuracy with which he had observed my movements. "What next?" I asked.

"I began by glancing at the address, and I could tell, even at the distance of six feet, that it was an unofficial communication. This I gathered from the use of the word 'Doctor' upon the address, to which, as a Bachelor of Medicine, you have no legal claim. I knew that University officials are pedantic in their correct use of titles, and I was thus enabled to say with certainty that your letter was unofficial. When on your return to the table you turned over your letter and allowed me to perceive that the enclosure was a printed one, the idea of a bazaar first occurred to me. I had already weighed the possibility of its being a political communication, but this seemed improbable in the present stagnant conditions of politics.

"When you returned to the table your face still retained its expression and it was evident that your examination of the photograph had not changed the current of your thoughts. In that case it must itself bear upon the subject in question. I turned my attention to the photograph, therefore, and saw at once that it consisted of yourself as a member of the Edinburgh University Eleven, with the pavilion and cricket-field in the background. My small experience of cricket clubs has taught me that next to churches and cavalry ensigns they are the most debt-laden things upon earth. When upon your return to the table I saw you take out your pencil and draw lines upon the envelope, I was convinced that you were endeavouring to realise some projected improvement which was to be brought about by a bazaar. Your face still showed some indecision, so that I was able to break in upon you with my advice that you should assist in so good an object."

I could not help smiling at the extreme simplicity of his explanation.

"Of course, it was as easy as possible," said I.

My remark appeared to nettle him.

"I may add," said he, "that the particular help which you have been asked to give was that you should write in their album, and that you have already made up your mind that the present incident will be the subject of your article."

"But how——!" I cried.

"It is as easy as possible," said he, "and I leave its solution to your own ingenuity. In the meantime," he added, raising his paper, "you will excuse me if I return to this very interesting article upon the trees of Cremona, and the exact reasons for their pre-eminence in the manufacture of violins. It is one of those small outlying problems to which I am sometimes tempted to direct my attention."

WAS SHERLOCK HOLMES AN AMERICAN?

By Christopher Morley

I think the fellow is really an American, but he has worn his accent smooth with years of London.

—THE THREE GARRIDEBS

A CAPRICIOUS SECRECY was always characteristic of Holmes. He concealed from Watson his American connection. And though Watson must finally have divined it, he also was uncandid with us. The Doctor was a sturdy British patriot: the fact of Holmes's French grandmother was disconcerting, and to add to this his friend's American association and sympathy would have been painful. But the theory is too tempting to be lightly dismissed. Not less than fifteen of the published cases (including three of the four chosen for full-length treatment) involve American characters or scenes. Watson earnestly strove to minimize the appeal of United States landscapes of which Holmes must have told him. The great plains of the West were "an arid and repulsive desert." [1] Vermissa Valley (in Pennsylvania, I suppose?) was "a gloomy land of black crag and tangled forest . . . not a cheering prospect." [2] Watson's quotation from the child Lucy [1]—"Say, did God make this country?"—was a humorous riposte to Holmes, spoofing the familiar phrase Watson had heard too often in their fireside talks. There is even a possible suggestion of Yankee *timbre* in the Doctor's occasional descriptions of the "well-remembered voice." The argument of rival patriotisms was a favorite topic between them. Watson never quite forgave Holmes's ironical jape when after some specially naïve Victorian imperialism by the Doctor (perhaps at the time of

[1] *A Study in Scarlet.*   [2] *The Valley of Fear.*

the '87 Jubilee) Sherlock decorated the wall with the royal
V.R. in bullet-pocks. (Or did the Doctor misread as V.R.
what was jocularly meant to be V.H.—because Watson too
insistently suggested a sentimental interest in Miss Violet
Hunter of *The Copper Beeches?* An H in bullet-pocks, if the
marksman's aim was shaken by a heavy dray in the street, or
by the neighboring Underground Railway, might well look
like an R.)

Why, again, does Watson write, "It was upon the 4th of
March, as I have good reason to remember," that the adventure of *A Study in Scarlet* began? And why was Holmes
still at the breakfast table? It was the 4th of March, 1881,
and Holmes was absorbed in reading the news dispatches
about the inauguration, to take place that day, of President
Garfield.

Was Holmes actually of American birth? It would explain
much. The jealousy of Scotland Yard, the refusal of knighthood, the expert use of Western argot, the offhand behavior
to aristocratic clients, the easy camaraderie with working
people of all sorts, the always traveling First Class in trains.
How significant is Holmes's "Hum!" when he notes that Irene
Adler was born in New Jersey.[3] And Watson's careful insertion of "U.S.A." after every American address, which always irritates us, was probably a twit, to tease his principal.
True, as Inspector MacDonald once said,[4] "You don't need
to import an American from outside in order to account for
American doings." But let us light the cherry-wood pipe and
examine the data more systematically.

* * * *

Holmes's grandmother was "the sister of Vernet, the French
artist."[5] This of course was Horace Vernet (1789–1863), the
third of the famous line of painters in that family. Horace

[3] *A Scandal in Bohemia.*   [4] *The Valley of Fear.*
[5] *The Greek Interpreter.*

"Lestrade and Holmes sprang upon him like so many staghounds"
("A Study in Scarlet," London, 1891, courtesy of J. B. Lippincott Co.)

Vernet's father (who had been decorated by Napoleon for his *Battle of Marengo* and *Morning of Austerlitz*) came from Bordeaux; and Horace's grandfather, the marine painter, from Avignon. Here we have an association with the South of France which he acknowledges by his interest in Montpellier [6] where he probably had French kindred, like Sir Kenelm Digby, who delivered there the famous discourse on the Powder of Sympathy.[7] Holmes knew Montpellier as an important center of scientific studies. It is deplorable that our Holmes researchers have done so little to trace his French relationship. It is significant that though he declined a knighthood in Britain he was willing to accept the Legion of Honor in France.[8]

Much might be said of Sherlock's presumable artistic and political inheritance from the Vernets. His great-uncle's studio in Paris was "a rendezvous of Liberals." [9] Surely the untidiness which bothered Watson at 221B is akin to the description of Horace Vernet "painting tranquilly, whilst boxing, fencing, drum and horn playing were going on, in the midst of a medley of visitors, horses, dogs and models." [10] Holmes's grandmother, one of this radical and bohemian and wide-traveling family, brought up among the harrowing scenes of the French Revolution and the Napoleonic wars, may quite possibly have emigrated to America.[11] It is not inconceivable then that at least one of Holmes's parents was an American. My own conjecture is that there was some distant connection with the famous Holmes household of Cambridge

---

[6] *The Empty House* Cf. also *The Disappearance of Lady Frances Carfax.*
[7] Anne Macdonell: (1910), p. xxxi.; *The Closet of Sir Kenelm Digby.*
[8] *The Golden Pince-Nez.*   [9] Encyclopaedia Britannica, article *Vernet.*
[10] *Ibid.* Perhaps Sherlock as a child got his first interest in boxing and fencing from Great-Uncle Horace.
[11] Turning to the telephone book, as Dr. Watson did for Garrideb, I find that several of the Vernet (Verner) family came to the U.S. There are two Vernets in Brooklyn, three Verners in Manhattan, one Verner in Floral Park, L.I.

(Mass.).   Every reader has noticed Holmes's passionate interest in breakfasts: does this not suggest the Autocrat of the
Breakfast Table?

I will not cloud the issue with futile speculation, though
certainly it is of more importance than many of the controversies (such as, was Holmes's dressing gown blue, purple,
or mouse colored?).[12] But before proceeding to recount some
specific passages which prove our hero's exceptional interest
in America let me add one more suggestion. The hopeless
muddle of any chronology based on *The Gloria Scott* and *The
Musgrave Ritual* is familiar to all students; Miss Dorothy
Sayers has done her brilliant best to harmonize the anomalies.
But all have wondered just what Holmes was doing between
the time he left the university and his taking rooms in
Montague Street. My own thought is that the opening of the
Johns Hopkins University in Baltimore in 1876, and the extraordinary and informal opportunities offered there for graduate study, tempted him across the water. He was certainly
familiar with papers in the chemical journals written by Ira
Remsen, the brilliant young professor who took charge of the
new laboratories in Baltimore. Probably in Baltimore he acquired his taste for oysters [13] and on a hot summer day noted
the depth to which the parsley had sunk into the butter.[14]
In that devoted group of young scholars and scientists and in
the musical circles of that hospitable city he must have been
supremely happy. His American-born mother (or father)
had often told him of the untrammeled possibilities of American life. The great Centennial Exposition in Philadelphia
(1876) was surely worth a visit; there he observed the mark

[12] Elementary. This particular gown was blue when new. (*The Twisted
Lip*) It had gone purple by the time of the *Blue Carbuncle*. During the long
absence 1891–94, when Mrs. Hudson faithfully aired and sunned it in the
backyard, it faded to mouse (*The Empty House*).

[13] *The Sign of the Four*.

[14] *The Six Napoleons*. Holmes's interest in the butter-dish is shown in
The Musgrave Ritual.

of the Pennsylvania Small Arms Company.[15] During his year or so in the States he traveled widely. He met Wilson Hargreave (who later became important in the New York Police Department) [16] perhaps in connection with the case of *Vanderbilt and the Yeggman*, a record of which he kept in his scrapbook.[17] He went to Chicago, where he made his first acquaintance with organized gangsterism.[18] I suggest that he perhaps visited his kinsmen the Sherlocks in Iowa—e.g. in Des Moines, where a younger member of that family, Mr. C. C. Sherlock, has since written so ably on rural topics.[19] He must have gone to Topeka; [20] and of course he made pilgrimage to Cambridge, Mass., to pay respect to the great doctor, poet and essayist. From Oliver Wendell Holmes, Jr., then a rising lawyer in Boston, he heard first-hand stories of the Civil War, which fired his interest in "that gallant struggle." Indeed he spoke to Watson so often about the Civil War that Watson repeated in the story of *The Resident Patient* the episode of the Henry Ward Beecher portrait which he had already told in *The Cardboard Box*.[21] It is interesting to note, in passing, that when Holmes spoke in that episode of having written two

[15] *The Valley of Fear.*   [16] *The Dancing Men.*   [17] *The Sussex Vampire.*
[18] "My knowledge of the crooks of Chicago," v. *The Dancing Men.* Cf. also allusions in *The Valley of Fear* and *The Three Garridebs.*
[19] C. C. Sherlock: *Care and Management of Rabbits* (1920); *The Modern Hen* (1922); *Bulb Gardening*, etc. (1922); v. *Who's Who in America*. Iowa is a great apiarian State; undoubtedly from the Sherlock side came the interest in roses, beekeeping, etc.
[20] Otherwise how could he know that there was no such person as Dr. Lysander Starr? (*The Three Garridebs*)
[21] There was no duplication in the stories as first printed: *The Cardboard Box* in the *Strand Magazine* of January 1893, *The Resident Patient* in August of the same year. In the latter story as it absurdly appears in the collected editions the description of the "blazing hot day in August" is repeated for "a close rainy day in October." The explanation is that Dr. Watson withheld *The Cardboard Box* from book publication for twenty-four years; perhaps it revealed some anti-American bias in his never having had the portrait of Beecher framed. But the Beecher incident showed Holmes's keen observation, and in compiling the *Memoirs* Watson carelessly spliced or trepanned it into *The Resident Patient*. Then, when he republished *The Cardboard Box* in *His Last Bow* (1917), he forgot this.

monographs on Ears in the *Anthropological Journal*, the alert
editor of the *Strand* at once took the hint. A few months
later, in October and November 1893, the *Strand* printed "A
Chapter on Ears," with photos of the ears of famous people—
including an ear of Dr. Oliver Wendell Holmes. Surely,
from so retiring a philosopher, then eighty-four years old, this
intimate permission could not have been had without the privileged intervention of Sherlock.

Speaking of the *Strand Magazine*, it is odd that our researchers do not more often turn back to those original issues which
solve many problems. The much belabored matter of
Holmes's university, for instance. There was never any
question about it, for in Sidney Paget's illustrations Holmes is
clearly shown sitting in Trevor's garden wearing a straw hat
with a *Light Blue* ribbon.[22] (He was, of course, a boxing
Blue.) Why has such inadequate honor been paid to those
admirable drawings by Paget?—Oxford was unthinkable to
Holmes; with what pleasure he noted that Colonel Moran[23]
and John Clay[24] were both "Eton and Oxford."

2

In *The Bruce-Partington Plans* one of our most suggestive
passages occurs. "You have never had so great a chance of
serving your country," cries Mycroft. But is Holmes moved
by this appeal? " 'Well, well!' he said, shrugging his shoulders." All emotions, we know, were abhorrent to that cold,
precise mind,[25] and certainly militant patriotism among them;
at any rate until many years later when bees, flowers, Sussex,

---

[22] *Strand Magazine*, Vol. V, p. 398. While speaking of the *Gloria Scott*, it
has been pointed out that Holmes never admitted to Watson why he chose
Mrs. Hudson's lodgings. She was the widow of the ruffian Hudson who
blackmailed old Mr. Trevor—and so more than ever "a long-suffering
woman." And of course the rapid disappearance of Watson's bull-pup was
because Holmes had been bitten by one in college days.

[23] *The Empty House.*   [24] *The Red-Headed League.*
[25] *A Scandal in Bohemia.*

and long association with the more sentimental Watson had softened him to the strange outburst about "God's own wind" on the terrible night of August 2nd, 1914.[26]—Plainly he resented Mycroft's assumption that England was his only country. Mycroft, seven years older, had earlier outgrown the Franco-American tradition of the family. If Mycroft had ever been in the States he had striven to forget it; indeed no one can think of Mycroft without being reminded (in more respects than one) of the great expatriate Henry James.[27]

That Holmes had a very special affection and interest in regard to the United States is beyond question. He had much reason to be grateful to American criminals, who often relieved him from the *ennui* of London's dearth of outrage. The very first case recorded by Watson was the murder of Enoch J. Drebber, the ex-Mormon from Cleveland. Irene Adler, *the* woman, was a native of New Jersey. In *The Red-Headed League* the ingenious John Clay represented The League as having been founded by the eccentric millionaire Ezekiah Hopkins of Lebanon, Pa., "U.S.A." In *The Five Orange Pips*, Elias Openshaw emigrated to Florida, rose to be a Colonel in the C.S.A. and made a fortune. Although Watson tries to prejudice the reader by painful allusions to the habits of these people, there is plentiful evidence that Holmes considered America the land of opportunity. (Watson preferred Australia.) Both Aloysius Doran[28] and John Douglas[29] had struck it rich in California. Senator Neil Gibson,[30] "iron of nerve and leathery of conscience," had also made his pile in gold mines. Hilton Cubitt, the Norfolk squire, had married a lovely American woman;[31] and Holmes was glad to be able to save Miss Hatty Doran from Lord St. Simon

[26] *His Last Bow.*
[27] It is possible that Mycroft's experience had been in Canada, not the U.S. Sherlock says Mycroft was known at the Foreign Office as an expert on Canada (*The Bruce-Partington Plans*).   [28] *The Noble Bachelor.*
[29] *The Valley of Fear.*   [30] *Thor Bridge.*   [31] *The Dancing Men.*

who was not worthy of her.[32]   He yawns sardonically at the
Morning Post's social item which implies that Miss Doran will
gain by becoming the wife of a peer. That case is a high
point in Holmes's transatlantic sympathy. He praises American slang, quotes Thoreau, shows his knowledge of the price
of cocktails, and utters the famous sentiment:

> "It is always a joy to meet an American, for I am one of those
> who believe that the folly of a monarch and the blundering of a
> minister in far-gone years will not prevent our children from
> being some day citizens of the same world-wide country under
> a flag which shall be a quartering of the Union Jack with the
> Stars and Stripes."

Which reminds one obviously of the fact that when Holmes
disguised himself as Mr. Altamont of Chicago, the Irish-
American agitator, to deceive Von Bork, he greatly resembled
the familiar cartoons of Uncle Sam.[33] He visited Chicago
again in 1912–13 to prepare himself for this rôle; I wish Mr.
Vincent Starrett would look up the details.

Holmes's fondness for America did not prevent him from
seeing the comic side of a nation that lends itself to broad
satiric treatment. In *The Man with the Watches*, one of the
two stories outside the canon,[34] Holmes remarks of the victim,
"He was probably an American, and also probably a man of
weak intellect."

(This rhetorical device for humorous purposes was a family
trait: we find it in Mycroft's description of the senior clerk at
the Woolwich Arsenal—"He is a man of forty, married, with
five children. He is a silent, morose man." [35]) After his long
use of American cant for Von Bork's benefit Sherlock

---

[32] *The Noble Bachelor.*   [33] *His Last Bow.*
[34] The other is *The Lost Special*; both are to be found in *The Conan
Doyle Stories*, London (John Murray) 1929. Holmes appears in both these
stories by obvious allusion, but Watson suppressed them, probably because
Holmes's deductions were wrong in both cases.
[35] *The Bruce-Partington Plans.*

says "My well of English seems to be permanently de-
filed." [36] But these japes are plainly on the principle "*On se
moque de ce qu'on aime.*" He kept informed of American
manners and events; when he met Mr. Leverton of Pinkerton's he said "Pleased to meet you" and alluded to "the Long
Island cave mystery." [37] He knew "the American business
principle" of paying well for brains.[38] He did not hesitate to
outwit a rascal by inventing an imaginary mayor of Topeka—
recalling for the purpose the name of the counterfeiter of
Reading years before.[39] (Those who escaped him were not
forgotten.) But nothing shows more convincingly his passionate interest in all cases concerning Americans than his
letter about the matter of the Man with the Watches, alluded
to above. Even in Tibet, where he was then travelling as a
"Norwegian named Sigerson," [40] he had kept up with the
news.

This was in the spring of '92; how Watson, after reading
the letter in the newspaper, can have supposed his friend was
really dead passes belief. There are frequent humorous allusions to American accent, the [41] shape of American shoes,[42]
American spelling.[43] I suspect that Holmes's travels in these
States never took him to the South or Southwest,[44] for he
shows a curious ignorance of Southern susceptibilities in the
matter of race, and [45] in spite of his American Encyclopaedia [46]
he did not know which was the Lone Star State. Let it be
noted that the part of London where he first took rooms

[36] *His Last Bow.*
[37] *The Red Circle.* The mystery, on true Sherlockian principles, is that
there are no caves on Long Island.
[38] *The Valley of Fear.*   [39] *The Three Garridebs, The Engineer's Thumb.*
[40] *The Empty House.*   [41] *The Hound of the Baskervilles.*
[42] *The Dancing Men, The Valley of Fear.*   [43] *The Three Garridebs.*
[44] The "remarkable case" of the venomous gila lizard (v. *The Sussex
Vampire*) need not suggest Arizona. It probably came from Number 3,
Pinchin Lane (*The Sign of the Four*).
[45] *The Yellow Face.*   [46] *The Five Orange Pips.*

(Montague Street, alongside the British Museum) is the region frequented more than any other by American students and tourists.

*   *   *   *

That Holmes was reared in the States, or had some school-ing here before going up to Cambridge, seems then at least arguable. His complete silence (or Watson's) on the subject of his parents suggests that they were deceased or not in Eng-land. A foreign schooling, added to his own individual tem-perament, would easily explain his solitary habits at college.[47] If he had gone to almost any English school the rugger jargon of Cyril Overton would have been comprehensible to him [48] —or he might have picked it up from Watson, who played for Blackheath.[49] Watson moreover, if he knew more about Holmes's family, may have been moved by jealousy to keep silent. Already he had suffered by the contrast between the corpulent Mycroft and his own older brother, the crapulent H.W.[50] Or his neglect to inform us may just have been the absent-mindedness and inaccuracy which we have learned to expect from good old Watson—and which were even ac-quired by his wife, who went so far as to forget her husband's first name and call him "James" in front of a visitor.[51] The Doctor has hopelessly confused us on even more important matters—that both Moriarty brothers were called James, for instance. Considering the evidence without prejudice, the idea that Holmes was at any rate partly American is enticing. As Jefferson Hope said,[52] "I guessed what puzzled the New

[47] The Gloria Scott.   [48] The Missing Three Quarter.
[49] The Sussex Vampire.   [50] The Sign of the Four.
[51] The Man with the Twisted Lip. This was probably the cause of the first rupture between Dr. and Mrs. Watson. Has it been pointed out, by the way, that there is a premonitory allusion to a second Mrs. Watson in The Disappearance of Lady Frances Carfax, where Watson evades Holmes's question as to who was his companion in the hansom? Also the Doctor had been bucking himself up with a Turkish bath.   [52] A Study in Scarlet.

Yorkers would puzzle the Londoners." So I leave it as a puzzle, not as a proven case, for more accomplished students to re-examine. But the master's own dictum [53] is apposite:— "When once your point of view is changed, the very thing which was so damning becomes a clue to the truth."

[53] *Thor Bridge*.

NUMMI IN ARCA
OR
THE FISCAL HOLMES

By R. K. Leavitt

In the early 70's of the last century there was at Cambridge [1] a long, lean young man of strange tastes and taciturn, not to say misanthropic, disposition. His name was Sherlock Holmes and he was so far from being a social success that during his first two years at that University he made only one friend, and that one through the accident of being bitten by a bulldog.[2]

But like so many youths whose early years are turned in upon themselves, Holmes had developed abilities—powers, he liked to have them called—of a most surprising order. And once the social ice had been broken by his acquaintance with Victor Trevor he made use of those talents to such good effect that by the time he left Cambridge he was not only known but admired by a considerable circle of friends and acquaintances including the suave, languid, dandified, and exceedingly aristocratic Reginald Musgrave.

Equally marked and comparably belated triumphs are, of course, common in every college generation on both sides of the Atlantic, though few of them are attained by the display of a methodology in observation and inference. But there is, to the psychologist interested in manifestation of the inferiority complex, little difference between a performance in deduction and one in legerdemain or in playing upon the saxophone. Holmes' early amateur displays were motivated by that potent admonition, invaluable to advertisers of cor-

[1] Sayers, Dorothy, "Holmes' College Career," in *Baker Street Studies*, London, 1934.   [2] *The Gloria Scott*.

respondence courses in piano-playing or in conversing with
waiters in French, "Astonish your Friends!"

That Holmes' séances created a sensation we know from his
account of young Musgrave's reference to "those powers with
which you used to amaze us." [3] At times he not only as-
tounded his friends but literally knocked them cold with his
demonstrations, as witness the elder Trevor's reaction to a
typical bit of Holmesian deduction.[4]

Indeed it was this involuntary tribute from Trevor père,
coupled with the old gentleman's extravagant, but all too obviously sincere verbal tribute which "was, if you will believe
me, Watson, the very first thing which ever made me feel
that a profession might be made out of what had been up to
that time the merest hobby." [5] "Mr. Holmes," Justice of the
Peace Trevor had said, "it seems to me that all the detectives of
fact and of fancy would be children in your hands. That's
your line of life, sir, and you may take the word of a man
who has seen something of the world."

It is not surprising, therefore, that the shrewd young
Holmes, on coming down from the University and up, as he
puts it, to London, should have essayed the career of consulting detective. He had, among his friends of the University
days, a group of young men whom he counted upon either
to get into trouble themselves or to spread the word of his
prowess among such of their friends in the well-bred and
moneyed world as might be embarrassed with adventures. He
had also, one must infer, sufficient capital to carry him
through the first and most difficult years of getting established in his chosen profession. And so, in 1876,[6] Mr. Sherlock Holmes set up in practice in Montague Street, just around
the corner from the British Museum. For some two years
the Holmesian practice was slim indeed. "Now and again,"

[3] *The Gloria Scott.*   [4] *The Gloria Scott.*
[5] *The Gloria Scott.*   [6] Sayers, op. cit.

he told Watson later, "cases come my way, principally through the introduction of fellow students." But these were fewer than the hopeful graduate had hoped. The Musgrave Ritual case, in 1878, was only the third of them.[7] And while these cases may well have yielded fees of considerable size, it may be conjectured that Holmes would hardly have been able to live upon his takings from the carriage trade. "You can hardly realize," he told Watson in narrating the affair of the Musgrave Ritual, "how difficult I found it at first, and how long I had to wait before I succeeded in making any headway."

It is true that the Musgrave Ritual case and the interest which was aroused by it put Holmes' fiscal legs under him. But for some years yet his leisure was all too abundant. He used much of it in study and some of it in writing, to eke out his slender earnings by the preparation of monographs and of articles for publication. These, however, can hardly even have kept so assiduous a smoker in pipe tobacco—his favorite and at that time his only smoking indulgence. (It is in later and more prosperous times that we see Holmes as the devotee of cigars and cigarettes).

By 1881, when the Holmes-Watson partnership came about (with such happy results for the world) Holmes "had already established a considerable, though not a very lucrative, connection."[8] The character of this early practice is admirably sketched by Watson in his introduction to the *Study in Scarlet:* "He had many acquaintances, and those in the most different classes of society. There was one little sallow, rat-faced, dark-eyed fellow, who was introduced to me as Mr. Lestrade, and who came three or four times in a single week. One morning a young girl called, fashionably dressed, and stayed for half an hour or more. The same afternoon brought a gray-headed, seedy visitor, looking like a Jew peddler, who

[7] *The Musgrave Ritual.*   [8] *The Musgrave Ritual.*

appeared to me to be much excited, and who was closely followed by a slipshod elderly woman. On another occasion an old white-haired gentleman had an interview with my companion; and on another a railway porter in his velveteen uniform." [9]

"These people," said Holmes to the puzzled Watson, when, on an occasion in their early days, he begged the use of their sitting-room, "are my clients . . . I depend on them for my bread and cheese . . . I listen to their story, they listen to my comments, and then I pocket my fee." [10]

"Bread-and-cheese" clients precisely describes the great run of those who called at 221B Baker Street. They were by no means to be compared, either in social status or in profitability, with the occasional toffs who were sent Holmes' way by his college friends. But it was they, and not the all-too-rare Reginald Musgraves, who kept the Holmesian flesh upon the Holmesian bones. And it is well to have a closer look at these, the clients of the early years, for Holmes very soon outgrew his dependence upon them, though he continued (be it said to his credit) to interest himself in such cases through all his years of affluence.

We have, of course, no explicit record in the Canon, of Holmes' fiscal transactions with these clients. Indeed, Watson, with a gentlemanly reticence in regard to the coarser affairs of life, avoids so much as mentioning any except the most spectacular of Holmes' fees. But it is possible to get a substantially accurate picture of the bread-and-cheese business of Mr. Sherlock Holmes, consulting detective, by consulting the memoirs of practitioners of another profession who, in their earlier years, depended upon exactly the same class of trade.

There is, as it happens, a most graphic account of the early struggles of a young medical man of that period, contained in

[9] *A Study in Scarlet.*   [10] *A Study in Scarlet.*

the autobiography of one Dr. A. C. Doyle, who set up in the general practice of medicine in Portsmouth and strove desperately to live on his earnings. His fees were customarily paid in one or two of the smaller silver coins of the realm, all hot from humble pockets and moist from troubled palms. So slender was the existence which he eked out on these meagre fees and upon his middleman's profits from the sale of medicines compounded with his own hands in his own dispensary, that every sixpence was a matter of household concern. On August 16, 1882, his younger brother, who lived with him, wrote to their mother:

"The patients are crowding in. We have made three bob this week. We have vaxenated a baby and got hold of a man with consumption, and today a gipsy's cart came up to the door . . . After he had rong two or three times Arthur yelled out at the pitch of his voice Go a way but the man rang again so I went down . . . and cried out go a way. The man began to swere at me and say that he wanted to see Arthur. All this time Arthur . . . was yelling Shut that door . . . so Arthur went down and opened the door and found out that the gipsy's child had measles . . . After all we got sixpence out of them and that is all ways something." [11]

The Dr. Doyle above referred to, records later the limitations of his annual income from this arduous, shilling-by-shilling life. "I made £154 the first year, and £250 the second, rising slowly to £300 which in eight years I never passed." [12]

We may conceive, then, of the early Holmes painfully gaining a livelihood from the even less wanted profession of consulting detective. His lucrative clients are still infrequent. But by dint of luck, labor, a discreet cultivation (probably involving the splitting of fees) of private inquiry agencies, and the recommendation of such satisfied customers as Mrs. Cecil

[11] A. Conan Doyle: *Memories and Adventures*, Doubleday Doran, New York, 1930, p. 71.   [12] *Ibid.*, p. 74.

The birthplace of Sherlock Holmes: doorway of "Doyle House,"
Southsea, Portsmouth

Forrester, he has managed to get cases of which the written records and other memorabilia in hardware form fill one-third of a large tin box.[13] Let us observe the still uncelebrated detective in the act of gaining a livelihood.

It is mid-morning. Watson, the slug-abed, has got up at last, has breakfasted in the customary silence of the newly-risen Englishman, has at length been mellowed by coffee and toast, and is caressing with liquid eye the picture of Henry Ward Beecher, which hangs upon the opposite wall. His hand steals from shoulder to leg trying absently to discover where that Old Jezail bullet may be *this* morning.

Holmes stands at the window, looking out. Business has been slow lately. A week or so has passed (as is not infrequently the case) without a single visitor. The eagle eyes rake the street, frisk every approaching pedestrian, peer into every oncoming cab or private carriage, on the lookout for cash customers. Oh for the sight of such an expensive equipage as caused Holmes some years later to exclaim, "A nice little brougham and a pair of beauties. A hundred and fifty guineas apiece. There's money in this case, Watson, if there is nothing else."[14] Oh, for a dashing hansom, with a distraught banker—or even a four-wheeler with a distraught anybody inside! Oh, for a breathless foot-passenger scanning the house-numbers in search of 221B! Oh, for *anything* that looks, however faintly, like a prospective client! But not even the obvious widowed cost-accountant with a borrowed umbrella and a passion for numismatics pauses before the expectant door. Holmes is just reflecting on the obstinacy of watched pots and weighing the attractions of a shot in the arm against those of a bout with the faithful Stradivarius.

But hold! The piercing eye picks out a figure from among the crowd at the far end of the block—a hurrying figure in pea-jacket, a curiously white-spotted bowler hat and blue

[13] *The Musgrave Ritual.*   [14] *A Scandal in Bohemia.*

trousers. There is no mistaking the urgency of the prospective client. Nor, upon inspection, is there any mistaking the assistant lighthouse-keeper—so obviously fresh from intimate association with sea-gulls, yet walking without the true sailor's roll. The lack of a complete air of authority marks the junior functionary, while the peculiarly one-sided wear of the boot-soles speaks of life on a circular stone stairway—a counter-clockwise stairway, evidently. Which lighthouses within a morning's run of London (for there are no wrinkles of an overnight journey in the man's attire) are left-handed? Surely none but the Farthingale and Manciple Rock. But the direction from which the man is approaching rules out Fenchurch Street Station, and hence the Farthingale. Quick, then! A stride, a long reach, a flick of the pages, and Holmes's invaluable scrapbook, Volume "T," is open at the Trinity House [15] list. Ah, here it is . . . Height 115 feet . . . Flashing white every . . . Principal Keeper James Pardoner . . . Assistant Keeper Matthew Muggridge. The slap of the closing books is followed by the peal of the bell downstairs. And by the time the visitor (directed from below by Mrs. Hudson) has knocked at the door, Holmes is disposed in his armchair, head thrown back, eyes half closed, finger-tips pressed together.

"Come in!"

"Mr. Holmes?"

"Good morning, Muggridge."

"Godalmighty, sir!" (a comment which registers in the curiously fallacious Watsonian memory as "For Heaven's sake, sir") "How did you . . ."

"One moment," says Holmes, "before you begin to tell me

[15] Parenthetically, the Holmesian method of indexing was an art, not a science. Watson relates, in *The Sussex Vampire*, that the great Index listed under the V's, "Victor Lynch the Forger" and "Venomous (sic) lizard or gila."

about the strange and inexplicable conduct of James Pardoner . . . Er, my dear Doctor . . . If you don't mind? . . ."

"Oh, not at all, not at all," says Watson, and picking up the morning papers he goes out into what for the purposes of his later record he describes as his bedroom. (If there are Modern Conveniences attached to the lodgings at 221B we shall never discover them from the writings of John H. Watson, M. D.) And there, in gentlemanly observance of his roommate's privacy, Watson remains immured, reading all through the Distressing Suburban Incidents, clear down to the Phenomenal Artichokes in Surrey, until he is at length released by a Holmes who mumbles further apologies as he absently bites a coin and puts it into the pocket of his dressing gown. Mr. Sherlock Holmes, consulting detective, has earned a shilling.

And so, with a sixpence here, a half crown there, and a more generous fee now and then from the occasional opulent client, Holmes made a net income of about £200 per annum. We may assume this figure from the fact that he and Watson found an ideal solution for the diggings problem in "going halves" [16] on the rental of Mrs. Hudson's rooms.

I say Holmes' income was £200 net, per annum. By net I mean the residue after deduction of necessary expenses in immediate connection with his cases.

For his humbler clients, of course, Holmes did not stir from the armchair. He was, so far as they were concerned, a consulting detective, pure and simple. His only operating expenses were wear-and-tear on the seat of his trousers and on the back of his dressing-gown. But let an affluent customer commission Holmes to do a job of detecting, and he was in the first hansom that came his way, flinging one sovereign to the driver and promising another for swift transportation, with equal prodigality and relish.

[16] *A Study in Scarlet.*

The reason for this open-handedness in the matter of expense-money goes far deeper than can be conceived by the ordinary, or salaried man who has, perhaps, taken a trip or two on expense-account. It lies, not in the joy of buying unaccustomed luxury and charging it to someone else, but in a careful calculation of the value of a fat expense-account as a tacit argument for unquestioning acceptance of an even fatter bill for professional services. Your own doctor knows this. He is spared the necessity of blushing when he licks the flap of the envelope containing his bill for a hundred dollars for snatching out your tonsils, because he knows that you have already got a bill for some $60 from the hospital for ambulance, operating-room, ether, wheel-chairs, nurses, anaesthetists, acolytes, helpers, henchmen, and file-closers.

So with Holmes as a professional man, dependent on the richness of a few fees to make up for the slimness of most of them, he made a consistent practice of running up good, impressive expense-accounts whenever a client looked promising. Let us take, as an example, Holmes' expenses in connection with the service of his client, Miss Mary Morstan, in *The Sign of the Four*. We can reconstruct it very nearly as Holmes must have sent it:

Sherlock Holmes
221B Baker Street, W.

Oct. 1, 1887 [17]

To Miss Mary Morstan, Dr.
   Talavera Villa
      Knatchbull Road, Lower Camberwell
      London, S.E.

To sundry expenses in connection with professional services rendered in the case at Pondicherry Lodge, on 27th–30th Sept., as follows:

[17] In the matter of this dating I accept the conclusions so admirably arrived at by the erudite Bell (*Baker Street Studies*, London, pp. 203 ff).

Four-wheeler, Baker St. to Lyceum Theatre

Cab from Pondicherry Lodge to Lower Camberwell, thence to
  Pinchin Lane and so to Upper Norwood (Nett after payment
  by Dr. Watson of pro rata for first part of ride, this being insisted on by him on score of pure pleasure) [18]

Hire of dog, Toby

Tip to Young Jack Smith

Wherry across river from Kennington

Hansom to Baker St.

Hire of Baker Street Irregulars

Searching-parties on either side of the river, including boat-hire

Advertisement, 74 words, in agony column of *Globe, St. James's,
  Westminster Gazette, Pall Mall Gazette, Standard, News, Star.*

Telegram to Inspector A. Jones, Scotland Yard, sent from Poplar,
  40 words

Miscellaneous expenses of self during one day along the water
  front visiting 16 boat yards, as follows:
    32 pts. beer @ 4 d. ea
    16 bets lost @ 1 s. ea

Cab fare to Westminster Wharf

  "   "   " Vauxhall Bridge, Lower Camberwell and back to
  Baker St. (Nett after Dr. Watson's contribution of his share)

Cab fare Westminster Wharf to Baker St.

Total

We may well imagine the gasp of dismay which the gentle
Miss Morstan—no longer in danger of being unhappily rich
—let out on receiving this formidable account. We can picture her unfolding with agitated fingers the other bill which
accompanied it—the bill for Professional Services. After such
enormous preliminary outlays on the part of Mr. Sherlock
Holmes almost anything might be expected in the way of
a detective's own fee. And while Miss Mary Morstan may

[18] It is inconceivable that the gallant Watson should accept reimbursement
from Holmes for that part of the ride which furnished him with the pleasure
of Miss Morstan's company. But it is equally inconceivable that Holmes
should have allowed his friend (whose moderate circumstances he well
knew) to pay all the expenses of a very long cab-ride at the high rates
prevailing for transportation in the small hours of the night.

have breathed a sigh of comparative relief upon discovering a bill of perhaps 20 guineas, it is not to be wondered at that during the rest of her all-too-short life she betrayed no more than a well-bred wife's dutifully polite interest in the company of Mr. Sherlock Holmes.

One other class of clients the detective had, even in these early days. These were the police. Lestrade was but the first of a long line of Scotland Yard inspectors who sought out Holmes and laid their cases before him. And these inspectors are the most puzzling of all the clients who made their way to Baker Street.

What was Holmes' interest in them and their cases? He never (except, of course, in the incident of Charles Augustus Milverton) turned down a case which one of them brought to him. On the contrary, he devoted considerable time to solving those cases, and spent sums for expenses in connection with them which he would never have been justified in disbursing if they came out of his own pocket. His expenses in the Lauriston Gardens mystery, for example, are nearly all of explicit record:

Hansom, Baker St. to Brixton Road
Cable to America and prepaid reply
Cab, Brixton Rd. to Kennington Pk. Gate
Half-sovereign tip to P. C. Rance
Advt. in Lost and Found Column of eight papers, 35 words
Telegram to each paper, transmitting advt.
Facsimile Wedding Ring
Cab from Baker St. to Houndsditch
Fee to Baker St. Irregulars, 6 boys @ 1 s. ea. per day, 2 days
Repairs to Mrs. Hudson's woodwork and glasses after struggle
  with Hope

Obviously Holmes must have been reimbursed for such an outlay. And with equal obviousness he must have got some return on the time he put so freely at the disposal of the

Regular Force. What was the nature of his arrangement with the Inspectors from Scotland Yard?

First, Holmes was not on the Yard's payroll. We know this from direct testimony as well as from inference. His Inspector clients refer to him always slightly as an amateur. The public prints are careful to avoid labeling him in any way as an official. He himself says repeatedly that he is not the police. In the case of the Crooked Man he makes a categorical [19] denial of police connection. In the Boscombe Valley mystery he says, "I am no official agent." In the case of the Blue Carbuncle he says, "I am not retained by the police to supply their deficiencies."

It may be argued that this remark implies that Mr. Holmes *was* retained by the police for some other purpose. It may be contended that in the cases just cited his status was that of a private detective, engaged by private citizens, while in such cases as that of the *Study in Scarlet* his connection with the police was indeed an official one. But in that event what of the Abbey Grange case? Here Holmes had been called in by Stanley Hopkins. He was acting in exactly the same capacity as in the *Study in Scarlet*. Nevertheless, we find him assuring a confessed murderer that the *police* haven't seen through the murderer's dodge and continuing, "I have so much sympathy for you that, if you choose to disappear in the next twenty-four hours I will promise you that no one will hinder you." Are those the words of one who is, however temporarily, in the official service of the police? [20] Yet Holmes had been

---

[19] "My God, are you in the police itself?" "No."

[20] P. 310. Holmes' habit of letting off criminals is by now, of course, notorious. In the 60 cases of record in the Writings, there are 37 definite felonies where the criminal was known to Mr. Sherlock Holmes. In no less than 14 of these cases did the celebrated detective take the law into his own hands and free the guilty person. In 23 cases the offender was taken by the police. In 7 cases justice was balked by suicide, by death at sea or by other acts of God. In 12 cases no crime was involved. And in 4 cases the criminal or criminals got away uncaught.

brought into this case by Inspector Stanley Hopkins, just as he had been brought into scores of cases by other inspectors beginning with Lestrade in the very early days at Baker Street. It is demonstrable, therefore, that Holmes had no official commission from Scotland Yard to act in any of the affairs of record in the Canon.

What, then, *was* the nature of Holmes' relation with the Inspectors from the Yard? Clearly this: he was a private detective engaged by each of them privately. For what purpose? For the enhancement of the Inspectors' professional reputations. And how was he paid? He was paid from the private pockets of his Inspector clients.

And how could they, subsisting as they did on a salary that was meagre even for those days, pay so much as the Holmesian expenses, to say nothing of the Holmesian fees? Obviously the worthy Inspectors got, as the saying goes, Theirs, by a discreet shaking-down of the underworld. And they were, in turn, shaken down by Mr. Sherlock Holmes, consulting detective. The substantial truth of these conclusions will, I am sure, be conceded by any fair-minded weigher of the evidence.

We have seen that Holmes had not—indeed *could* not have had any official standing. Therefore he was neither engaged by nor paid by the official force as such. But he was engaged by the Inspectors. Therefore he was engaged by each as an individual. Their interest was in catching criminals, or at least in getting themselves well known as dangerous potential catchers of criminals. They were careful to see that Holmes got none of the public credit for their apprehensions. And Holmes, on his part, respected the bargain he had with them, by refraining from seeking or even accepting this credit. What recompense, then, could Holmes have got? Jealous as he was of approbation, he had to forego it in these cases. Keenly as he enjoyed the chase, he could not, particularly in

his early days, afford to hunt at such extravagant expense as
we have noted in the case of the *Study in Scarlet*. He must
have been paid in money.[21] And, indeed, he himself told
Watson as much when, at the close of that very case he quoted
Horace to the effect that the public hissing meant nothing to
him so long as he could sit in the privacy of his home and
count over his takings.[22] Whence, then, these fees? The pay
of an Inspector of those days probably was not large. Even
if the "testimonials" presented to the force at the satisfactory
conclusion of some cases[23] may have found their ways into
the Holmesian pockets they could not have been counted
upon as means of paying off the detective's fees. Obviously,
then, the Inspector must have had other sources of income.
What other income is a humble officer of police most likely to
have? Is it necessary to ask this question of any realist? No.
Obviously Lestrade, Gregson, the various Joneses and others
must have made a fairly good thing out of their relations with
the underworld of London. And, as obviously, their ability
to keep on exacting tribute, and perhaps to increase it, depended upon their reputations as sleuths. Hence, it was the
part of a good business man to engage Mr. Sherlock Holmes
at whatever might be his price, to help maintain this reputation.

Parenthetically, Lestrade appears to have been the steadiest
of all Holmes' Inspector customers. The others came and
went—even Stanley Hopkins, who brought seven cases to

[21] Watson says that Holmes helped Inspector Alec McDonald (*Valley
of Fear*) "his own sole reward being the intellectual joy of the problem."
Either this is one of the numerous cases in which Holmes deliberately mis-
informed Watson, or more likely the canny McDonald was clever enough
to get for nothing (and to get *repeatedly*) those eminent services which
cost others so dear. Perhaps this latter hypothesis explains in part Mc-
Donald's later attainment of "national fame." Space forbids the minute
examination of this brilliant Scot's career. It is humbly suggested as a subject for the learned researches of that eminent Holmesian commentator,
Mr. A. G. Macdonell.
[22] *A Study in Scarlet*.   [23] *Ibid*.

Holmes [24] grew discouraged after Holmes let off their prey in the Abbey Grange case and was heard from no more. Yet Lestrade, already a client of long standing in 1881, continued throughout Holmes' professional career to be an habitual seeker of the great detective's assistance. Presumably it must have been profitable assistance to Lestrade. Otherwise he would hardly have come back so often to Holmes. One is tempted, then, to speculate upon the professional and the private careers of Inspector Lestrade. The former was long and, if not distinguished (for Lestrade was still an Inspector in 1901 [25] after more than twenty years in that grade) at least it was a career not ruined by public exposure of malfeasance. To be sure, we have record of Lestrade's being in private practice for a time. In the case of the Boscombe Valley mystery in 1889 [26] he had been retained by Miss Turner and the other neighbors to prove young McCarthy's innocence, and was the means of bringing Holmes into that case. This would indicate the possibility that the worthy Lestrade had been more than half detected in his extortions, and had been rusticated by the authorities. But either the case against him was not well established or (as is more likely) he himself possessed usable knowledge of the private life of some person in authority, for we find him, later, respectably re-installed as an Inspector of the regular force.

Tempting as it is to follow the career of Lestrade, however, we are immediately concerned with that of Mr. Sherlock Holmes. We have seen that he started in practice in an exceedingly modest way, that his early clients were for the most part folk of humble station, that a few more distinguished customers and an occasional Inspector or private detective brought him a net income of some £200 a year in 1881.

From that year on Mr. Holmes was never headed in his

[24] *The Abbey Grange.*
[25] *The Six Napoleons; Charles Augustus Milverton.*   [26] Bell, *op. cit.*

pursuit of a competence. We see him expanding the scale of his living as the years go by—smoking not merely the economical pipe but cigars and cigarettes, dining on fancy game and vintage wine and delighting in the exhibition of other signs of solvency.

By the time of the adventure of the *Beryl Coronet,* which was certainly not later than 1887, Holmes was able to write his check for £3000. By 1890, the date of the Dying Detective, Holmes' payments to Mrs. Hudson were "princely." By 1891 Holmes was able to drop out of practice altogether and, after having pretended to drop into the Reichenbach Fall, to spend three years in travel and exploration of a fairly costly nature, while still keeping up the princely payments on the Baker Street quarters. Nor was the Holmesian exchequer depleted by this drain. He was able to buy Watson's practice in 1893 for the mere pleasure of having the Doctor once again with him. By 1895 he was maintaining "at least five small refuges in various parts of London, in which he was able to change his personality."

All through these years he was able to afford the luxury of playing with cases in which there was obviously no profit. For example, the Red Circle case was undertaken in the first instance to please the humble Mrs. Warren, and was carried through partly to "tidy it up," partly for the sake of "education" and partly on an "Art for Art's Sake" basis. Hall Pycroft, in *The Stock Broker's Clerk,* Scott Eccles, in *Wisteria Lodge,* the unhappy John Hector McFarlane of *The Norwood Builder* and Miss Violet Smith of *The Solitary Cyclist,* among others, could hardly have excited the cupidity of a detective whose clients were increasingly sprinkled with royalty, nobility, cabinet-ministers, millionaires, and foreign governments. Indeed, Watson says of him in 1895 [27] that he practiced Art for Art's Sake to the point of eccentricity. "So

[27] *Black Peter.*

unworldly was he—so capricious—that he frequently refused his help to the powerful and wealthy—while he would devote weeks—to the affairs of more humble clients."

The sources of an affluence which would allow the indulgence of such tastes are not at first evident. True, Holmes received large fees in certain of the cases of record in the Canon. The *Beryl Coronet* yielded him a profit of £1000, thanks to his clients' fear of disgrace if the story in Holmes' keeping ever came out. From the *Scandal in Bohemia* Holmes undoubtedly made a very good fee. It is interesting to note the righteous indignation with which Holmes in the first instance refused both the hand of His Bohemian Majesty and the King's "emerald snake ring," [28] and yet how, a few weeks later, he turned up with a splendid "snuffbox of old gold with a great amethyst in the centre of the lid," confiding " 'It is a little souvenir from the King of Bohemia.' " [29] One would give much to know precisely the tactics which the haughty Holmes employed to preserve his pose of austere dignity and yet secure not only the snuffbox but the fat fee to which the snuffbox was only an additional tip. Undoubtedly Holmes' return of the unexpended balance of the King's £1000 advance for expenses paved the way for an adjustment satisfactory to both parties. It is not beyond the range of reasonable speculation to suppose that the ring referred to in the same story as coming from the reigning family of Holland in connection with a matter of great delicacy was also accompanied by a good-sized check. The *Blue Carbuncle,* a case taken up at first in mere caprice earned a reward of £1000 for its finder who, we may be sure, split generously with Mr. Sherlock Holmes. Lord Robert St. Simon, the Noble Bachelor, was undoubtedly charged a more-than-adequate fee for Mr. Holmes' services, particularly since he refused the detective's invitation to supper. But the noble lord undoubtedly paid

[28] *A Scandal in Bohemia.*   [29] *A Case of Identity.*

without a murmur. Aware that he was in Holmes' power, he was also aware that Holmes was a man of judgment and discretion, for he had been recommended by Lord Backwater. And this Lord Backwater, as one of those concerned in the shady affair of Silver Blaze (to which we shall refer later) would undoubtedly have counseled his friend that Holmes was no man to trifle with. The Naval Treaty case in 1888 [30] undoubtedly cost the "extremely well connected" Tadpole Phelps a tidy sum, and it is probable that Sir Henry Baskerville paid generously for the extended services of the great detective in the Fall of '89. Senator Neil Gibson, the Gold King, was in all likelihood charged all that the traffic would bear, in spite of Holmes' bare-faced falsehood that his professional charges were upon a fixed scale. Holmes' reasons for making this extravagant and uncalled-for statement to the American are, of course, clear. First, he wanted to put the blustering purse-proud Yankee in his place, and second, he was at the moment calculating how much Gibson would stand for, and he was astute enough to lay the foundations for an unquestioning acceptance of the account he meant to render. In this case, at least, Holmes did not deceive his bearer out of mere sport. [31]

[30] I adopt Mr. Christopher Morley's ingenious dating; *Saturday Review of Literature*, Dec. 22, 1934.

[31] A considerable article might be written on the subject of Holmes' deliberate deceptions. He seems to have taken a delight in gulling the credulous Watson. Of course the classic example is his assuring the Doctor in the first days of their acquaintance that he was entirely ignorant of the Copernican theory. Watson, simple-minded soul, never thought to question this, even when, not many years later, the talk of the two roamed "from golf clubs to the causes of the change in the ecliptic" (*Greek Interpreter*). Many of the so-called inconsistencies in the Canon are traceable directly to Watson's unhesitating acceptance of everything Holmes told him. Holmes appears to have filled Watson full of a great deal of assorted misinformation partly out of mere impishness and partly as a defensive measure. Watson was, according to our brash Yankee standards, a man of almost superhuman ability to keep his nose out of other people's business. But Holmes' secretiveness was even more marked and he probably considered Watson a busybody, to be kept at a distance. For example, Watson

There are other cases mentioned, but not described in the Canon—cases which hint by their very names at rich fees. The year 1887 was distinguished by the extensive operations in connection with the Netherland-Sumatra Company and the colossal schemes of Baron Maupertuis. The next year Holmes served the King of Scandinavia. The following year saw the cases involving both the reigning house of Holland and that of Bohemia, as well as the affair of the Vatican Cameos. Business was poor from then until after the Great Return in 1893. But then, beginning with the case of the papers of ex-President Murillo and the arrest of Huret, the Boulevard Assassin, Holmes was constantly active in affairs which brought him decorations, gifts from royalty, offers of knighthood—and, by inference, considerable fees. It is no wonder that he was able to retire in 1903 to follow the gentlemanly pursuit of farming. Raising blooded stock—even if it is only bees—has never been a lucrative occupation for gentlemen, and Holmes had need of a comfortable fortune to pursue his hobby.

This fortune was built up, as I have shown, by an extraordinary combination of shrewdness and showmanship, not unspiced with chicanery. And it is this admixture of trickiness which puts Holmes in a class by himself among detectives. I have already alluded to his lifelong habit of shaking down the detective force. Let me close with a brief reference to two of the cases particularized in the Writings.

The first of these is the case of Silver Blaze, a most reprehensible proceeding, in which Holmes was not only party to the running of a nobbled horse but probably also to a much

did not find out until the date of the *Greek Interpreter* that Holmes had a brother. Nor, even then, though their acquaintance had been "long and intimate" did Holmes think it safe to tell Watson more than the barest facts about Mycroft. "I did not know you quite so well in those days," chuckled Holmes when, in 1895, he again mentioned the fact of his brother's existence.

Sherlock Holmes as "a plump and dapper blade" (*Harper's Weekly*, 1893)

more serious offense. All facts point to the conclusion that Holmes with the connivance of Mr. Silas Brown, and probably with that of Lord Backwater, whose horse, Desborough, ran in the same race (and who is implicated by the fact that he later recommended Mr. Holmes to the Noble Bachelor) deliberately framed the Wessex Plate. Between them they bet large sums of money on Silver Blaze, so that the odds shortened from 15-to-1 to 3-to-1 and then, as the conspirators became certain that Silver Blaze would run and that Backwater's jockey actually could be trusted to pull Desborough as arranged—as, in the closing moments, they put their last farthing on the nose of Silver Blaze—to 5-to-4. It is probable that no small portion of the Holmes fortune could be traced to this operation, and one would give much to know what he, Backwater and Brown had to say to one another when Holmes excused himself from Col. Ross and (pleading that he wanted to put five shillings on the next race) went to meet his guilty co-operators behind the grandstand.

The other case is that in which Holmes received the largest fee mentioned specifically in the Canon: the adventure of the *Priory School*. In this affair Holmes was engaged in the first instance by one client, Dr. Thorneycroft Huxtable, headmaster of the school in question. Yet he wound up by accepting his principal fee for the compounding of a felony from His Grace the Duke of Holdernesse. It is true that his first claim upon that nobleman was for two rewards, totaling £6000 for information as to the whereabouts of the missing child and the names of the persons who had him in custody. But Holmes allowed the Duke to buy for an *additional* £6000 his complete acquiescence in a scheme not only to conceal the guilt and aid the escape of James Wilder as an accessory before the fact of murder, but to conceal the guilt of the Duke himself as accessory after the fact. More, Holmes even went so far as to counsel His Grace of Holdernesse to further crime in purchasing the silence of the actual striker of the blow. Surely it will be conceded that in this case, at least, Mr. Sherlock Holmes justified the prediction of Justice of the Peace Trevor, "It seems to me that all the detectives of fact or of fiction would be children in your hands."

And if Mr. Holmes, pausing by chance in the labors of bee keeping on the downs near Eastbourne to favor an octogenarian rheumatic twinge, should see these lines, I know he will not mind. He has only to console himself with that Horatian [82] maxim which he once quoted to Dr. Watson:

> *"Populus me sibilat; at mihi plaudo*
> *Ipse domi, simul ac nummos contemplor in arca."*

[82] *Satires,* I, 66–67.

ON THE EMOTIONAL GEOLOGY
OF BAKER STREET

By ELMER DAVIS

THE CASUAL READER may feel that a chapter on the emotions, the gentler emotions, in Baker Street should resemble the well known chapter on the snakes in Iceland. There can be no doubt that to Sherlock Holmes, from any practical viewpoint, Mrs. Hudson was always The Woman; and during a large part of his life to Dr. Watson as well. But the research of scholars has demonstrated that the casual and superficial reader of the sacred writings often misses something of paramount importance; and such may well be the case with Holmes's well known indifference to women.

S. C. Roberts has shown [1] that Holmes could be not only courteous but cordial to women, and has noted the significant fact that the women who particularly elicited his sympathetic attention were usually named Violet. The romance with Victor Trevor's sister which he infers, a romance frustrated by her incautious visit to diphtheritic Birmingham, is plausible enough; but does it explain all? I think not. How often does a man remain faithful all his life to the memory of the lost sweetheart of his youth? The thing has happened; Washington Irving, I believe, was thus faithful (in his fashion), and granted Holmes's coldly intellectual temperament, one might suppose that it happened in his case too.

But on this point Holmes was not coldly intellectual. "He never spoke of the softer emotions," Watson records, "save with a gibe and a sneer." [2] The implications of this remark have been strangely overlooked; such bitterness is not the

[1] *Baker Street Studies*, London, 1934.　　　[2] *A Scandal in Bohemia*.

fruit of mere indifference. It has a definitely neurotic flavor; and it may be that Roberts has done the memory of Violet Trevor a grave disservice by exhuming her from the oblivion in which Holmes charitably left her.

For the landscape of the emotions, it must be remembered, is usually of volcanic origin. Modern realistic novelists, in their preoccupation with the slow erosions and sedimentations of married life, have tended to obscure this truth. These more gradual forces have their effect, greater or less in individual cases; but the average man or woman lives (often without realizing it) in an emotional realm whose topography has been determined by some great explosion of the past—some earth-shaking eruption of white-hot lava which slowly cooled and hardened into basalt cliffs that form the dominant features of the terrain for years after. Erosion may slowly and slightly soften their craggy outlines, but only a subsequent eruption can really change the landscape, and even then the lava of the earlier flow remains, a stubbornly indestructible foundation, shaping in some degree the outline of the superstructure.

Holmes seems to have been a one-eruption man; and the nature of that volcanic upheaval, which left him with nothing but gibes and sneers for the softer passions, may perhaps be inferred from his tremendous and unique admiration for Irene Adler.[3] Her intelligence, her coolness, her resource, her sportsmanship and good humor—all these captivated him; that her reputation was "dubious and questionable," by the standards of the eighties, disturbed him not at all. Watson, true to the *mores* of his time, was less tolerant. But Holmes was also, in many respects, a man of his time; his charitable attitude toward the erring Irene is explicable only on the hypothesis of some emotional experience which had disgusted him with mere "virtue," and had burned into him the great truth that

[3] *Ibid.*

desire is no guarantee of intellectual compatibility, or indeed of any intellect at all.

That the Violet Trevor whom Roberts posits may have been the vehicle of this experience is not, on the face of things, improbable. Her brother Victor was no ball of fire; and her father, though his early life had been adventurous enough, seems to have been only a passive plaything of Chance. Violet, brought up in the peaceful rural life of Donnithorpe by a father who had had all the excitement and irregularity in life that he ever wanted, was quite possibly an attractive and blameless nitwit; and Holmes's discovery of her stupidity or lack of spirit may well have disgusted him with an emotion which such a woman—even such a woman—could inspire. From this viewpoint his apparently irrelevant reference to the circumstances of her death may have been no mere sentimental reminiscence, but a prayer of thanksgiving. The epidemic of diphtheria in Birmingham was a godsend to Holmes, who certainly could never have become the Holmes of history if hampered by such a wife.

There remains the more obscure, perhaps the more sinister problem of the love life of Watson.

Roberts's *Doctor Watson* [4] is the fullest and best, but not yet the definitive biography of this enigmatic figure—in some aspects perhaps the most typical of late-Victorian middle-class Englishmen—behind whose commonplace and stodgy front research reveals depths of psychological complexity still unplumbed. The notorious untrustworthiness of his memory does not explain all the discrepancies in the autobiographical data which he has furnished; the man seems to have been capable not only of deception but of self-deception. Father Knox remarks on some of Holmes's explanations as good

[4] *Doctor Watson*, by S. C. Roberts, London, 1931.

enough for Watson, but absurd to the more penetrating eye.[5] What then shall be said of Watson's explanations? Good enough for Holmes—nay more, good enough for Watson, or for the moral censor in Watson's consciousness; too damnably good for the investigator, who after he has probed his deepest still feels doubtful if he has really come upon the truth. What was too uncomfortable Watson could forget, and forget convincingly; it is hardly too much to say that latent in his character, held in check only by his incurable predilection for respectability, there was a potential Poderjay.

Accordingly it is difficult to accept the charitable explanation offered by Miss Helen Simpson [6] of the scandal which cut short Watson's promising career at St. Bartholomew's Hospital, and drove him into the Indian Army. "Watson himself is silent," she concedes; and when Watson is silent, there is usually a reason. She visualizes "some frailer member of the other sex making charges against Watson, either with a view to blackmail or revenge." Revenge for what—seduction, or disinclination to seduce? The geologist of the emotions will prefer a different hypothesis; in this affair Watson was the frailer member, and he never forgot the lesson that it taught him.

Several times he mentions some lovely young girl who was "completely under the influence" of some scoundrel—a phrase whose abhorrent implication, half a century ago, needs no underlining. Manners were different then; yet those with even juvenile or hearsay memories of that time cannot quite believe that women who were completely under masculine influence could have been very numerous. Does not the poorly concealed relish of Watson's references to such a situation disguise a nostalgic longing for some woman who would be completely under Watson's influence, as some woman in the past had not? May not his cold aloofness to-

[5] *Baker Street Studies.*   [6] *Ibid.*

ward Irene Adler reflect incurable distrust and hostility toward a woman who could deal as she chose with men and, even in the eighties, come off with all the honors? *Had not some such woman dealt with Watson?* Had not the house man at Bart's fallen insanely in love with some actress or singer who presently tired of him; and was it not his continued pursuit of her—undissuadable, shameless, ridiculous, and above all unconcealed—that cost him his position and his career? Once bitten, he was twice shy.

Years later Watson found solace—for a time—with a more tractable woman. But it is impossible to agree with the view that Watson's first marriage was unusually happy. For a year or so it may have been; but thereafter there enters the problem of what Roberts terms the "intermittent resumption of partnership with Holmes." Mrs. Watson, as any married man must realize, would have called it something much stronger, if by that time she had still been at all interested in her husband. Most commentators agree that Mrs. Watson "maintained a continuous sympathy" with this friendship and collaboration; which if true would prove her more inhuman than the misogynist Holmes. What woman who loves her husband would gladly acquiesce in his repeated absences from home, of indefinite duration and on the shortest notice? The conclusion is inescapable that the romance engendered by the pursuit of the Agra treasure [7] was soon worn away by the stresses of domesticity; that either Mary Morstan Watson was always glad enough to see her husband leave home, or that he was deliberately and cruelly blind to her dissatisfaction, and was careful to leave no hint of it in the record.

The evidence is indeed susceptible of a darker interpretation. Mrs. Watson's increasingly frequent absences from home after a year or two of marriage may suggest that home life had become intolerable to her; possibly, even, that she (or

[7] *The Sign of the Four.*

her husband) had been attracted elsewhere. Of such an irregularity, had it befallen his wife or *a fortiori* himself, we
may be sure that Dr. Watson would have said not a word, as
becomes the strong silent Englishman. But this is no more
than a possibility; the logic of the case points to increasing
boredom rather than active estrangement; and if Watson
showed the "ravages of grief and worry" after his wife's
death, as Roberts suggests, his dominant emotion may have
been remorse rather than bereaved desolation.

Some years after Mary Morstan Watson's death her husband remarried, an event which seems to have taken place
about the end of 1902. Who was the lady? Roberts suggests that she was Miss Violet de Merville, one-time fiancée
of the wicked Baron Adelbert von Gruner, and protégée of
that Illustrious Client [8] whose identity, if it was ever in any
doubt, is in doubt no longer. But the evidence adduced in support of this theory is mere inference, and the probabilities are
powerfully against it. Watson, at the time of his second
marriage, was at least fifty. Miss de Merville, with "the
ethereal other-world beauty of a fanatic" and a "will of iron,"
was not the woman to attract a prudent middle-aged widower
who liked domestic comfort. If Watson really had that "experience of women extending over many nations and three
separate continents" of which he boasts in *The Sign of the
Four* (Roberts has managed to cast grave doubt on two of the
continents) he must have known that she was more dangerous
than dynamite, supremely a woman to avoid. Moreover, so
solidly conventional a late Victorian would have been unlikely to want to marry a woman who had "doted upon"
and "been obsessed by" the infamous von Gruner; nor, perhaps, would he have felt too comfortable about her enlist-
ment of the interest, however chivalrous and paternal, of his
sovereign, when that sovereign was Edward VII.

[8] *The Illustrious Client.*

A two-minute sketch of Sherlock Holmes, by Frederic Dorr Steele
(by permission of the artist)

But there is direct evidence which renders this theory completely untenable. When Sir James Damery, having reported to Holmes the successful disenchantment of Miss de Merville, left the rooms on Baker Street, Watson left with him, "as I was myself overdue." Overdue where? Not at the bedside of a patient; since Holmes's distant cousin Dr. Verner had bought up his practise, eight years earlier, he had not returned to his profession. Overdue, obviously (in view of his marriage soon after) in the drawing-room of a fiancée who did not take his involvement in Holmes's affairs as lightly as did Mary Morstan Watson. And now appears the significance of a detail which Roberts unaccountably dismisses as of small importance—Watson's departure from Baker Street in September 1902 to quarters of his own.

This happened before Watson met Miss de Merville—if indeed he ever met her at all, of which we have not the slightest proof. Can it be doubted that the second Mrs. Watson put her foot down well in advance of the ceremony? That she made it a condition precedent of her acceptance that her husband should have no more to do with "the sort of people you knew before we were married"—*i.e.* conspicuously with Sherlock Holmes? The probability is supported by Holmes's own words in *The Blanched Soldier:* "The good Watson had lately deserted me for a wife, the only selfish action which I recall in our association." The date makes it clear that this refers to the second marriage; the first could hardly have been called selfish from Holmes's point of view because Mary Morstan Watson was always glad, for whatever reason, to have her husband out of the house. The second Mrs. Watson was obviously made of sterner stuff, and readers with a taste for the morbid may speculate, if they like, on what she said to the Doctor when at last he appeared that evening, overdue, and confessed that he had been detained by one of Sherlock Holmes's cases, involving another woman.

Who was this resolute female? Obviously some one who had known the first Mrs. Watson, and who had herself observed and pondered on the Doctor's frequent dartings away from the fireside. Not a relative, for Mary Morstan "had no relatives in England"; and presumably a younger woman. Men in the forties marry women near their own age, if they are wise; but widowers in the fifties are more likely to be attracted to youth. Was she not, most plausibly, one of the daughters of that Mrs. Cecil Forrester in whose household Mary Morstan was the governess when Watson met her? [9] Mr. Cecil S. Forester, the English novelist and historian, is possibly related to the family, and might clear up the uncertainty for us. At any rate, it was certainly a woman who knew enough about the first marriage to tell the amorous doctor, "I don't intend to go through what poor Mary suffered"; or, on the alternative hypothesis that it was the first Mrs. Watson rather than her husband whose love grew cold, "I care enough for you to want you to stay at home."

Watson, then, ultimately paid the price of his failure to make his first marriage a success; Watson and more than Watson. For this was the end of the world-famous partnership. Vincent Starrett shows [10] that Roberts is in error in dating Holmes's retirement to bee-keeping in Sussex in 1907; it happened in 1904, within two years of Watson's remarriage. Is it not probable that after a quarter of a century of practise Holmes had found his cases increasingly monotonous, history repeating itself (the close resemblance between *The Three Garridebs* and *The Red-Headed League* is not the only instance); that he was no longer inclined to go on with his work when it could no longer be set down in that public record which he always (but with what transparent insincerity!) pretended to scorn? It is significant that the final adventure of the two (*His Last Bow*, the events of which occurred in

[9] *The Sign of the Four.*   [10] *Baker Street Studies.*

August 1914) is chronicled by an unknown third person, who doubtless received from Watson a story which Watson dared not write himself; and that (as has been noted by various students who apparently missed the implication) Holmes and Watson had not met for some years previously.

There is a corollary of the highest importance. What became of that famous tin dispatch box in the vaults of Cox & Company, bankers, of Charing Cross, in which were preserved the records of the unpublished cases of Sherlock Holmes? [11] Presumably on Watson's death it passed to his wife; so strong-minded a woman would hardly have permitted him to will anything out of the family, even if in her eyes it had no value. What did she do with it? In a fit of unreasoning emotion she may have burned the papers; possibly she even sold them to the rag man. If we are never to hear the story of the politician, the lighthouse, and the trained cormorant; of the singular adventure of the Grice Patersons in the island of Uffa; of the giant rat of Sumatra, for which a world so largely dominated by giant rats of one sort or another is perhaps at last prepared—if all that is lost to mankind forever, the fault lies with the second Mrs. Watson . . . Or, just possibly, does that collection of papers still exist, gathering dust in an attic somewhere? If Mr. Cecil S. Forester has any influence with his female relatives, we soon may know.

[11] *Thor Bridge.*

DR. WATSON'S SECRET

By Jane Nightwork

ONE OF MY fellow members has spoken of the secret in Sherlock Holmes's life, his American connection. Perhaps it is permissible now to remark upon an even more carefully hidden arcanum, Dr. Watson's clandestine marriage.

The infuriating inconsistencies of Watsonian chronology have cost scholars many a megrim. The more carefully we examine them the more deeply confused they seem. Some authorities (*e. g.* Miss Dorothy Sayers) have attempted to account for slips on the theory that Watson misread his own handwriting in his notes.[1] Others (*e. g.* Mr. S. C. Roberts) have fallen back upon the regrettable hypothesis that occasionally the Doctor was not "in his normal, business-like condition." [2] Still others (*e. g.* Mr. R. E. Balfour) reject from the canon stories that appear incompatible.[3] It is true that *The Sign of the Four* begins with neither Holmes nor Watson in completely rational state. Watson had had Beaune for lunch, which affected him so that he thought it was his leg that pained him (instead of his shoulder). Holmes had taken a 7 per cent solution of cocaine. Holmes's addiction to the drug was (at that period) habitual; but why had Watson taken the Beaune on that particular day? We shall see. It was to screw up his courage for an imminent ordeal.

Let me digress a moment, at the risk of repeating matter familiar to all genuine Holmesians, to note a few of the outstanding anomalies which must be reconciled. The case of

[1] The Dates in *The Red-Headed League*, *Colophon*, vol. v, pt. 17, 1934.
[2] *Doctor Watson*, by S. C. Roberts, London, 1931.
[3] New Light on Dr. Watson's Early Works, *Cambridge Review*, 2 Nov., 1934.

The Noble Bachelor is dated (by the hotel bill, the high autumnal winds, and the age of Lord St. Simon) as October 1887. This, Watson says, was "a few weeks before my own marriage." And the somewhat elastic time-allusions in *The Stockbroker's Clerk* also imply that the wedding took place late in the year. On the other hand both *The Crooked Man* and *The Naval Treaty* distinctly suggest that the marriage was in the spring or early summer.

How may these contradictions be reconciled? Surely not by the assumption that good old methodical Watson ("the one fixed point in a changing age") [4] was simply careless or muddled. Watson wove a tangled web in his chronology because he was deliberately trying to deceive. Why not adopt the reiterated thesis of the master himself: when you have excluded the impossible, whatever remains, *however improbable*, must be the truth. The truth must be that Watson had contracted a secret marriage with Mary Morstan, some time before the adventure of *The Sign of the Four*. His allusions are perfectly comprehensible if we realize that he is sometimes referring to the actual date of that union; and sometimes to the purely fictitious occasion (late in the autumn) which he and his wife agreed to represent to their friends as the time of the nuptial.

The extraordinary year 1887 is crucial in any study of Holmes-Watson history. All scholars have noted the exceptional number of important cases assigned to this year. Particularly, beginning early in February, there was the business of the Netherland-Sumatra Company [5] which took Holmes abroad. Watson, now in full health and vigor, did not spend his entire life sitting in Baker Street, or even at his club playing billiards with Thurston. How and when he first met Mary Morstan we do not know; probably in connection with the earlier case when Holmes was "of some slight service" to

[4] *His Last Bow.*   [5] *The Reigate Squires.*

her employer, Mrs. Cecil Forrester.[6]   (I like to think, incidentally, that Mrs. Forrester's "tranquil English home," with the stained glass in the front door, the barometer and the bright stair-rods, was in Knatchbull Road, Camberwell, for which Boucicault named the villain in *After Dark*.)   At any rate, both Watson and Miss Morstan were lonely and financially insecure.   Their romance was immediate, but both were afraid to admit it to their associates.   Miss Morstan would lose her position; Watson would incur the annoyance of the misogynist Sherlock.

I will be as brief as possible, for once this hypothesis is grasped, all experienced Watsonians will observe the wealth of corroborating circumstances.   Let us reexamine the chronology of the year 1887.

First of all, we cannot accept Mr. Roberts's conclusion that *The Sign of the Four* belongs to 1886.   The facts are positive: Mary Morstan had received six pearls, one every year, beginning in May '82.   She calls that "about six years ago"; in reality it was only just over five years, but she thought of it as six because she had that number of pearls.   Also she says her father disappeared in "December 1878—nearly ten years ago." From the beginning of the year '87 her grieving heart would naturally think of the bereavement as in its tenth year.   Even in her sorrow her precise mind could not reckon it so until the calendar year '87.   I accept July 1887 as the date of *The Sign of the Four* adventure—preferring to follow the postmark on Sholto's letter rather than Watson's subsequent reference to a "September evening."   As for the yellow fog (rare in July, surely?) seen by Holmes, it was at least 7 per cent cocaine.   But mark well: we now have for the first time an explanation of Watson's mysterious telegram that morning. He and Mary Morstan Watson, weary of meeting by stealth, had at last decided to break their news to Holmes.   The mys-

[6] *The Sign of the Four.*

tery of the pearls, which they had often discussed, was an additional motive. Watson had gone to the Wigmore Street Post Office (as a matter of fact isn't it just around the corner in Wimpole Street?) not primarily to *send* a wire but to receive one. Addressed *Poste Restante* was a message from Mary. She had received the puzzling letter from Thaddeus Sholto and appealed to her husband for advice. He wired back telling her to come to Baker Street. And the Beaune for lunch was his attempt to fortify himself for the revelation to come. Observe, throughout the narrative, how slyly old Watson concealed from Sherlock the fact that he and Mary were already intimate.

Recapitulate, then, the events of 1887. Early in the year, probably February or March, while Holmes was absent in the Netherland-Sumatra business, Watson and Mary Morstan were secretly married. They met as and when they could, but told no one. Their anxious and surreptitious bliss was interrupted by the news (April 14) that Holmes was ill in Lyons. Watson hurried to France, he and Sherlock returned together, and spent April 25–27 at Reigate.[1] Perhaps this was followed by the matter of the Grice Patersons in the island of Uffa—where *is* Uffa, by the way? But if it is (as it sounds) in the Hebrides, Shetlands or Orkneys, the Grice Patersons would have sense enough not to go there until midsummer.

Holmes was in aggressive spirits after the Reigate visit; Watson was gloomy. His secret preyed on his mind; he wrote many letters to Mary. (He had in his desk "a sheet of stamps and a thick bundle of postcards.") At the time of the Jubilee (June 21) it was the shooting of the V. R. into the wall that finally convinced Watson he must make a break. "With me there is a limit," he said in *The Musgrave Ritual*. He made up his mind to take charge of his own check-book, find a home, and resume practice. *The Sign of the Four*, coming just when

[1] *The Reigate Squires.*

it did (July 8) was a happy coincidence. His anxieties about Miss Morstan becoming heiress of the Agra treasure were just as sincere as if he had really been only a suitor. Since their marriage had been concealed, everyone would be sure to think him a fortune-hunter.

After the excitement was over, the pair went through the appearance of a formal engagement for the benefit of Holmes and Mrs. Forrester (not to say Mrs. Hudson.) May it not have been Watson's now frequent visits to Knatchbull Road that brought the Camberwell Poisoning to Holmes's attention? No doubt soon after *The Sign of the Four* Mary had her summer vacation, and she and the Doctor used this for a furtive honeymoon—perhaps in "the glades of the New Forest"; Southsea would have been a little too public. So when the elated husband, narrating the *Five Orange Pips*, speaks of his wife he forgets that she was not at that time known as such. It was not until November that he found a home of his own, left Baker Street and set up housekeeping in Paddington. *The Noble Bachelor* affair in October preceded by a few weeks what they agreed to call their "marriage." They simply told their friends, about Guy Fawkes Day, that they were going to slip off quietly to a registry office. Probably the medical practice was bought as of January 1, 1888.

Sitting on a pile of cushions with plenty of shag tobacco, and following the master's cardinal principle, the preceding seems to me the only possible solution. This chronology harmonizes many apparently conflicting statements. It makes intelligible the allusions at the beginning of *A Scandal in Bohemia* (March 20–22, 1888). It gives sense to Watson's eagerness that Sherlock should become interested in Violet Hunter; how delightful, the Doctor thought naïvely, if he and Holmes should both marry governesses—and alumnæ of the same agency, for undoubtedly Mary, too, had been a client

of Westaway's. When the case of *The Stockbroker's Clerk*
came along in June '88, Watson jumped at the chance to go to
Birmingham with Holmes. He thought he might be able to
persuade Sherlock to run out to Walsall (only 8 miles away)
to see Miss Hunter at the school where she was headmistress.

I must not weary you in the matter of Dr. Watson's private
affairs; but there is just one more point which is essential to
mention. We were arguing that the correct date of *The Sign
of the Four* is July (1887) rather than September. The most
apparently damning evidence against July has been ingeniously
pointed out by Mr. H. W. Bell in that indispensable little
volume *Baker Street Studies*.[8] Holmes insisted on Athelney
Jones staying for dinner—for which he had ordered "oysters
and a brace of grouse." Neither of these are in season in July.
But is not this precisely what Holmes meant by his following
remark to Watson: "You have never yet recognized my
merits as a housekeeper." Surely he was calling attention to
his cunning in being able to procure these luxuries when they
were impossible for most people.

If my suggestion is acceptable that Dr. Watson and Miss
Morstan had been secretly married in the spring but agreed
to pretend that it didn't happen until autumn, other chronological reconciliations are possible. We now see that the
Naval Treaty (in "the July which immediately succeeded my
marriage"—viz., the next July after their collusive wedding-
date in November) must have been in July '88. The treaty
had been drawn up in May of that year, obviously in view of
the illness of Frederick III of Germany and the probable
succession of the young Kaiser—whose temperament was only
too likely to necessitate readjustments of the European balance
of power. There were two other cases in that month, you remember: *The Second Stain* and *The Tired Captain*. Watson's ingrained mixture of duplicity and naïveté in regard to

[8] *Baker Street Studies*, London, 1934.

the date of the Morstan marriage is delightfully shown when years later he sets down the story of *The Second Stain*. It happened, he says, "in a year, and even in a decade, that shall be nameless"—quite oblivious that in his earlier reference he had unmistakably dated and identified the episode.

From here on the succession of events is fairly plain. *A Case of Identity* is evidently late spring of '88. *The Crooked Man* is the summer of '88. Myself I should prefer to place *The Engineer's Thumb* in '88 ("not long after my marriage," he says), but Watson positively assigns it to summer '89. *The Valley of Fear* must have been in January '89; followed in June by *The Man with the Twisted Lip* and that autumn by the great *Hound of the Baskervilles*. Watson's long absence from home and practice while visiting Baskerville Hall may well have been another trial of Mrs. Watson's disposition; but we find her in June 1890 generously urging the Doctor to accompany Holmes to Boscombe Valley. Immediately after returning from Boscombe Valley Holmes became interested in *The Lost Special* (one of the cases outside the legitimate canon, never recorded by Watson).[9] And 1890 closes with *The Red-Headed League* and *The Blue Carbuncle;* it is pleasant to think of Holmes and Watson sitting down cheerfully to the post-Christmas goose: their last intimacy before the tragic events of April and May 1891.

It is also possible to believe that Watson's innocent and timid subterfuge of the secret marriage quite escaped Holmes's attention. Sherlock had grown into the habit of regarding Watson as a lay figure who would never do the unexpected; the great detective was intensely absorbed in his own ideas and except on those mischievous occasions when he turned the full focus of his observation upon his companion he was not likely to speculate much on Watson's private thoughts. And a man of Watson's upright, simple and candid nature, once

[9] *Round the Fire Stories*, by A. Conan Doyle, London, 1908.

Sidney Paget's Holmes and Watson (from "The Adventure of the Blue Carbuncle," courtesy of Harper & Brothers)

driven in upon himself, can develop surprising foxiness. It pleases me to think that the self-sacrificing Doctor was dashing enough to seize the romance that came his way. His pangs, his honorable yearnings, his necessities for concealment, gave him (every student has noticed) a special tenderness for women in distress. In brooding the problem of his later marriage one could be tempted to wish that the superb Grace Dunbar of *Thor Bridge* might have been the second Mrs. Watson. (She also had been a governess.) But knowing Senator Neil Gibson, it is unlikely.

Having caused endless embarrassment by his transparent attempts to disguise the facts of his first marriage, no wonder Watson said nothing whatever about the second. And apropos the second matrimony (which all scholars agree to place about the end of 1902) it is interesting to note that Watson chose to establish his renewed ménage in Queen Anne Street. It crosses Harley Street, is only a stroll from 221B, and still very near the Wigmore Street Post Office. The other most famous resident of that immediate neighborhood is *The Young Man with the Cream Tarts*.

THE CARE AND FEEDING
OF SHERLOCK HOLMES

By Earle F. Walbridge

His diet was usually of the sparest.

—The Yellow Face

I had very clear recollections of days and nights without a thought of food.

—The Valley of Fear

Breakfast, to paraphrase one of the lesser poets, was Sherlock Holmes's best meal.   There are at least two dozen references to it in the saga.   Breakfast was frequently the only meal he permitted himself when the game was afoot, and the long-suffering Watson was obliged, as usual, to take the consequences.   While it is true that Mrs. Hudson's cuisine was a little limited, she had—in the words of Holmes's perfect tribute—as good an idea of breakfast as a Scotchwoman.[1]   She may have extended herself a bit on this particular morning, what with curried chicken, ham and eggs, toast, tea and coffee all on one occasion (an occasion, be it remembered, on which Percy Phelps was moved to unseemly antics, though his plate was as empty as a Barmecide's), but she could always be depended on for fresh relays of rashers and eggs. ("Your breakfast has completed the cure," muttered the epollicate engineer to Holmes gratefully.[2])   He once cabled all the way from Montpellier to Mrs. Hudson to put forth her best efforts for two hungry travellers next day at 7:30;[3] whether ante- or post-meridian was not indicated.   Of course

[1] *The Naval Treaty.*   [2] *The Engineer's Thumb.*
[3] *Lady Frances Carfax.*

this was long before the era of European skyways, and Holmes may have had dinner in mind.

These, however, were the good days. On others, breakfast was likely to be a sketchy and interrupted affair, not conducive to proper digestion. Watson was surprised and resentful, early in April of 1883, to be roused at 7:15 A.M., probably considering Holmes's excuse—that Mrs. Hudson had been knocked up—as worse than frivolous;[4] nor, probably, did he find Dr. Grimesby Roylott's poker-twisting feats the most calming of morning *apéritifs*. There was never any guaranty that breakfast would be followed by the usual sequence of meals. Holmes might go charging down to Dartmoor, for instance, and there would be nothing to eat until nightfall—not, in this case, even a forkful of Ned Hunter's soporific curried mutton.[5] On at least one occasion Holmes must have felt that apologies were in order, when he had ravished Watson by telegram from Mrs. Watson's bed and breakfast board, to accompany him to Boscombe Valley. He blamed Lestrade, who had referred the case to him—"and hence it is that two middle-aged gentlemen are flying westward at fifty miles an hour instead of quietly digesting their breakfasts at home."[6] Compunction seized him occasionally; he saw to it once that cocoa was brewed (probably Epps', grateful and comforting) and poured down Watson's throat at daybreak; foreseeing that there would be no more nourishment until they had a meal of sorts, perhaps as forbidding and squalid as the inn itself, in the kitchen of The Game Cock.[7] He brewed coffee for Watson and Stanley Hopkins over a spirit lamp before they set out for Yoxley Old Place, where they undoubtedly lunched on cutlets—provided that The-Professor-It-Was-She did not consume them

[4] *The Speckled Band.*   [5] *Silver Blaze.*
[6] *The Boscombe Valley Mystery.*   [7] *The Priory School.*

all *in camera*.[8] It was not that Holmes did not appreciate good food. Victor Trevor's father had a tolerable cook at his place in Donnithorpe, Norfolk,[9] and it was Holmes's opinion that "he would be a fastidious man who could not put in a pleasant month there." (This was the Victor Trevor whose bullpup froze onto Holmes's undergraduate ankle). In the way of catering in the Baker Street rooms, he could do it when he chose, as though Mrs. Hudson had been Mrs. Todgers herself. Witness his stuffing Athelney Jones with oysters and grouse, and something a little choice in white wines;[10] or the "quite epicurean little cold supper"[11] (of grouse, pheasant, *pâté-de-foie-gras*, and a couple of ancient and cobwebby bottles[12]) into which the Noble Bachelor refused to sink so much as one ducal tooth. Oysters, in fact, were one of Holmes's little weaknesses. He babbled of them after a three-day fast ("Shall the world, then, be overrun by oysters? No, no; horrible!");[13] and they may have been responsible for the "occasional indiscretions" which led to his breakdown and his involving Watson in the Cornish horror.[14] Vegetables he apparently considered an even worse horror. He knew nothing of practical gardening,[15] and evidently cared less. Some experience with British beetroot, vegetable marrow or boiled potato must have seared his soul. The roast beef of old England was something else again; he once repaired to Simpson's-in-the-Strand to recoup his energies with

---

[8] *The Golden Pince-Nez.*   [9] *The "Gloria Scott."*
[10] *The Sign of the Four.*   [11] *The Noble Bachelor.*
[12] Probably a comet vintage. Cf. *The Stock-Broker's Clerk.* Judging from the amount of time they spent in Turkish baths, a good deal of unrecorded tippling must have gone in Baker Street. It is likely that Mary Morstan Watson abolished the tantalus in short order. Holmes and Watson sat in the Strasburg *salle-à-manger* arguing for half an hour during "The Final Problem." But was it solicitude for Watson, or the prospect of more *pâté*, that detained Holmes so long?
[13] *The Dying Detective.*   [14] *The Devil's Foot.*
[15] *A Study in Scarlet.* But he evidently has a kitchen-garden on the Sussex downs now.

a cut off the joint.[16] A cold side of beef always reposed on the sideboard,[17] and the pseudo-landlady, the false Dmitri, Mrs. Turner (*sic*) makes her sole appearance in the saga with a tray of beef and beer.[18]

Food was renounced altogether when he was keen on a case. "When will you be pleased to dine, Mr. Holmes?", Mrs. Hudson would ask. "Seven-thirty, the day after tomorrow," said he.[19] Less epigrammatically, he would snap "At present I cannot spare energy and nerve force for digestion" to Watson's medical remonstrances. "You are knocking yourself up, old man," Watson pleaded,[20] and a flush probably dyed Sherlock's sallow cheeks.[21] But he remained firm. In hiding on the Baskerville moors, he commissioned young Cartwright to bring him a clean collar and a loaf of bread. Cartwright, apparently on his own responsibility, added a tinned tongue and two tins of preserved peaches. They remained untouched.[22]

On the other hand, business and breakfast sometimes mingled harmoniously. After a healthful session of pig-sticking he returned with an excellent appetite.[23] "There can be no question, my dear Watson, of the value of exercise before breakfast," he exclaimed.

Holmes would have been no true-born Englishman had he not wanted his tea occasionally. He accepted a 5:30 cup from Watson;[24] helped himself to a cup on another occasion;[25] and fortified Watson with tea one hot afternoon before taking him to meet his brother,[26] warning the doctor that the Diogenes Club was the queerest club in London, and Mycroft one of the queerest men. The sight of him at high tea, demolishing four eggs and filling his mouth with toast, warmed the cockles of

[16] *The Dying Detective.* [17] *The Beryl Coronet.*
[18] *A Scandal in Bohemia.* [19] *The Mazarin Stone.*
[20] *The Sign of the Four.* [21] *The Five Orange Pips.*
[22] *The Hound of the Baskervilles.* [23] *Black Peter.*
[24] *The Sign of the Four.*
[25] *The Beryl Coronet.* This is the only recorded instance in English fiction in which tea was not drunk "thirstily." [26] *The Greek Interpreter.*

Watson's foolish heart.[27] Nor did he refuse Mrs. St. Clair's cold supper at The Cedars, Kent, where a large and comfortable double-bedded room had been placed at their disposal, and Watson was quickly between the sheets.[28]

At times Holmes would twit his faithful companion humorously, attributing to him his own shortcomings. "By Jove! my dear fellow," he exclaimed. "It is nearly nine, and the landlady babbled of green peas at seven-thirty. What with your eternal tobacco, Watson, and your irregularity at meals, I expect that you will get notice to quit, and that I shall share your downfall." [29] But then he would regale the doctor with coffee and *curaçao* at Goldini's in Kensington; [30] or with carboniferous roast goose, although even then he postponed the feast from dinner to supper-time. (The bird was really the property of Mr. Henry Baker, but Mr. Baker was satisfied when Holmes gave him a fresh goose and restored his lost hat).[31]

On what meat does our Sherlock feed, at his villa on the southern slope of the Sussex downs—or on what besides the honey from his bees? He is ninetyish, now, and Mrs. Hudson must be a centenarian. But honey is a bland food, and spreads easily on toast from her never-failing rack. Stands the Church clock at ten to three, and there is honey still for tea.

[27] *The Valley of Fear.*   [28] *The Man With the Twisted Lip.*
[29] *The Three Students.*   [30] *The Bruce-Partington Plans.*
[31] *The Blue Carbuncle.*

Watson as *Boobus Britannicus* (drawing by Arthur I. Keller for "The Valley of Fear," New York, 1914, courtesy of Doubleday, Doran & Co.)

THREE IDENTIFICATIONS:
LAURISTON GARDENS, UPPER SWANDAM LANE, SAXE-COBURG SQUARE

By H. W. Bell

DR. WATSON WHEN writing his reminiscences was often at pains to conceal the locality of a crime. His works contain many instances of such consideration for the feelings of others. We can imagine the annoyance of Mr. Jabez Wilson, for example, if his working hours had been disturbed and his clients frightened away by the irruption of sightseers eager to inspect the tunnel which Vincent Spaulding had laboriously driven under the vaults of the City and Suburban Bank. And the sentiments of the bank-directors themselves are not pleasant to contemplate. Although as a physician Watson might well have been indifferent to resentment on the part of the proprietor of Lauriston Gardens, whose houses were untenanted because of his insanitary neglect of the drains, he did consider the effect of notoriety upon the innocent neighbours. If in the case of Donnithorpe such caution may seem at first thought unnecessary, the elder Trevor being dead and Victor permanently in India, it must be remembered that the house had undoubtedly been sold, and that the new owners would have suffered from the resulting publicity. As for Hurlstone, it is as certain as anything can be that Reginald Musgrave, M.P., would have been offended to the depths of his feudal soul by any mention of the primitive passions to which his house had furnished the setting.

Nowadays, however, the special reasons for Watson's reticence are no longer operative, and a good murder is more likely to enhance property-values than to depress them. The

City and Suburban Bank, if it still maintains its separate
identity, will no longer shudder at reference to an almost
successful robbery of its vaults; rather will it point with pride,
in our more enterprising times, to the fact that its gold was
not stolen. Jabez Wilson has long since left his premises in
Saxe-Coburg Square, and the square itself is much changed.
Donnithorpe has in all likelihood become either a school or a
country club. Birlstone is in ruins. We need therefore feel
no reluctance at the call of duty to identify, so far as we are
able, the localities which Watson has been at such pains to
conceal.

I

NO. 3, LAURISTON GARDENS [1]

This, the scene of Watson's initiation, will always be of
exceptional interest to the student. So far as we are aware,
no attempt has hitherto been made to identify it.

Gregson, in his letter to Holmes, describes No. 3, Lauriston
Gardens as being 'off the Brixton Road.' [2] Although this expression might seem to indicate a location in an intersecting
street, such a notion is negatived by Jefferson Hope's twice
mentioning it as *in* the Brixton Road. [3] Watson's account
should be read:

'. . . this is the Brixton Road, and that is the house . . .' We
were still a hundred yards or so from it, but he insisted upon our
alighting, and we finished our journey upon foot. Number 3,
Lauriston Gardens . . . was one of four which stood back some
little way from the street, two being occupied and two empty.
The latter looked out with three tiers of vacant melancholy windows . . . A small garden . . . separated each of these houses
from the street, and was traversed by a narrow pathway . . .

[1] References in the notes are to the Collected Edition published by John
Murray (vol. I, *Short Stories* [1928], and vol. II, *Long Stories* [1929]).
[2] II, 26.   [3] II, 126, 128.

The garden was bounded by a three-foot brick wall with a fringe of wood rails upon the top . . .[4]

It is clear that although the row of four houses was actually *in* the Brixton Road, yet in a sense it was *off* it, being set back some distance from the pavement. And in fact there is no such group of four houses in any of the streets intersecting the Road. Furthermore, though there are in that thorough-fare itself several pairs of houses, a few groups of three and five, and many more extensive, there is only one which consists precisely of four.

These four houses, it is pleasant to observe, correspond with almost perfect accuracy to Watson's description. They are three storeys in height, and are set back about thirty feet from the pavement, from which one mounts a few steps to the pathway leading to the front door. The gardens are bounded by a three-foot brick wall, upon which, however, the old wooden railing has been replaced by a more durable affair in iron. Some subsequent landlord has apparently made the necessary improvements, for all four houses are now occupied. They are numbered from 314 to 320. Since Watson specified No. 3, we may suppose that No. 318, the third in the row, was the scene of the death of Enoch J. Drebber.

Lest the name 'Lauriston Gardens' should arouse any mis-givings, we reprint here the list of 'Abolished Subsidiary Names' which have in the past diversified the suburban uni-formity of the Brixton Road:

Hamilton place, Holland place, Commerce place, Bowhill terrace, Minerva terrace, Vassall place, Castle terrace, Claremont place, Alfred place, Loudoun place, St. John's grove, The Willows North, Gloucester place, Brixton villas, Berkeley villas, St. John's villas, Agell terrace, Gresham villas, Brixton place, Spencer place, Brighton place, Elizabeth place, Carlton place, Carlton terrace, St. George's place, Ilchester place, St. Ann's terrace, Lawn place,

[4] II, 28.

Grove place, Firgrove place, Woodhall place, Loughboro'
place, Park place, Park terrace, Grosvenor place, Manor terrace,
Manor rise, Commercial place.[5]

Somewhere among the names of these thirty-eight ghostly
terraces, villas, places, and groves, innocent victims of the
passion for uniformity, must be sought the original of which
'Lauriston Gardens' is the alias.

About sixty yards up the Brixton Road from No. 318, and
on the same, or western, side, there was a post-office [6] at least
as late as 1896;[7] and at about an equal distance above the post-
office, across the road, is the Old White Horse, which is undoubtedly the White Hart where, according to P.C. Rance,
there had been a fight at eleven o'clock on the night of
March 3, 1881.[8]

2

UPPER SWANDAM LANE, AND ITS VICINITY

Watson describes Upper Swandam Lane as 'a vile alley
lurking behind the high wharves which line the north side of
the river to the east of London Bridge.' [9] In this sentence the
word 'north' should read 'south,' as we hope to show.[10]

A casual reading of *The Man with the Twisted Lip* undoubtedly gives the impression that Upper Swandam Lane
was situated on the north of the Thames. We are told that
Neville St.Clair was in the habit of returning home every
night 'by the 5.14 from Cannon Street.' [11] Therefore, when
we read that Mrs. St.Clair 'started for the City' after lunch

---

[5] *List of the Streets and Places within the Administrative County of London*, 3rd. ed., 1929, p. 615.   [6] II, 37.
[7] Ordnance Survey Map, London, XI.44 (scale 1:1056, or 5 feet = one
statute mile) ed. 1894–6.   [8] II, 41.   [9] I, 126.
[10] The error was probably deliberate, for he describes the lane as being
'in the furthest east of the City.' Perhaps he was anxious to conceal its
whereabouts from drug-addicts. This would account for the elaborate
pseudonymity in which he veils all the district.   [11] I, 131.

to make some purchases, and then visited the shipping company's office before going back to Lee, we naturally assume
that, since she must have arrived at Cannon Street, she must
have taken the down train at the same station. An examination of the map,[12] however, makes it evident that our assumption is unwarranted.

There is, in fact, no alley on the north side of the Thames
east of London Bridge [13] which in any way satisfies the conditions. The alley must be practicable for a cab, for Watson
drove up to the door of the Bar of Gold, and it must lead to a
railway station, for there is no suggestion that Mrs. St.Clair
had lost her way.[14] All the alleys in the district which Watson indicates run down at right-angles from Lower Thames
Street, and would not be entered except by persons bound for
some definite address in them. Furthermore, it is stated that
Fresno Street, where the shipping office was situated,
'branches out of Upper Swandam Lane', whereas none of the
streets near the river, from Blackfriars Bridge to the Tower,
can be described as branching out of these waterside alleys.

When, however, we cross to the Surrey side we find that
all the requirements in the narrative, except for Paul's Wharf,
are fulfilled. Here, to the east of London Bridge, are two
streets, Pickle Herring Street, and its continuation, Shad
Thames, which, half a century ago, contained a number of
small shipping offices. Walking westwards along these
streets, one passes through an alley, Stoney Lane, leading into
Tooley Street, which, in turn, is the direct approach to London
Bridge Station, on the same railway-line as Cannon Street
Station. The houses at the lower end of Stoney Lane over-
look the river. From a back window of any of them St.Clair
could easily have hurled his weighted coat on the mud.[15]

[12] Ordnance Survey Map, London, VII, 76, 86, 87.
[13] That is, within the City. It is not to be supposed that Mrs. St.Clair
patronised the shopkeepers of Wapping.   [14] I, 132.   [15] I, 135, 149.

It seems probable, then, that Mrs. St.Clair, after lunching at home, took a train to Cannon Street, did her shopping in the City, and afterwards crossed the river to collect her parcel from Scotland, intending to return to Lee from the nearby London Bridge Station.

There remains the minor difficulty of 'Paul's Wharf.' We venture the suggestion that, as Pickle Herring Street, or Shad Thames, has been altered in Watson's narrative to 'Fresno Street,' and as Stoney Lane has become 'Upper Swandam Lane,' so 'Paul's Wharf,' though bearing the same name as a wharf on the north bank of the river,[16] here serves to mask the identity of one on the south bank. The coincidence, though slightly confusing, is of no consequence.[17]

3

SAXE-COBURG SQUARE

Watson records that when Holmes and he travelled by the Underground to reconnoitre the neighbourhood of Jabez Wilson's pawnbroking establishment, and incidentally to inspect the knees of his assistant's trousers, they alighted at Aldersgate. From there, 'a short walk'[18] brought them to the square. He describes it as

a pokey, little, shabby-genteel place, where four lines of dingy two-storied brick houses looked out into a small railed-in enclosure.[19]

[16] The real Paul's Wharf is *west* of London Bridge, and can have had no connexion with the events described.

[17] A further source of confusion is the name 'Aberdeen Shipping Co.' There was an Aberdeen Steam Navigation Co., with offices at No. 102, Queen Victoria Street. But unless we are prepared to accept the equation: Cannon St. + East Cheap = Upper Swandam Lane, that 'vile alley,' and are able to credit Neville St.Clair with the notable feat of hurling his jacket from East Cheap over the tops of the intervening houses and into the Thames, a distance of over 200 yards, we must recognise the presence of another coincidence.   [18] I, 43.   [19] I, 43.

Wilson's establishment occupied a corner site.[20]   Back of it,
'one of the main arteries which convey the traffic of the City
to the north and west' [21] presented a bustling contrast to the
somnolent decay of the square.

Aldersgate, then, must have been the nearest Underground
station to Saxe-Coburg Square, since Holmes had no reason
to make a circuitous approach.   There are only two squares
in the neighbourhood, and one of them, Charterhouse Square,
is eliminated by its extent, shape (it is five-sided), and lack of
seclusion.   The other is Bridgewater Square.   It satisfies almost all the requirements, being poky, little, shabby, and
rectangular, and containing a small railed-in enclosure.
Furthermore, the buildings on its western side abut upon
premises approached from two passages leading out of Aldersgate Street, which, in turn, is 'a main artery . . . to the north
and west.' [22]

On the evening of Saturday, October 4, 1890,[23] Holmes
and Watson, accompanied by Inspector Jones and Mr. Merryweather, drove from Baker Street to the bank through an
'endless labyrinth' of streets, emerging at last into Farringdon
Street, when Holmes remarked that they were near their ob-
jective.[24]   On arriving, they passed down a narrow passage,
and entered the bank by a side door.[25]

Our proposed identification might be questioned on two
grounds: a) the buildings in the square are not now two-
storeyed dwellings, but warehouses and business premises of
various kinds; b) it is actually within the City limits, whereas
Wilson spoke of being 'near the City.' [26]   To these we reply,
in the first place, that forty-nine years, with their inevitable
changes, have passed since Watson's visit; and, secondly, that
to Wilson 'the City' meant rather the financial and banking

[20] I, 43.   [21] I, 44.   [22] Ordnance Survey Map, London, VII, 55.
[23] H. W. Bell: *Sherlock Holmes and Dr. Watson*, 1932, pp. 70–1; D. L.
Sayers: 'The Dates in *The Red-Headed League*,' *Colophon*, vol. V, pt. 17,
1934, no pagination.   [24] I, 48.   [25] I, 49.   [26] I, 33.

centre than the administrative area, and that, in short, his reference was not topographical but metaphysical.

There are two further possible objections which must be anticipated. Watson records that, after rattling through 'an endless labyrinth of gas-lit streets' they 'emerged into Farringdon Street.' [27] This is merely a slip of the pen. To reach Farringdon Street their best and most natural route would have been via Oxford Street and Holborn, an itinerary that cannot be described as an 'endless labyrinth.' It is evident that the street referred to is Farringdon *Road*, the approach to which from Baker Street might well appear tortuous, especially at night. The second point concerns Vincent Spaulding's reply to Holmes's question. 'Third right, fourth left,' [28] does not lead to the Strand from any square in London, and Holmes and Watson did not put the direction to the test. They examined the 'main artery,' had a sandwich and a cup of coffee, and, since it was already afternoon and they were booked for a concert at which Sarasate was playing, returned by cab or Underground to St. James's Hall.

We do not know whether Spaulding made the first answer that came into his head, in order to save time and return to his excavating, or whether Watson has inadvertently misquoted him in his notes. But it is a fact that, if we alter the phrase to 'third left, fourth right,' we do obtain a route by which any-one not wholly deficient in a sense of direction could readily reach the Strand. [29]

Thus it seems probable that Jabez Wilson's pawnbroking

---

[27] I, 48.   [28] I, 44.

[29] Spaulding would assume that Holmes and Watson were emerging from Bridgewater Square into Barbican and its continuation, Long Lane. Omitting alleys and the narrow, smaller streets, 'first left' is Australian Avenue, 'second,' Aldersgate Street, 'third,' West Smithfield. Thereafter, 'first right' is Hosier Lane, 'second,' Cock Lane, 'third,' Holborn Viaduct, and 'fourth,' Ludgate Hill, from which a straight course leads through Fleet Street to the Strand.

business was carried on at No. 5, Bridgewater Square, a corner site, which abuts on premises served by two passages: Aldersgate Buildings, and another unnamed. These, in turn, lead into Aldersgate Street.[30]

[30] It is probable that 'Pope's Court' (I, 32, 36, 39) is a transparent alias for Mitre Court, which connects Fleet Street with the Temple.

THE OTHER BOARDER

By JAMES KEDDIE

WE COME NOW to the Mystery of the Other Boarder at 221B
Baker Street. We know a good deal else about him, but we
do not know his name. We know that he was brought into
the world by a certain Dr. James Winter who also took care
of him during his infancy. Dr. Winter vaccinated the Other
Boarder, opened an abscess for him, and blistered him for
mumps.

Dr. Winter must have been a remarkable man. When his
little charge grew up and himself took a medical degree, it is
recorded that Dr. Winter was "the same as ever." Dr. Winter's age was impossible to discover, and his chronicler can
only state that he "struck his stream as high up as George the
Fourth, and even the Regency, but without ever getting quite
to the source." For Dr. Winter, the death of Robert Peel
"brought the history of England to a definite close."

To the Other Boarder (whose personality we must catch
from its reflection in his description of the old doctor), Dr.
Winter was clearly a survival of "a past generation." He had
learned medicine under an "obsolete and forgotten system."

Dr. Patterson, on the other hand, was contemporaneous
with the Other Boarder; yet it was Dr. Winter who, invited
out of courtesy to watch a delicate operation on Sir John
Sirwell, saved their reputations for these young men by
stepping in where they had failed and bringing the operation
to a successful issue. Dr. Winter had received Patterson and
the Other Boarder most cordially when they settled into his
neighborhood, but the patients' reception had been less warm.

An epidemic of influenza broke out: "One morning I met

The house of Sherlock Holmes and Dr. Watson, Baker Street, in the Eighteen-nineties (photograph by Dr. Gray Chandler Briggs)

Patterson on my round," writes the Other Boarder, "and found him looking rather pale and fagged out. He made the same remark about me."

Both young doctors came down with influenza. "It was of Patterson naturally that I thought," continues the Other Boarder, "but somehow the idea was repugnant to me. I thought of his cold critical attitude. . . . I wanted something more soothing—something more genial.

" 'Mrs. Hudson,' said I to my housekeeper, 'would you kindly run along to old Dr. Winter and tell him I should be obliged to him if he would step around.'

"She was back with her answer presently. 'Dr. Winter will come round in an hour or so, sir, but he has just been called in to attend Dr. Patterson.' "

Mrs. Hudson! "My Housekeeper"!

This incident is recorded by one A. C. Doyle [1] (an authority, by the way, frequently overlooked by students of Baker Street lore) who, as might readily be established, was in Edinburgh University Medical College when Dr. John Watson was a student there.

Doyle undoubtedly knew Watson. Equally undoubtedly he knew the Other Boarder. But there are problems to be solved and questions to be answered before the Mystery of the Other Boarder can be cleared up. First of all, we must be sure that it was at 221B Baker Street that the Mysterious Surgeon whom we must still call the Other Boarder had Mrs. Hudson for his housekeeper. We must approach this question with caution, for much more than the Identity of the Other Boarder depends upon our findings.

Remember, my dear fellow, we do not know that Mrs. Hudson was even in charge at 221B Baker Street when Holmes and Watson took rooms there at the time of "the dark incidents

---

[1] "Behind the Times," a story in *Round the Red Lamp*, London, 1894; now contained in *Tales of Medical Life*.

of the *Study in Scarlet*." "The Housekeeper's" name is not mentioned in Watson's narrative of these singular and stirring events. "Mrs. Hudson, our landlady," comes out of her anonymity at the time of the shocking affair at Pondicherry Lodge, which ended so romantically for Watson. Some time later (on the twentieth of March, 1888, according to *A Scandal in Bohemia*) we know that Mrs. Hudson had been supplanted as "our housekeeper" at 221B by a Mrs. Turner.

What had become of Mrs. Hudson during the time between Watson's marriage and the now historic affair of Irene Adler and the Royal Personage who preferred to be addressed as the Count Von Kramm? Did Mrs. Hudson sell her rooming house at 221B Baker Street as a going concern? Was it while she was absent from that memorable address that she kept house for Dr. Winter's protégé? But Mrs. Hudson returned to Baker Street. Did Mrs. Turner find her distinguished guest too much for her? Did Mrs. Hudson, on the other hand, on her return to Baker Street, find it necessary, now that Dr. Watson had departed to a home of his own, to take on the Other Boarder?

It is a reasonable hypothesis, but one not capable of proof, that A. C. Doyle (who knew Watson intimately although he did not seem fully to understand him) recommended the Other Boarder to Mrs. Hudson. It is highly probable that he saw him there when he called at 221B. Perhaps it was there that he heard the gently amusing and faintly pathetic anecdote, "Behind the Times," which gives us our sole clue to the Other Boarder's existence. Undoubtedly, and for literary effect, he retold the story in the first person just as he had heard it.

Doubtless, time and the deliberation of the scholar will eventually disentangle every knot in Baker Street History.

SHERLOCK HOLMES AND MUSIC

By HARVEY OFFICER

VERY EARLY IN the relationship between Dr. John Watson and Mr. Sherlock Holmes, the former gentleman drew up a series of deductions about his newly acquired friend. It will be remembered that Watson never formally altered or criticised these deductions. Nevertheless, since Holmes himself so often deplored his friend's limited powers of observation, perhaps we may take a similar liberty. I propose therefore, in this brief paper, to show that there was a side of Holmes' character and attainments which, though hinted at in various places, was never really understood or appreciated.

The tenth item of the list, entitled, somewhat erroneously, "Sherlock Holmes, His Limits"—reads, "Plays the violin well." [1] One cannot help wishing that Dr. Watson knew a little more about music, for shortly afterwards he writes, "Leaning back in his armchair of an evening he would close his eyes and scrape carelessly at the fiddle which was thrown across his knees." Now anyone who knows the violin can do that. But Watson goes further and betrays a lamentable lack of attention to detail, for he writes, "Sometimes the chords were sonorous and melancholy; occasionally they were fantastic and cheerful." I submit that you can do sonorous or melancholy chords or fantastic and cheerful chords on a piano with a certain degree of carelessness, but I defy any violinist to produce such chords on a violin that is lying carelessly across his knees. Chords on a violin are always a *tour de force*. They are not natural to the instrument. They can only be played when the violin is held strongly in its accus-

[1] *A Study in Scarlet.*

tomed position, and even then they are not the violin's most expressive sounds. It is pre-eminently the instrument of melody, not of harmony.

When Dr. Watson gives details of what was actually played he is on surer ground. Probably when he gave the above somewhat highly colored and romantic description of his friend's performance, he was attempting to say something about music which was unfamiliar to him. But on other occasions he mentions Mendelssohn's "Lieder," which are of course the *Songs Without Words;* and he speaks also of "a whole series of favorite airs" which were probably selected in deference to the good doctor's limited musical tastes.

We may note some further details—a concert by Sarasate; [2] another by Madame Norman-Neruda, [3] a distinguished violinist to whom, in 1901, Queen Alexandra gave the title "Violinist to the Queen"; and on one occasion Holmes' appreciation of music is evidenced by his taking a box at the opera in order to hear the two de Reszkes in *The Huguenots.* [4]

But all these details fade into insignificance before the amazing revelation of Holmes' knowledge of music which is given us in the story entitled *The Bruce-Partington Plans.* Here we read that the great detective was at this time immersed in the study of mediaeval music; that the results of his study eventually appeared in a monograph upon the Polyphonic Motets of Orlando di Lasso; and that this monograph, printed for private circulation only, was the last word on the subject.

It will be necessary, perhaps, to set down exactly what this implies. The motets of di Lasso number five hundred and ten, filling eleven volumes of the great Breitkopf and Härtel edition. They are written for voices ranging in number from two to twelve. One cannot hear these motets today anywhere in the world. One cannot play them, for they are

---

[2] *The Red-Headed League.*   [3] *A Study in Scarlet.*
[4] *The Hound of the Baskervilles.*

meant for voices only, and would be meaningless if played on instruments. One can only do what Sherlock Holmes must have been able to do, *i.e.*, read them, and then with the ear of the mind hear their complicated web of sounds.

There is an ancient wheeze about a toastmaster presiding over a large gathering and wishing in his opening address to include all his audience. He began, "Ladies and gentlemen, musicians and singers." He might with equal truth have said, "Musicians and violinists." It is unfortunately true that a man or woman who can sing, or play upon an instrument, is not always a musician. Now Holmes played the violin and was a lover of music. But this by no means makes him a musician. Nevertheless a musician he was, as we learn from this one passing reference. He knew the only kind of music which one can know only if one is very really a musician. His violin-playing would help him hardly at all. There are few victrola records of di Lasso, and these few are the motets which groups of people like the English Singers have performed. But the vast mass of his works is never heard. In spite of all this Holmes could write a monograph on these five hundred motets which was the last word on the subject!

Diligent search has failed to unearth a copy of that precious monograph. The name of Sherlock Holmes does not occur in Grove's *Dictionary of Music*. In spite of these facts we are clearly justified in ranking Holmes among the great musicologists of our time.

SUSSEX INTERVIEW

By P. M. STONE

"COME, COME, MR. HOLMES," I countered in a final desperate effort to ward off a curt dismissal. "After all, you must admit, you owe it to posterity that these base insinuations, aimed to discountenance your former exploits, should be checked. Again," I added, gathering courage as I observed that the venerable detective had reseated himself by the fire, "this matter of dates in the Watson chronology. A fine mess he has made of them it seems and a brief statement from you might close an interminable controversy."

"Quite true, young man, quite true," came the slow response, as Sherlock Holmes relighted his pipe and gazed reflectively across the low fender into the fire. I exulted with relief that I had in some manner touched a responsive chord and waited eagerly for his final pronouncement upon my singular quest.

It had been, indeed, a momentous day. Brett, my chief, had finally assented to what he termed a preposterous mission, and I had set forth that morning at 10 o'clock from Victoria, determined that before nightfall I would secure for my paper an interview with Sherlock Holmes. I had, through devious influential channels at Scotland Yard, finally ascertained his address; and upon arrival at Crown Lydgate, just beyond Amberley, a brisk three mile walk across the downs by way of a well-defined drover's path had brought me at length to my goal.

The spot selected by the renowned detective for his retirement was one of remote seclusion. Situated far from the teeming centre of his several crime investigations, the remodeled Tudor farm-house rested in a hollow of the Sussex downs; a winding private roadway was visible westward leading towards Chichester, and in the foreground, at the summit of the slope, stood a small latticed pavilion which afforded a magnificent view of the distant sea.

Upon arrival at a stone gate-house which marked the termination of my upland course I was admitted to the precincts of Faraway by an aged retainer of dour countenance who had evidently been apprized of my coming. Telford at the Yard held, I knew, intermittent communication with Holmes and the Inspector had promised to telephone a brief message by way of introduction.

On being ushered into the spacious library of the house, a few moments later, I was at once impressed with its close resemblance to the picture so familiar to all students of the Baker Street menage. A large oval table, littered with an accumulation of books, manuscript paper and other writing material, occupied the centre of the room; at one side of the wide hearth stood a huge oaken settle, and through the open doorway at my right I caught sight of what was evidently a laboratory, for the shelves revealed rows of bottles and chemical apparatus, while the presence of a small, brick-coated blast furnace indicated that Holmes had not entirely renounced his fond proclivity for research.

A moment later Sherlock Holmes rose from his high-backed arm chair at the farther side of the table and extended to me a cordial welcome. Time had, in fact, touched him with a gentle hand. His spare figure, tall and with the slight stoop at the shoulders, revealed to the unprofessional eye no indication of declining vigor, and a glance at the pile of manuscript gave evidence of those astonishing intellectual forces which had brought him to the pinnacle of a distinguished career.

Within the range of my vision I presently detected one or two other reminders of the London lodgings in Baker Street, long familiar to me through a close study of the Watson chronicles. In a corner of the settle by the fireside stood the worn violin case; the Persian slipper, once the favored receptacle for Holmes' tobacco (one wonders to what use its mate was ever destined), was fastened to the wall close by the bell rope, and carelessly thrown over the end of a long couch I noted a blue dressing gown which had probably been worn by the detective during the early morning hours of work upon his manuscript.

"Great Heavens," I observed, inwardly, "can this be the same garment about which such heated controversy has been waged? And, if such be the case, where is the equally famous mouse-colored gown that figured so prominently in the adventure of *The Empty House?* But, after all," I reflected, "Mrs. Hudson may have held one in reserve, for her lodger was notoriously careless when engaged with his chemical experiments."

A modern touch was added to the room's equipment by the presence of a tall, steel filing cabinet placed in the deep window alcove. This contained, I surmised, a complete card reference pertaining to his innumerable investigations.

Of the familiar morocco case and the syringe which once drew Watson's indignant protests, there was no sign whatever. Long since, no doubt, the detective had renounced this avenue of escape from physical exhaustion, and a solution of 7 per cent. cocaine held for him no further allurements.

It was easily observed that I had interrupted him at some laborious task; possibly, I judged from the array of papers and note-books before him, his long awaited compendium of Crime and Detection. He evinced, however, no irritability at being for the moment turned aside from this monumental task and, asking me to be seated, gave a tug at the long bell rope which hung at one side of the fire-place. An elderly

woman responded presently and my host requested that sherry
and biscuits be brought in, since luncheon was not to be served
until an hour later.

"Mrs. Hudson is, I regret to say, no longer in service here,"
Holmes remarked a moment later, noting my inquiring glance
as the door closed behind the housekeeper's retreating figure.
"Martha did in fact come to my assistance shortly after my
retirement, but a year or more ago I pensioned her off and
the good woman is now residing with a niece in Cumberland.
A loyal, devoted supporter she was, indeed," he added with
feeling, "and it required the disposition of a saint to cope
with the irregular course of my existence in Baker Street.

"But, I note," he continued, after seating himself opposite
me near the fire-side and subjecting me to a rather searching
glance, "that you came down by way of Crown Lydgate and
followed the lower drover's track across the downs. Also,"
he added, smiling, "you showed good judgment in choosing
the left hand corner of the compartment on your journey, for
the vista is far more enjoyable and you probably caught sight
of the ruined castle on the ridge as you passed through Amberley."

"Yes," I responded with enthusiasm, "and it appears a delightful, inviting region to a city man, I assure you. But
how——?"

"Elemen— that is to say, quite simple, Mr. Godfrey," he
answered with a smile. "One's mind photographs these trifles
after long practice, and my own experience has perhaps extended beyond the apprenticeship stage."

"Even so," I interrupted, "how did——?"

"It is certain that you approached Faraway along the drover's path from Crown Lydgate, for I can see strong evidence
of the chalky soil upon your upturned shoe. Had you come
down by way of Ferriby Junction—an equally attractive

route—and then followed the main highway to my western entrance, the turf path leading in from the gate would have very quickly removed such traces.

"As for the other matter," he resumed, aware that he held my fixed attention, "perhaps I am upon less solid ground, but a strong suspicion of grey dust upon the left elbow of your dark suit tells me that you rested it upon the window sill of the railway carriage."

"Ah! Mr. Holmes," I retorted quickly, "but perhaps I seated myself back to the engine, in which case——"

"Hardly possible, young man," came the ready response as Sherlock Holmes extended to me a glass of sherry and indicated the biscuit box within reach on the table. "You see, I am familiar with these trains and the ten o'clock from Victoria is sparsely patronized. Never have I found difficulty securing a smoking compartment to myself for the journey down—or at the most with two companions. And it would only be natural for you to seat yourself facing the course of your journey. Finally, once leaving the terminal, I believe the sun reflection would strongly favor such a choice."

"Correct you are, sir," I replied, laughing, "and I wonder that Doctor Watson ever caught you napping."

"Poor Watson," Holmes responded. "I badgered him continually, but he always took it in good nature. You will be interested to learn that he is resting at a nursing home in Kensington. That Jezail bullet wound at Maiwand in 1880, you know, brought him a chronic disorder of the leg——"

"You mean the left shoulder?" I interjected, suddenly.

"That's so, young man," the detective replied, directing at me another sharp glance as he refilled his pipe and settled back more comfortably in his chair. "I observe that you are aware of Watson's amazing inconsistencies. First, it's a shoulder, then a leg; and I often wonder," he added with a chuckle, "if he received a cranial fracture during the same engagement."

It was at this juncture of our interview that I barely escaped dismissal for I now—all too abruptly—approached the delicate topic of conflicting dates in the Watson records and their challenge to all devoted students of the saga.

Holmes stiffened at once as I reminded him of the protracted controversies waged over the chronology of his exploits; his long, tapering fingers drummed on the table and I surmised that my injudicious remarks had aroused in him unpleasant recollections.

My appeal to reason, however, quickly mollified him, for he presently suggested another glass of sherry. We moved closer to the fireside, where I reclined against the cushioned settle and my host turned upon me an enquiring, more conciliatory glance.

"Dates—dates—dates," he exclaimed vehemently. "One might add, a fig for dates. And, after all, Watson, poor chap, had some excuse; his practice and the urgent demands of my investigations gave him little time for an accurate, chronological record of events."

"That is so, Mr. Holmes," I agreed. "You will understand, sir, that none among the vast throng of your admirers desires to intrude upon your privacy at this late stage; it is merely that we seek elucidation upon certain phases of your professional work and early training."

"That will come in due season, Mr. Godfrey," Holmes responded slowly as he stooped to throw a fresh log on the glowing embers of the fire. "I might add that these critical surveys have not always brought me vexation or dismay at Watson's inaccuracies. Some of them are amusing and highly ingenious.

"For instance," he resumed, after a moment of reflection, "that episode of my college career which featured Trevor and his damnable pup. The fact is, he smuggled the animal inside the gates after nightfall—a certain porter at the lodge could amplify my brief statement—and in consequence Trevor was given a rare old dust-up, I assure you, by the authorities.

"My own college career ran full circle, so to speak, and I took up residence in Montague Street during the year 1876. That is a long time ago, young man, and criminal investigation has undergone vast changes during that period. My own methods are now, perhaps, antiquated, though I have upon certain occasions been sought by Yard officials who are kindly disposed to look upon me as one keeping abreast of the times."

"I can well understand that, sir," I interposed. "But," I added, "to return for a moment, with your permission, to the moot question of dates in Doctor Watson's records. Are you willing to present a brief statement that might serve to clear away some of the inconsistencies that have provoked discussion?"

"Willing enough," Sherlock Holmes responded readily, a smile stealing across his thin, smoothly shaven features. "But I do believe our critics, even though they employ ingenious methods which indicate exhaustive research, lay undue stress upon what are, after all, inconsequential matters of detail.

"I assure you," he continued, "that all the cases so ably recorded by my confrère will bear the most rigid scrutiny so far as my own participation in their solution is concerned; but both Watson and myself were grossly delinquent in the matter of chronological memoranda. Again, I have never, alas, been awarded medals in the art of calligraphy and the doctor did not at all times consult me while engaged in his laborious deciphering of my hurried notes.

"Watson is determined," the detective concluded, "to present an extended reply to these persevering investigators of our adventures; but I have counseled him against precipitate action, and, furthermore, I wish first to consult an old diary that is lodged in a battered tin box at Cox's bank."

At this point announcement was made by Holmes' house-

The Reichenbach Fall: scene of Holmes' supposed death in Switzerland

keeper that luncheon was served, and presently we repaired
to a small, oak-raftered dining room which immediately ad-
joined the library on the west. Through the wide casement
windows one caught an inviting view of the rolling downs,
along the upper ridge of which a flock of sheep were sharply
outlined against the crystal blue skyline. Closer at hand my
eye followed the course of a turf path winding down to the
western entrance of Faraway, and strung overhead I observed
the telephone wire which served as almost his only means of
communication with the outside world.

During the following three quarters of an hour Holmes
proved himself an extremely courteous and genial host. My
fears concerning a possible reluctance on his part to answer
my queries, had been dispelled by the warmth of his manner,
and cautiously now I broached one or two topics which
would, I hoped, bring me some astonishing revelation.

Concerning the period of his wanderings in Central Asia,
following the Reichenbach affair, he had little to say. "I appreciate," he agreed, "that my own published records covering
this pilgrimage are both sketchy and tantalizing. Some day,
however, the complete document may be released; as a matter
of fact I have long since approved of such a course, but my
brother Mycroft's executors up to now have been unable to
find all the note-books that were left, you recall, in his custody. I believe that my report on the geology of Central
Tibet may hold more than casual interest for certain among
our learned societies.

"You realize," he continued, "that the preparation of this
monograph will draw heavily upon my time and energy; furthermore, both Watson and the local medico, who have my
health in charge, caution me to devote only a few hours each
day to such labors."

"Let us hope, sir, that many years of rest and enjoyment
remain for you," I interjected. "And many of us are equally

hopeful that you and Doctor Watson may offer us at least one more volume devoted to certain unrecorded cases that were mentioned in the earlier chronicles. Many conjectures have been advanced concerning them and the precise nature of your own participation."

"Such an event may eventually materialize," Sherlock Holmes responded, smiling, "and I trust you may feel no disappointment at the results." As he spoke we rose to return once more to our former seats by the library fireside, and within a moment or two the housekeeper brought in the coffee urn which she placed, together with cups and saucers, upon a low smoking stand.

"Am I overpresumptuous, Mr. Holmes," I inquired, "if I ask you for further details concerning this work?"

"Not at all; there is no secret about it, I assure you. During the past year I have spent a portion of each day compiling additional episodes of my professional career from my own note-books and those other records so carefully preserved by Watson. The doctor, let me add, took no active part in some of these adventures; consequently, although he has consented to write a foreword of explanation, the main task of editing falls upon me. And I hope," he added with humorous severity, "that the dates, in all instances, may stand beyond suspicion."

In reply to my further queries, the detective informed me that it was first intended to delay publication of the volume until after his decease, but continued pressure from a London publisher had finally brought permission to announce it for the forthcoming year.

"It is practically ready now," he confessed, as he refilled his pipe and extended a long arm towards the match box on the smoking stand. "You will understand, however, that my other venture—the compendium of Crime and Detection—has consumed a vast amount of energy, and I could not allow less important matters to interrupt my progress on the major work. I have now arrived midway in the final volume and, please God, I may be spared to bring it to completion."

"Naturally one is extremely interested," I hazarded, "to learn just which cases you have selected from that famous tin box at Cox's bank."

"The book will record only six more of my early cases," Holmes readily responded. "They are cases of supreme interest and importance, I assure you; and it is only because of my dilatory methods that these episodes were not entrusted to Watson's editorship years ago.

"First of all I deal at some length with the Arnsworth Castle affair, in Derbyshire, in 1888. Then follows an account of my experiences with the Camberwell poisoning gang; the singular affair of the aluminium crutch which, by the way, appears to have stirred up some amusing conjectures; the Tankerville Club scandal which involved among others a high cabinet official; the long drawn out chase across Yorkshire in pursuit of the Tarleton murderers; and, finally, a case of unusual importance which I shall refer to as the affair of the Bermondsey Dwarf."

At this point in his statement Sherlock Holmes paused and gazed for a moment or two into the fire. "That case," he resumed at length, "introduced to me the most malevolent figures ever to cross my path, with the possible exceptions of Professor Moriarty and Doctor Grimesby Roylott. You will be amazed at the account I have presented of human depravity. It forms a fitting conclusion to the volume, for in certain respects my resources were taxed as in no other instance, and the case possesses also a singular pathological interest.

"I am going up to town tomorrow to visit Watson," the detective concluded, briskly rising to knock the ashes from his pipe. "His birthday comes along shortly and I must secure somewhere a pound or two of the abominable shag tobacco which he favors as of yore. But on second thought," he added with a chuckle, "perhaps I would confer a favor upon posterity if I were to present him with a bound volume of almanacks covering the active period of our associations together."

A glance at my watch now informed me that I should give immediate thought to my return journey, and I crossed the room to reclaim my hat and stick from the couch where I had deposited them upon my arrival. There were, to be sure, many matters which I had not touched upon: the confusion of dates in the chronicle of the Red-Headed League; Mycroft's final illness; further particulars concerning Mrs. Hudson's affairs; and more comprehensive details relative to Holmes's apprenticeship in the art of detection at the time he resided in Montague Street. But time did not permit a continuation of the interview; and, furthermore, I surmised from a glance or two which he had directed towards the table, that he was anxious to resume work upon his famous *magnum opus*.

There was, nevertheless, one inquiry which I was determined to pursue. As I stood at the threshold and assisted Sherlock Holmes with his top-coat—for he had announced his intention to accompany me to the gate—I exclaimed, "Oh! a final question, sir. There have been many queer statements made, as you know, about Professor Moriarty. Some of your critics have dared to advance the theory that he never existed; others have suggested that he escaped death at the Reichenbach and later returned to London, where he resumed his nefarious operations."

The detective gazed at me long and silently, and for a moment I suspected that I would carry away with me no fresh enlightenment. Then he turned suddenly, crossed to the window alcove, and swung open the heavy door of a small safe which I had previously noted beyond the filing cabinet.

From an upper compartment he withdrew an object wrapped in tissue paper, and this he handed to me.

"My one and only souvenir of Moriarty as he is generally known," Sherlock Holmes remarked slowly, "and you are the only individual—with the exception of Watson—who has ever inspected it."

I removed the wrapping and examined curiously a short fragment of heavy watch chain, from the centre portion of which was suspended a gold medal, measuring in diameter about one and one half inches. One side bore the inscription, *St. Andrews 1869*, and on the other side I read the words, *Jasper Mariott—Highest Award Of Merit*, and then the single word *Mathematics* in slightly larger lettering beneath.

"I picked this up from the pathway immediately after the struggle at the Reichenbach," Sherlock Holmes said gravely as I handed the memento back to him. "Upon my return to England, three years or more later, I took occasion to journey northward and eventually unearthed a number of revealing facts pertaining to Mariott's student days and subsequent career.

"You will recall, of course, that he was forced to resign the chair of mathematics at one of our smaller universities, where he had established himself quickly in the highest educational circles and issued several monographs based on exhaustive scientific research. I shall not dwell upon the circumstances of his dismissal, but merely repeat that they led to his later adoption of the name Moriarty and his spectacular rise to a commanding position in the London underworld of that day."

"The legend persists, Mr. Holmes," I interruped, "that Moriarty was alive at the time of the European war, and that even now no definite news of his death ever has been recorded."

"Nonsense, sheer nonsense," the detective replied, with

some indication of annoyance. "You may take my word for it that his influence has long since been removed from the world. Moriarty—Mariott—call him by any name you desire—lies at the foot of the Reichenbach Fall, and no mumbo-jumbo of modern science or sorcery can bring him back to life again."

Warm sunlight flooded the landscape as we followed a gravel pathway up the slope towards the pavilion which I had observed that morning. A glance towards my right afforded me a view of the southerly exposed garden area where the elderly retainer, who had admitted me to the precincts of Faraway, was engaged in trimming a hedge. Beyond him I caught sight of a stone sun-dial, and arranged along the farther border of the enclosure were a number of conical bee hives.

Presently we stood together at the summit of the ridge and gazed across the tremendous rolling expanse of the downs, upon which racing shadows were cast from a small cluster of billowing white clouds. Sheep were grazing a quarter of a mile away; a heavy tractor was toiling upward along one of the winding roads below us; and westward I observed the square tower of a parish church just beyond the main highway.

"This is my world," Holmes said with deep emotion, after a long silence during which I had been captivated by the full sweep of a magnificent prospect extending to the distant sea.

"Elemental," I responded, somewhat dreamily, as I mentally compared the glorious scene before me with the more familiar urban environment of my daily duties.

"That will do, young man," said the detective sharply, "and you had better step along if you plan to catch the 4:12 from Crown Lydgate. Just keep to the lower path after you pass the water tower on the first ridge—it will save you a quarter hour."

Chagrined at having offended my distinguished host at this

final stage of a long-sought interview, I glanced at my watch and extended a hand in farewell. But as Sherlock Holmes turned to descend the slope toward his cottage I thought I heard a subdued chuckle; and then there came to me unmistakably—though I doubt they were intended for my ears—the words, "Elemental, indeed!"

THE ADVENTURE OF THE UNIQUE HAMLET

By Vincent Starrett

"Holmes," said I, one morning as I stood in our bay window, looking idly into the street, "surely here comes a madman. Someone has incautiously left the door open and the poor fellow has slipped out. What a pity!"

It was a glorious morning in the spring, with a fresh breeze and inviting sunlight, but as it was early few persons were as yet astir. Birds twittered under the neighboring eaves, and from the far end of the thoroughfare came faintly the droning cry of an umbrella-repair man: a lean cat slunk across the cobbles and disappeared into a courtway; but for the most part the street was deserted save for the eccentric individual who had called forth my exclamation.

My friend rose lazily from the chair in which he had been lounging, and came to my side, standing with long legs spread and hands in the pockets of his dressing gown. He smiled as he saw the singular personage coming along; and a personage indeed he seemed to be, despite his curious actions, for he was tall and portly, with elderly whiskers of the variety called mutton-chop, and eminently respectable. He was loping curiously, like a tired hound, lifting his knees high as he ran, and a heavy double watch-chain bounced against and rebounded from the plump line of his figured waistcoat. With one hand he clutched despairingly at his silk, two-gallon hat, while with the other he made strange gestures in the air in an emotion bordering upon distraction. We could almost see the spasmodic workings of his countenance.

"What under heaven can ail him?" I cried. "See how he glances at the houses as he passes."

"He is looking at the numbers," responded Sherlock Holmes, with dancing eyes, "and I fancy it is ours that will bring him the greatest happiness. His profession, of course, is obvious."

"A banker, I should imagine, or at least a person of affluence," I ventured, wondering what curious bit of minutiæ had betrayed the man's vocation to my remarkable companion, in a single glance.

"Affluent, yes," said Holmes, with a mischievous twinkle, "but not exactly a banker, Watson. Notice the sagging pockets, despite the excellence of his clothing, and the rather exaggerated madness of his eye. He is a collector, or I am very much mistaken."

"My dear fellow!" I exclaimed. "At his age and in his station! And why should he be seeking us? When we settled that last bill—"

"Of books," said my friend, severely. "He is a book collector. His line is Caxtons, Elzevirs, and Gutenberg Bibles; not the sordid reminders of unpaid grocery accounts. See, he is turning in, as I expected, and in a moment he will stand upon our hearthrug and tell the harrowing tale of an unique volume and its extraordinary disappearance."

His eyes gleamed and he rubbed his hands together in satisfaction. I could not but hope that his conjecture was correct, for he had had little recently to occupy his mind, and I lived in constant fear that he would seek that stimulation his active brain required in the long-tabooed cocaine bottle.

As Holmes finished speaking the doorbell echoed through the house; then hurried feet were sounding on the stairs, while the wailing voice of Mrs. Hudson, raised in protest, could only have been occasioned by frustration of her coveted privilege of bearing up our caller's card. Then the door burst violently inward and the object of our analysis staggered to the center of the room and, without announcing his intention by word or sign, pitched headforemost to our center rug. There he lay, a magnificent ruin, with his head on the fringed border and his feet in the coal scuttle; and sealed within his lifeless lips was the amazing story he had come to tell—for that it was amazing we could not doubt in the light of our client's extraordinary behavior.

Sherlock Holmes ran quickly for the brandy bottle, while I knelt beside the stricken man and loosened his wilted neckband. He was not dead, and when we had forced the nozzle of the flask between his teeth he sat up in groggy fashion, passing a dazed hand across his eyes. Then he scrambled to his feet with an embarrassed apology for his weakness, and fell into the chair which Holmes invitingly held towards him.

"That is right, Mr. Harrington Edwards," said my companion, soothingly. "Be quite calm, my dear sir, and when you have recovered your composure you will find us ready to listen."

"You know me then?" cried our visitor. There was pride in his voice and he lifted his eyebrows in surprise.

"I had never heard of you until this moment; but if you wish to conceal your identity it would be well," said Sherlock Holmes, "for you to leave your bookplates at home." As Holmes spoke he returned a little package of folded paper slips, which he had picked from the floor. "They fell from your hat when you had the misfortune to collapse," he added whimsically.

"Yes, yes," cried the collector, a deep blush spreading across his features. "I remember now; my hat was a little large and I folded a number of them and placed them beneath the sweatband. I had forgotten."

"Rather shabby usage for a handsome etched plate," smiled my companion; "but that is your affair. And now, sir, if you are quite at ease, let us hear what it is that has brought you, a collector of books, from Poke Stogis Manor—the name is on

Sherlock Holmes: bust by Wilkins in the possession of the Doyle family

the plate—to the office of Mr. Sherlock Holmes, consulting expert in crime. Surely nothing but the theft of Mahomet's own copy of the Koran can have affected you so strongly."

Mr. Harrington Edwards smiled feebly at the jest, then sighed. "Alas," he murmured, "if that were all! But I shall begin at the beginning.

"You must know, then, that I am the greatest Shakespearean commentator in the world. My collection of *ana* is unrivaled and much of the world's collection (and consequently its knowledge of the veritable Shakespeare) has emanated from my pen. One book I did not possess: it was unique, in the correct sense of that abused word; the greatest Shakespeare rarity in the world. Few knew that it existed, for its existence was kept a profound secret between a chosen few. Had it become known that this book was in England—anyplace, indeed—its owner would have been hounded to his grave by wealthy Americans.

"It was in the possession of my friend—I tell you this in strictest confidence—of my friend, Sir Nathaniel Brooke-Bannerman, whose place at Walton-on-Walton is next to my own. A scant two hundred yards separate our dwellings; so intimate has been our friendship that a few years ago the fence between our estates was removed, and each roamed or loitered at will in the other's preserves.

"For some years, now, I have been at work upon my greatest book—my *magnum opus*. It was to be my last book also embodying the results of a lifetime of study and research. Sir, I know Elizabethan London better than any man alive; better than any man who ever lived, I think—" He burst suddenly into tears.

"There, there," said Sherlock Holmes, gently. "Do not be distressed. Pray continue with your interesting narrative. What was this book—which, I take it, in some manner has disappeared? You borrowed it from your friend?"

"That is what I am coming to," said Mr. Harrington Edwards, drying his tears, "but as for help, Mr. Holmes, I fear that is beyond even you. As you surmise, I needed this book. Knowing its value, which could not be fixed, for the book is priceless, and knowing Sir Nathaniel's idolatry of it, I hesitated before asking for the loan of it. But I had to have it, for without it my work could not have been completed, and at length I made my request. I suggested that I visit him in his home and go through the volume under his eyes, he sitting at my side throughout my entire examination, and servants stationed at every door and window, with fowling pieces in their hands.

"You can imagine my astonishment when Sir Nathaniel laughed at my precautions. 'My dear Edwards,' he said, 'that would be all very well were you Arthur Bambidge or Sir Homer Nantes (mentioning the two great men of the British Museum), or were you Mr. Henry Hutterson, the American railway magnate; but you are my friend Harrington Edwards, and you shall take the book home with you for as long as you like.' I protested vigorously, I can assure you; but he would have it so, and as I was touched by this mark of his esteem, at length I permitted him to have his way. My God! If I had remained adamant! If I had only—"

He broke off and for a moment stared blindly into space. His eyes were directed at the Persian slipper on the wall, in the toe of which Holmes kept his tobacco, but we could see that his thoughts were far away.

"Come, Mr. Edwards," said Holmes, firmly. "You are agitating yourself unduly. And you are unreasonably prolonging our curiosity. You have not yet told us what this book is."

Mr. Harrington Edwards gripped the arm of the chair in which he sat. Then he spoke, and his voice was low and thrilling:

"The book was a 'Hamlet' quarto, dated 1602, presented

by Shakespeare to his friend Drayton, with an inscription four lines in length, written and signed by the Master, himself!"

"My dear sir!" I exclaimed. Holmes blew a long, slow whistle of astonishment.

"It is true," cried the collector. "That is the book I borrowed, and that is the book I lost! The long-sought quarto of 1602, actually inscribed in Shakespeare's own hand! His greatest drama, in an edition dated a year earlier than any that is known; a perfect copy, and with four lines in his own handwriting! Unique! Extraordinary! Amazing! Astounding! Colossal! Incredible! Un—"

He seemed wound up to continue indefinitely; but Holmes, who had sat quite still at first, shocked by the importance of the loss, interrupted the flow of adjectives.

"I appreciate your emotion, Mr. Edwards," he said, "and the book is indeed all that you say it is. Indeed, it is so important that we must at once attack the problem of rediscovering it. Compose yourself, my dear sir, and tell us of the loss. The book, I take it, is readily identifiable?"

"Mr. Holmes," said our client, earnestly, "it would be impossible to hide it. It is so important a volume that, upon coming into its possession, Sir Nathaniel Brooke-Bannerman called a consultation of the great binders of the Empire, at which were present Mr. Rivière, Messrs. Sangorski and Sutcliffe, Mr. Zaehnsdorf, and certain others. They and myself, with two others, alone know of the book's existence. When I tell you that it is bound in brown levant morocco, with leather joints and brown levant doublures and fly-leaves, the whole elaborately gold tooled, inlaid with seven hundred and fifty separate pieces of various colored leathers, and enriched by the insertion of eighty-seven precious stones, I need not add that it is a design that never will be duplicated, and I mention only a few of its glories. The binding was personally done by Messrs. Rivière, Sangorski, Sutcliffe, and Zaehnsdorf, working alternately, and is a work of such enchantment that any man might gladly die a thousand deaths for the privilege of owning it for twenty minutes."

"Dear me," quoth Sherlock Holmes, "it must indeed be a handsome volume, and from your description, together with a realization of importance by reason of its association, I gather that it is something beyond what might be termed a valuable book."

"Priceless!" cried Mr. Harrington Edwards. "The combined wealth of India, Mexico, and Wall Street would be all too little for its purchase."

"You are anxious to recover this book?" asked Sherlock Holmes, looking at him keenly.

"My God!" shrieked the collector, rolling up his eyes and clawing at the air with his hands. "Do you suppose—?"

"Tut, tut!" Holmes interrupted. "I was only testing you. It is a book that might move even you, Mr. Harrington Edwards, to theft—but we may put aside that notion. Your emotion is too sincere, and besides you know too well the difficulties of hiding such a volume as you describe. Indeed, only a very daring man would purloin it and keep it long in his possession. Pray tell us how you came to lose it."

Mr. Harrington Edwards seized the brandy flask, which stood at his elbow, and drained it at a gulp. With the renewed strength thus obtained, he continued his story:

"As I have said, Sir Nathaniel forced me to accept the loan of the book, much against my wishes. On the evening that I called for it, he told me that two of his servants, heavily armed, would accompany me across the grounds to my home. 'There is no danger,' he said, 'but you will feel better;' and I heartily agreed with him. How shall I tell you what happened? Mr. Holmes, it was those very servants who assailed me and robbed me of my priceless borrowing!"

Sherlock Holmes rubbed his lean hands with satisfaction. "Splendid!" he murmured. "This is a case after my own heart. Watson, these are deep waters in which we are adventuring. But you are rather lengthy about this, Mr. Edwards. Perhaps it will help matters if I ask you a few questions. By what road did you go to your home?"

"By the main road, a good highway which lies in front of our estates. I preferred it to the shadows of the wood."

"And there were some two hundred yards between your doors. At what point did the assault occur?"

"Almost midway between the two entrance drives, I should say."

"There was no light?"

"That of the moon only."

"Did you know these servants who accompanied you?"

"One I knew slightly; the other I had not seen before."

"Describe them to me, please."

"The man who is known to me is called Miles. He is clean-shaven, short and powerful, although somewhat elderly. He was known, I believe, as Sir Nathaniel's most trusted servant; he had been with Sir Nathaniel for years. I cannot describe him minutely for, of course, I never paid much attention to him. The other was tall and thickset, and wore a heavy beard. He was a silent fellow; I do not believe he spoke a word during the journey."

"Miles was more communicative?"

"Oh yes—even garrulous, perhaps. He talked about the weather and the moon, and I forget what all."

"Never about books?"

"There was no mention of books between any of us."

"Just how did the attack occur?"

"It was very sudden. We had reached, as I say, about the halfway point, when the big man seized me by the throat—to prevent outcry, I suppose—and on the instant, Miles snatched the volume from my grasp and was off. In a moment his companion followed him. I had been half throttled and could not immediately cry out; but when I could articulate, I made the countryside ring with my cries. I ran after them, but failed even to catch another sight of them. They had disappeared completely."

"Did you all leave the house together?"

"Miles and I left together; the second man joined us at the porter's lodge. He had been attending to some of his duties."

"And Sir Nathaniel—where was he?"

"He said good-night on the threshold."

"What has he had to say about all this?"

"I have not told him."

"You have not told him!" echoed Sherlock Holmes, in astonishment.

"I have not dared," confessed our client miserably. "It will kill him. That book was the breath of his life."

"When did all this occur?" I put in, with a glance at Holmes.

"Excellent, Watson," said my friend, answering my glance. "I was about to ask the same question."

"Just last night," was Mr. Harrington Edwards' reply. "I was crazy most of the night, and didn't sleep a wink. I came to you the first thing this morning. Indeed, I tried to raise you on the telephone, last night, but could not establish a connection."

"Yes," said Holmes, reminiscently, "we were attending Mme. Trentini's first night. You remember, Watson, we dined later at Albani's."

"Oh, Mr. Holmes, do you think you can help me?" cried the abject collector.

"I trust so," answered my friend, cheerfully. "Indeed, I am certain I can. Such a book, as you remark, is not easily hidden. What say you, Watson, to a run down to Walton-on-Walton?"

"There is a train in half an hour," said Mr. Harrington Edwards, looking at his watch. "Will you return with me?"

"No, no," laughed Holmes, "that would never do. We must not be seen together just yet, Mr. Edwards. Go back yourself on the first train, by all means, unless you have further business in London. My friend and I will go together. There is another train this morning?"

"An hour later."

"Excellent. Until we meet, then!"

2

We took the train from Paddington Station an hour later, as we had promised, and began our journey to Walton-on-Walton, a pleasant, aristocratic little village and the scene of the curious accident to our friend of Poke Stogis Manor. Sherlock Holmes, lying back in his seat, blew earnest smoke rings at the ceiling of our compartment, which fortunately was empty, while I devoted myself to the morning paper. After a bit I tired of this occupation and turned to Holmes to find him looking out of the window, wreathed in smiles, and quoting Horace softly under his breath.

"You have a theory?" I asked, in surprise.

"It is a capital mistake to theorize in advance of the evidence," he replied. "Still, I have given some thought to the interesting problem of our friend, Mr. Harrington Edwards, and there are several indications which can point to only one conclusion."

"And whom do you believe to be the thief?"

"My dear fellow," said Sherlock Holmes, "you forget we already know the thief. Edwards has testified quite clearly that it was Miles who snatched the volume."

"True," I admitted, abashed. "I had forgotten. All we must do then, is to find Miles."

"And a motive," added my friend, chuckling. "What would you say, Watson, was the motive in this case?"

"Jealousy," I replied.

"You surprise me!"

"Miles had been bribed by a rival collector, who in some manner had learned about this remarkable volume. You remember Edwards told us this second man joined them at the lodge. That would give an excellent opportunity for the substitution of a man other than the servant intended by Sir Nathaniel. Is not that good reasoning?"

"You surpass yourself, my dear Watson," murmured Holmes. "It is excellently reasoned, and as you justly observe the opportunity for a substitution was perfect."

"Do you not agree with me?"

"Hardly, Watson. A rival collector, in order to accomplish this remarkable coup, first would have to have known of the volume, as you suggest, but also he must have known upon what night Mr. Harrington Edwards would go to Sir Nathaniel's to get it, which would point to collaboration on the part of our client. As a matter of fact, however, Mr. Edwards' decision to accept the loan, was, I believe, sudden and without previous determination."

"I do not recall his saying so."

"He did not say so, but it is a simple deduction. A book collector is mad enough to begin with, Watson; but tempt him with some such bait as this Shakespeare quarto and he is bereft of all sanity. Mr. Edwards would not have been able to wait. It was just the night before that Sir Nathaniel promised him the book, and it was just last night that he flew to accept the offer—flying, incidentally, to disaster also. The miracle is that he was able to wait an entire day."

"Wonderful!" I cried.

"Elementary," said Holmes. "If you are interested, you will do well to read Harley Graham on *Transcendental Emotion;* while I have myself been guilty of a small brochure in which I catalogue some twelve hundred professions and the emotional effect upon their members of unusual tidings, good and bad."

We were the only passengers to alight at Walton-on-Walton, but rapid inquiry developed that Mr. Harrington Edwards had returned on the previous train. Holmes, who had disguised himself before leaving the coach, did all the talking. He wore his cap peak backwards, carried a pencil behind his ear, and had turned up the bottoms of his trousers; while from one pocket dangled the end of a linen tape measure. He was a municipal surveyor to the life, and I could not but think that, meeting him suddenly in the highway I should not myself have known him. At his suggestion, I dented the crown of my hat and turned my jacket inside out. Then he gave me an end of the tape measure, while he, carrying the other, went on ahead. In this fashion, stopping from time to time to kneel in the dust and ostensibly to measure sections of the roadway, we proceeded toward Poke Stogis Manor. The occasional villagers whom we encountered on their way to the station bar paid us no more attention than if we had been rabbits.

Shortly we came in sight of our friend's dwelling, a picturesque and rambling abode, sitting far back in its own grounds and bordered by a square of sentinel oaks. A gravel pathway led from the roadway to the house entrance and, as we passed, the sunlight struck fire from an antique brass knocker on the door. The whole picture, with its background of gleaming countryside, was one of rural calm and comfort; we could with difficulty believe it the scene of the sinister tragedy we were come to investigate.

"We shall not enter yet," said Sherlock Holmes, passing the

gate leading into our client's acreage; "but we shall endeavor to be back in time for luncheon."

From this point the road progressed downward in a gentle incline and the trees were thicker on either side of the road. Sherlock Holmes kept his eyes stolidly on the path before us, and when we had covered about one hundred yards he stopped. "Here," he said, pointing, "the assault occurred."

I looked closely at the earth, but could see no sign of struggle.

"You recall it was midway between the two houses that it happened," he continued. "No, there are few signs; there was no violent tussle. Fortunately, however, we had our proverbial fall of rain last evening and the earth has retained impressions nicely." He indicated the faint imprint of a foot, then another, and still another. Kneeling down, I was able to see that, indeed, many feet had passed along the road.

Holmes flung himself at full length in the dirt and wriggled swiftly about, his nose to the earth, muttering rapidly in French. Then he whipped out a glass, the better to examine something that had caught his eye; but in a moment he shook his head in disappointment and continued with his exploration. I was irresistibly reminded of a noble hound, at fault, sniffing in circles in an effort to reëstablish a lost scent. In a moment, however, he had it, for with a little cry of pleasure he rose to his feet, zigzagged curiously across the road and paused before a hedge, a lean finger pointing accusingly at a break in the thicket.

"No wonder they disappeared," he smiled as I came up. "Edwards thought they continued up the road, but here is where they broke through." Then stepping back a little distance, he ran forward lightly and cleared the hedge at a bound, alighting on his hands on the other side.

"Follow me carefully," he warned, "for we must not allow our own footprints to confuse us." I fell more heavily than my companion, but in a moment he had me by the heels and helped me to steady myself. "See," he cried, lowering his face to the earth; and deep in the mud and grass I saw the prints of two pairs of feet.

"The small man broke through," said Sherlock Holmes, exultantly, "but the larger rascal leaped over the hedge. See how deeply his prints are marked; he landed heavily here in the soft ooze. It is significant, Watson, that they came this way. Does it suggest nothing to you?"

"That they were men who knew Edwards' grounds as well as the Brooke-Bannerman estate," I answered; and thrilled with pleasure at my friend's nod of approbation.

He lowered himself to his stomach, without further conversation, and for some moments we crawled painfully across the grass. Then a shocking thought occurred to me.

"Holmes," I whispered in horror, "do you see where these footprints tend? They are directed toward the home of our client, Mr. Harrington Edwards!"

He nodded his head slowly, and his lips were tight and thin. The double line of impressions ended abruptly at the back door of Poke Stogis Manor!

Sherlock Holmes rose to his feet and looked at his watch.

"We are just in time for luncheon," he announced, and brushed off his garments. Then, deliberately, he knocked upon the door. In a few moments we were in the presence of our client.

"We have been roaming about the neighborhood," apologized the detective "and took the liberty of coming to your rear door."

"You have a clue?" asked Mr. Harrington Edwards, eagerly.

A queer smile of triumph sat upon Holmes' lips.

"Indeed," he said, quietly, "I believe I have solved your little problem, Mr. Harrington Edwards."

"My dear Holmes!" I cried, and "My dear sir!" cried our client.

"I have yet to establish a motive," confessed my friend; "but as to the main facts there can be no question."

Mr. Harrington Edwards fell into a chair; he was white and shaking.

"The book," he croaked. "Tell me!"

"Patience, my good sir," counseled Holmes, kindly. "We have had nothing to eat since sunup, and we are famished. All in good time. Let us first dine and then all shall be made clear. Meanwhile, I should like to telephone to Sir Nathaniel Brooke-Bannerman, for I wish him also to hear what I have to say."

Our client's pleas were in vain. Holmes would have his little joke and his luncheon. In the end, Mr. Harrington Edwards staggered away to the kitchen to order a repast, and Sherlock Holmes talked rapidly and unintelligibly into the telephone and came back with a smile on his face. But I asked no questions; in good time this extraordinary man would tell his story in his own way. I had heard all that he had heard, and had seen all that he had seen; yet I was completely at sea. Still, our host's ghastly smile hung heavily in my mind, and come what would I felt sorry for him. In a little time we were seated at table. Our client, haggard and nervous, ate slowly and with apparent discomfort; his eyes were never long absent from Holmes' inscrutable face. I was little better off, but Sherlock Holmes ate with gusto, relating meanwhile a number of his earlier adventures—which I may some day give to the world, if I am able to read my illegible notes made on the occasion.

When the sorry meal had been concluded we went into the library, where Sherlock Holmes took possession of the easiest chair with an air of proprietorship that would have been amusing in other circumstances. He screwed together his long pipe and lighted it with almost malicious lack of haste, while Mr. Harrington Edwards perspired against the mantel in an agony of apprehension.

"Why must you keep us waiting, Mr. Holmes?" he whispered. "Tell us, at once, please, who—who—" His voice trailed off into a moan.

"The criminal," said Sherlock Holmes, smoothly, "is—"

"Sir Nathaniel Brooke-Bannerman!" said a maid, suddenly, putting her head in at the door; and on the heels of her announcement stalked the handsome baronet, whose priceless volume had caused all this commotion and unhappiness.

Sir Nathaniel was white, and he appeared ill. He burst at once into talk.

"I have been much upset by your call," he said, looking meanwhile at our client. "You say you have something to tell me about the quarto. Don't say—that—anything—has happened—to it!" He clutched nervously at the wall to steady himself, and I felt deep pity for the unhappy man.

Mr. Harrington Edwards looked at Sherlock Holmes. "Oh, Mr. Holmes," he cried, pathetically, "why did you send for him?"

"Because," said my friend, "I wish him to hear the truth about the Shakespeare quarto. Sir Nathaniel, I believe you have not been told as yet that Mr. Edwards was robbed, last night, of your precious volume—robbed by the trusted servants whom you sent with him to protect it."

"*What!*" screamed the titled collector. He staggered and fumbled madly at his heart, then collapsed into a chair. "My God!" he muttered, and then again: "My God!"

"I should have thought you would have been suspicious of evil when your servants did not return," pursued the detective.

"I have not seen them," whispered Sir Nathaniel. "I do not mingle with my servants. I did not know they had failed to return. Tell me—tell me all!"

"Mr. Edwards," said Sherlock Holmes, turning to our client, "will you repeat your story, please?"

Mr. Harrington Edwards, thus adjured, told the unhappy tale again, ending with a heartbroken cry of "Oh, Nathaniel, can you ever forgive me?"

"I do not know that it was entirely your fault," observed Holmes, cheerfully. "Sir Nathaniel's own servants are the guilty ones, and surely he sent them with you."

"But you said you had solved the case, Mr. Holmes," cried our client, in a frenzy of despair.

"Yes," agreed Holmes, "it is solved. You have had the clue in your own hands ever since the occurrence, but you did not know how to use it. It all turns upon the curious actions of the taller servant, prior to the assault."

"The actions of—?" stammered Mr. Harrington Edwards. "Why, he did nothing—said nothing!"

"That is the curious circumstance," said Sherlock Holmes.

Sir Nathaniel got to his feet with difficulty.

"Mr. Holmes," he said, "this has upset me more than I can tell you. Spare no pains to recover the book and to bring to justice the scoundrels who stole it. But I must go away and think—think—"

"Stay," said my friend. "I have already caught one of them."

"What! Where?" cried the two collectors together.

"Here," said Sherlock Holmes, and stepping forward he laid a hand on the baronet's shoulder. "You, Sir Nathaniel, were the taller servant; you were one of the thieves who throttled Mr. Harrington Edwards and took from him your own book. And now, sir, will you tell us why you did it?"

Sir Nathaniel Brooke-Bannerman toppled and would have fallen had not I rushed forward and supported him. I placed him in a chair. As we looked at him we saw confession in his eyes; guilt was written in his haggard face.

"Come, come," said Holmes, impatiently. "Or will it make it easier for you if I tell the story as it occurred? Let it be so, then. You parted with Mr. Harrington Edwards on your doorsill, Sir Nathaniel, bidding your best friend good-night with a smile on your lips and evil in your heart. And as soon as you had closed the door, you slipped into an enveloping raincoat, turned up your collar, and hastened by a shorter road to the porter's lodge, where you joined Mr. Edwards and Miles as one of your own servants. You spoke no word at any time, because you feared to speak. You were afraid Mr. Edwards would recognize your voice, while your beard, hastily assumed, protected your face and in the darkness your figure passed unnoticed.

"Having strangled and robbed your best friend, then, of your own book, you and your scoundrelly assistant fled across Mr. Edwards' fields to his own back door, thinking that, if investigation followed, I would be called in, and would trace those footprints and fix the crime upon Mr. Harrington Edwards—as part of a criminal plan, prearranged with your rascally servants, who would be supposed to be in the pay of Mr. Edwards and the ringleaders in a counterfeit assault upon his person. Your mistake, sir, was in ending your trail abruptly at Mr. Edwards' back door. Had you left another trail, then, leading back to your own domicile, I should unhesitatingly have arrested Mr. Harrington Edwards for the theft.

"Surely you must know that in criminal cases handled by me, it is never the obvious solution that is the correct one. The mere fact that the finger of suspicion is made to point at a certain individual is sufficient to absolve that individual from guilt. Had you read the little works of my friend and colleague, Dr. Watson, you would not have made such a mistake. Yet you claim to be a bookman!"

A low moan from the unhappy baronet was his only answer.

"To continue, however: there at Mr. Edwards' own back door you ended your trail, entering his house—his own house —and spending the night under his roof, while his cries and ravings over his loss filled the night and brought joy to your unspeakable soul. And in the morning, when he had gone forth to consult me, you quietly left—you and Miles—and returned to your own place by the beaten highway."

"Mercy!" cried the defeated wretch, cowering in his chair. "If it is made public, I am ruined. I was driven to it. I could not let Mr. Edwards examine the book, for that way exposure would follow; yet I could not refuse him—my best friend—when he asked its loan."

"Your words tell me all that I did not know," said Sherlock Holmes, sternly. "The motive now is only too plain. The work, sir, was a forgery, and knowing that your erudite friend would discover it, you chose to blacken his name to save your own. Was the book insured?"

"Insured for £100,000, he told me," interrupted Mr. Harrington Edwards, excitedly.

"So that he planned at once to dispose of this dangerous and dubious item, and to reap a golden reward," commented Holmes. "Come, sir, tell us about it. How much of it was forgery? Merely the inscription?"

"I will tell you," said the baronet, suddenly, "and throw myself upon the mercy of my friend, Mr. Edwards. The whole book, in effect, was a forgery. It was originally made up of two imperfect copies of the 1604 quarto. Out of the pair I made one perfect volume, and a skillful workman, now dead, changed the date for me so cleverly that only an expert of the first water could have detected it. Such an expert, however, is Mr. Harrington Edwards—the one man in the world who could have unmasked me."

"Thank you, Nathaniel," said Mr. Harrington Edwards, gratefully.

"The inscription, of course, also was forged," continued the baronet. "You may as well know everything."

"And the book?" asked Holmes. "Where did you destroy it?"

A grim smile settled on Sir Nathaniel's features. "It is even now burning in Mr. Edwards' own furnace," he said.

"Then it cannot yet be consumed," cried Holmes, and dashed into the cellar. He was absent for some time and we heard the clinking of bottles and, finally, the clang of a great metal door. He emerged, some moments later, in high spirits, carrying a charred leaf of paper in his hand.

"It is a pity," he cried, "a pity! In spite of its questionable authenticity, it was a noble specimen. It is only half consumed; but let it burn away. I have preserved one leaf as a souvenir of the occasion." He folded it carefully and placed it in his wallet. "Mr. Harrington Edwards, I fancy the decision in this matter is for you to announce. Sir Nathaniel, of course, must make no effort to collect the insurance."

"Let us forget it, then," said Mr. Harrington Edwards, with a sigh. "Let it be a sealed chapter in the history of bibliomania." He looked at Sir Nathaniel Brooke-Bannerman for a long moment, then held out his hand. "I forgive you, Nathaniel," he said, simply.

Their hands met; tears stood in the baronet's eyes. Powerfully moved, Holmes and I turned from the affecting scene and crept to the door unnoticed. In a moment the free air was blowing on our temples, and we were coughing the dust of the library from our lungs.

3

"They are a strange people, these book collectors," mused Sherlock Holmes, as we rattled back to town.

"My only regret is that I shall be unable to publish my notes on this interesting case," I responded.

"Wait a bit, my dear Doctor," counselled Holmes, "and it will be possible. In time both of them will come to look upon it as a hugely diverting episode, and will tell it upon themselves. Then your notes shall be brought forth and the history of another of Mr. Sherlock Holmes's little problems shall be given to the world."

"It will always be a reflection upon Sir Nathaniel," I demurred.

"He will glory in it," prophesied Sherlock Holmes. "He will go down in bookish chronicle with Chatterton, and Ireland, and Payne Collier. Mark my words, he is not blind even now to the chance this gives him for a sinister immortality. He will be the first to tell it." (And so, indeed, it proved, as this narrative suggests.)

"But why did you preserve the leaf from *Hamlet?*" I inquired. "Why not a jewel from the binding?"

Sherlock Holmes laughed heartily. Then he slowly unfolded the leaf in question, and directed a humorous finger to a spot upon the page.

"A fancy," he responded, "to preserve so accurate a characterization of either of our friends. The line is a real jewel. See, the good Polonius says: *'That he is mad, 'tis true: 'tis true 'tis pittie; and pittie it is true.'* There is as much sense in Master Will as in Hafiz or Confucius, and a greater felicity of expression. . . . Here is London, and now, my dear Watson, if we hasten we shall be just in time for Zabriski's matinee!"

MR. SHERLOCK HOLMES AND
DR. SAMUEL JOHNSON

By RICHARD D. ALTICK

ALL SHERLOCKIANISM IS based upon one's willingness to abandon sober considerations of established scientific and historical fact, and to allow oneself to dwell unrestricted in the pleasant realm of the imagination. Therefore, I think, it entirely suits the spirit of Holmesian speculation to dispute the popular belief that Sir Arthur Conan Doyle sternly suppressed his interest in the supernatural when he wrote the Holmes tales. Though in each of the famous cases in which, for a time, a supernatural explanation seems to be the only possible one, Holmes's cold scientific reasoning is finally triumphant, yet spirits do walk through the stories: not in such a way as to impair one's faith in the unshakable rationality of the Science of Deduction, but rather to warm the hearts of those enthusiasts who divide their allegiance between two pairs of literary comrades.

Some day the tablet which Mr. Morley has proposed actually will be erected in the Criterion bar in London to mark the site of the first meeting of Holmes and Watson. The formal unveiling will be the occasion for a great international gathering of Holmes addicts; and during the ensuing celebration we may well expect the Johnsonians among them to make a special pilgrimage to a certain spot on the Suffolk coast, near Harwich, there to commemorate what was not only the last recorded meeting of the immortal pair but also the occasion upon which the two genial spirits in eighteenth-century garb who hovered near Holmes and Watson during the entire period of their companionship came nearest, perhaps, to revealing themselves.

It was on the fateful night of August 2, 1914, that the aquiline-faced reasoner and the stodgy ex-army surgeon met at Harwich after a separation of some years. Holmes had just brought to a conclusion his brilliant plot against the German arch-spy, Count von Bork; and while the Count reposed, securely bound and cursing fluently in German, in Watson's car, the two friends wandered down to the beach and "chatted in intimate converse for a few minutes, recalling once again the days of the past." As they turned back to the car the detective pointed to the moonlit sea and shook a thoughtful head.

" 'There's an east wind coming, Watson.'

" 'I think not, Holmes. It is very warm.'

" 'Good old Watson! You are the one fixed point in a changing age. . . .' " [1]

Both men were naturally moved by their reunion after the lapse of years. Furthermore, Holmes's mind was occupied with the problem of the disposition of the Count; and Watson's delicious, true-to-form failure to grasp the significance of Holmes's remark about the east wind, in the face of the events that were then rocking the world, shows us that his wits had grown no sharper with the passage of years. So it was easy for the ghosts lurking in their vicinity to go unnoticed.

If Boswell, eager as ever for good copy, suggested to Dr. Johnson that they introduce themselves to the other pair, the Doctor must have vetoed the idea, his own deep bias on many questions making him entirely sympathetic with Holmes's impatience with such rubbish as ghosts or rumors of ghosts. But Watson, ever the more credulous and sentimental member of the Baker Street household, would have understood their

[1] *His Last Bow.*

presence there; for Boswell and Johnson were on a sentimental journey of their own. They had come to revisit the scene of the first affectionate leave Boswell had taken of his new-found mentor. Almost exactly one hundred and fifty-one years before (August, 1763) young Boswell had embarked for Helvoetsluys from this very spot. "My revered friend," as he recorded later, "walked down with me to the beach, where we embraced and parted with tenderness, and engaged to correspond with letters." [2]

Holmes and Watson climbed into the car and drove off, and Boswell and Dr. Johnson were left alone under the stars. Thus two pairs of men whose comradeships have become the everlasting property of literature never met; but so long as we have Watson's engrossing memoirs, reminiscences of Boswell and Johnson will continue to float, as hazy, perhaps, yet as thoroughly agreeable as Holmes's cigarette smoke, through the chambers in Baker Street.

If one were so humorless as to launch a formal professorial inquiry into the matter, it would be important to know that Sir Arthur was a thorough-going and enthusiastic Johnsonian, as is evidenced by an appreciative essay in his book *Through the Magic Door*.[3] But so pleasant a fancy as this shrinks from solemn research and documentation. We need only utter a word of gratitude that the ways of the imagination are sufficiently devious to allow an author, as he goes about the business of creating a criminologist of great intellect and somewhat eccentric personal habits, and a devoted companion-biographer, to draw upon half-lost memories of a real genius and of the disciple whose single-minded service to him resulted in the world's greatest biography. Then we are ready to ponder alluring questions: Was it during his college days that Holmes first became acquainted with Dr. Johnson? Surely it must have been, for Holmes was more plastic then,

[2] *Life of Samuel Johnson*, by James Boswell.   [3] London, 1908.

more ready to adopt—as he undoubtedly did—certain of Johnson's temperamental traits and idiosyncrasies. When, then, did Dr. Watson read Boswell? It is reasonable to suppose that he carried the *Life of Johnson* in his box when he campaigned in Afghanistan; during those long interims between fights and the longer period of his convalescence he would have had ample time to absorb Boswell's biographical ideals and methods as thoroughly as he did.

It is not for me to attempt an extensive survey of the traces we find of Johnsonianism in Holmes and Boswellism in Watson: that, some day, will be the happy task of a man like Mr. S. C. Roberts, who knows his Boswell, as well as his Sherlock Holmes, by heart. But it is a diverting pastime to select, almost at random, familiar aspects of those two great personalities and conjecture how they were influenced by the *Life of Johnson*—a book which, handsomely bound, must have occupied an honored place among the huge case-books and the treatises on surgery on the shelves at Baker Street.

It must be admitted that it would require considerable stretching of the imagination (even that of the most ingenious Holmesian) to fit Dr. Johnson's corpulence into Holmes's tall thin figure, and to accommodate his shambling gait, his awkwardness, his convulsive gestures to Holmes's swift, sure, tiger-like movements. The Doctor, who had an unashamed aversion toward clean linen, would have been sorely at a loss to explain why Holmes, while living in a prehistoric hut at Dartmoor, should have "contrived, with that catlike love of personal cleanliness which was one of his characteristics, that his chin should be as smooth and his linen as perfect as if he were in Baker Street." [4] And on the other hand, it is difficult to imagine Holmes, who "never spoke of the softer passions, save with a gibe and a sneer," expressing a naïve desire to "spend my life in driving briskly in a post-chaise with a pretty

[4] *The Hound of the Baskervilles.*

woman." [5]. But their many dissimilarities make the parallels we find between them all the more interesting.

Take for example the interesting coincidence of the chemical table. If Boswell and Watson ever had been able to arrange a meeting between their respective mentors in the Baker Street rooms, any doubts which Dr. Johnson might have had upon meeting the lithe, nervous reasoner would have been resolved immediately upon seeing, in the living-room corner, the acid-charred bench, the Bunsen burners, and the "formidable array of bottles and test-tubes" to which Holmes repaired for his not infrequent all-night philosophical sessions. Boswell would have reminded Watson that on his first visit to Johnson's library he "observed an apparatus for chymical experiments, of which Johnson was all his life very fond," and that Johnson, as late as 1782, had found amateur chemistry a means of mental relaxation after a severe paralytic stroke. Watson in reply would have recounted to Boswell how, when Holmes reached an impasse in the matter of the Norwood tragedy, he sought a complete change of occupation, and "busied himself all the evening in an abstruse chemical analysis which involved much heating of retorts and distilling of vapors, ending at last in a smell which fairly drove me out of the apartment. Up to the small hours of the morning," he would tell the sympathetic Boswell, "I could hear the clinking of his test-tubes which told me that he was still engaged in his malodorous experiment." [6] Indeed, they might have made quite a little game of quoting parallel passages. When Boswell recalled how that same experimental curiosity led Johnson, at the age of seventy, to shave the hair from part of his right arm and breast merely to see how long it would take to grow again, Watson might have countered with the remark of Stamford, the dresser who was to Holmes and Watson what Tom Davies was to Johnson and Boswell: "Holmes is

[5] *Life of Samuel Johnson.*   [6] *The Sign of the Four.*

a little too scientific for my tastes—it approaches to cold-bloodedness. I could imagine his giving a friend a little pinch of the latest vegetable alkaloid, not out of malevolence, you understand, but simply out of a spirit of inquiry, in order to have an accurate idea of the effects." [7]

And then, the intolerable positiveness of the two thinkers! A conversational dictator—a layer-down of dogma—a stater of what he conceived to be and what he unapologetically offered as indisputable fact—a man from whose judgment no appeal was possible: I happened to be thinking of Dr. Johnson, but the description applies with equal accuracy, does it not, to Holmes. (Johnson's pistol missed fire, sometimes; but, as Goldsmith said, when that happened he knocked you down with the butt end of it. Were the truth to be confessed, Holmes's automatic missed fire too; only his self-assurance was so great that Watson was persuaded into believing he was being shot when Holmes in reality was futilely clicking the trigger.) "Detection is, or ought to be, an exact science, and should be treated in the same cold and unemotional manner. You have attempted to tinge it with romanticism, which produces much the same effect as if you worked a love-story or an elopement into the fifth proposition of Euclid." [8] This is the manner of the Great Cham laying down the law before the Literary Club as much as it is Holmes lecturing to a solitary hearer. "But the romance was there," Watson timorously objects from across the fire, in defense of *A Study in Scarlet*. "I could not tamper with the facts." But the lecturer is impatient of such irrelevant interruptions, and swings his bludgeon again. "Some facts should be suppressed," he goes on, Johnsonian-like, full steam ahead; "or, at least, a just sense of proportion should be observed in treating them. The only point in the case which deserved mention

[7] *A Study in Scarlet.*   [8] *The Sign of the Four.*

was the curious analytical reasoning from effects to causes, by
which I succeeded in unravelling it. . . ."

It would be instructive to make a comparative list of the
subjects on which Holmes and Johnson were deeply preju-
diced; but we can stop only long enough to note one of their
most outstanding temperamental biases. Both were men of
utter rationality, who scorned every suggestion of the emotional. Recall the famous little scene which occurs just after
Mary Morstan has left Holmes's sitting-room:

"What a very attractive woman!" I exclaimed, turning to my
companion.

He had lit his pipe again and was leaning back with drooping
eyelids. "Is she?" he said languidly; "I did not observe."

"You really are an automaton—a calculating machine," I cried.
"There is something positively inhuman in you at times."

He smiled gently.

"It is of the first importance," he said, "not to allow your
judgment to be biassed by personal qualities. A client is to me
a mere unit, a factor in a problem. The emotional qualities are
antagonistic to clear reasoning. I assure you that the most win-
ning woman I ever knew was hanged for poisoning three little
children for their insurance-money, and the most repellent man
of my acquaintance is a philanthropist who has spent nearly a
quarter of a million upon the London poor." [9]

And when at the conclusion of the grim business of the *Sign
of the Four* Watson happily announces, "Miss Morstan has
done me the honour to accept me as a husband in prospective,"
Holmes cavalierly dashes his enthusiasm by refusing to con-
gratulate him: "Love is an emotional thing," he says, "and
whatever is emotional is opposed to that true cold reason I
place above all things."

Sometimes (as Watson so neatly puts it) I found myself regarding
him as an isolated phenomenon, a brain without a heart, as de-

[9] *Ibid.*

ficient in human sympathy as he was preëminent in intelligence. His aversion to women and his disinclination to form new friendships were both typical of his unemotional character, but not more so than his complete suppression of every reference to his own people.[10]

If, in some moment of self-searching, the youthful Sherlock Holmes had sought distinguished precedent for his almost unnatural emotionlessness, he would have been immeasurably heartened to find this passage in his Boswell, a passage which perhaps Watson had in the back of his mind as he wrote the sentences just quoted:

In drawing Dryden's character, Johnson has given, though I suppose unintentionally, some touches of his own. Thus:—"*The power that predominated in his intellectual operations was rather strong reason than quick sensibility.* Upon all occasions that were presented, he studied rather than felt; and produced sentiments not such as Nature enforces, but meditation supplies. With the simple and elemental passions as they spring separate in the mind, he seems not much acquainted. He is, therefore, with all his variety of excellence, not often pathetick; and *he had so little sensibility of the power of effusions purely natural, that he did not esteem them in others.*"

But even the most rational of men are sometimes bundles of contradictions. Certainly it was so in the case of Holmes and Johnson, for hand in hand with their scorn of the normal human emotions went an extreme susceptibility to praise. Behind Holmes's deprecatory "Elementary, my dear Watson!" lay a strong pleasure in being the object of genuine admiration. Indeed, his defense of his toleration of Watson, though accurate so far as it goes, is incomplete: "A confederate who foresees your conclusions and course of action is always dangerous, but one to whom each development comes as a perpetual surprise, and to whom the future is always a closed

[10] *The Greek Interpreter.*

book, is indeed an ideal helpmate." He might have added that it was his love of basking in the sunlight of Watson's honest praise after the closed book was opened that kept the friendship intact through those memorable years. Take that supremely dramatic moment when Holmes breaks the plaster bust of Napoleon and produces the famous black pearl of the Borgias:

Lestrade and I sat silent for a moment, and then, with a spontaneous impulse, we both broke out clapping, as at the well-wrought crisis of a play. A flush of colour sprung to Holmes's pale cheeks, and he bowed to us like the master dramatist who receives the homage of his audience. It was at such moments that for an instant he ceased to be a reasoning machine, and betrayed his human love for admiration and applause. *The same singularly proud and reserved nature which turned away with disdain from popular notoriety was capable of being moved to its depths by spontaneous wonder and praise from a friend.*[11]

To which one need only add for comparison this singularly apposite sentence of Boswell's: "He loved praise when it was brought to him; but he was too proud to seek for it."

It was not merely professional pride, either, that made Holmes "more depressed and shaken than I had ever seen him" when Watson discovered in the morning paper the news of the death of John Openshaw: "It becomes a personal matter with me now," he declared, "and if God gives me health, I shall set my hand upon this gang. That he should come to me for help, and that I should send him away to his death—!"[12]   And his very human sympathy for young Captain Croker, which extended even to breaking the law,[13] leads us to echo in his praise Goldsmith's remark, "Johnson, to be sure, has a roughness in his manner; but no man alive has a more tender heart."

Such little anomalies in their characters result sometimes in

[11] *The Six Napoleons.*
[13] *The Abbey Grange.*
[12] *The Five Orange Pips.*

our seriously suspecting Holmes, with all his intolerance of sham, of occasional dissembling. Piquantly enough, both he and Dr. Johnson strove to deceive their friends on the same point. Let us imagine Johnson enjoying a Baker Street breakfast, seated at the table with the morning newspapers and the polished silver coffee pot which once gave Watson the idea that Holmes had eyes in the back of his head: [14] when Mrs. Hudson enters with the rashers and the steaming, fragrant coffee he turns to her and ponderously remarks (as he once did to a lady with whom he was about to sup): "I, madam, who live at a variety of good tables, am a much better judge of cookery than any person who has a very tolerable cook, but lives much at home, for his palate is gradually adapted to the tastes of his cook, whereas, madam, in trying by a wider range, I can more exquisitely judge." Mrs. Hudson no doubt would deliver him a pregnant look; and if he dined in Baker Street very often she would discover, as his friends soon did, that independent observation of his table-manners and his excessive appetite would by no means bear out his pretensions to exquisite taste. Now Holmes, in order to be as consistent as possible in his character of the detached, almost bodiless intellect, made it very clear that he had no interest in food: "Why, surely, as a doctor, my dear Watson, you must admit that what your digestion gains in the way of blood supply is so much lost to the brain. I am a brain, Watson. The rest of me is a mere appendix." [15] But independent observation would no more confirm that statement than it would Dr. Johnson's: not so long as we are constantly encountering appetizing references in the stories to "oysters and a brace of grouse, with something a little choice in white wines" (the dinner-prelude to the wild chase down the Thames in the steam-launch *Aurora*) [16] and "a couple of brace of cold wood-

[14] *The Hound of the Baskervilles.*   [15] *The Mazarin Stone.*
[16] *The Sign of the Four.*

cock, a pheasant, a *pâté de fois gras* pie with a group of ancient and cobwebby bottles" (over which Holmes—his idealism fired, no doubt, by his success in the case of the Noble Bachelor—relieved himself of the somewhat oratorical but no less laudable hope that "the folly of a monarch and the blundering of a minister in far-gone years will not prevent our children from being some day citizens of the same world-wide country under a flag which shall be a quartering of the Union Jack with the Stars and Stripes").[17] Holmes would have writhed at Johnson's blunt dictum, "For my part, I mind my belly very studiously and very carefully, for I look upon it that he who does not mind his belly will hardly mind anything else;" and yet, if the Baker Street menus are an accurate indication, epicure that he was he too minded his belly very studiously.

Watson's affinity with James Boswell began at birth; for (if we may accept the attractive hypothesis of Mr. James Keddie) he was as much of a Scotchman as Boswell. And his history, up to the time he met Holmes, was essentially that of the earlier chronicler; for both "naturally gravitated to London, that great cesspool into which all the loungers and idlers of the Empire are irresistibly drained," and, having "neither kith nor kin in England," were therefore as free as air. Boswell met Johnson in the first place because, as a professional sycophant, he had definite designs upon him. Watson's biographical impulse, on the other hand, came after the friendship was well begun, when it dawned upon him that fate had thrown him into a situation felicitously like the eighteenth-century one he had read so much about while he was campaigning in Afghanistan.

"I am lost without my Boswell!" exclaimed Holmes as Watson, with unwonted delicacy, made to leave the room before the entrance of the King of Bohemia.[18] By those six words Holmes shows us that he recognized how closely the relation-

[17] *The Noble Bachelor.*   [18] *A Scandal in Bohemia.*

ship between him and his companion followed the distinguished literary model. He knew he was playing Dr. Johnson to Watson's Boswell, and he accepted the rôle good-humoredly. He did not, it is true, approve of Watson's methods ("You have degraded what should have been a course of lectures into a series of tales"),[19] but he was pleased to supply him with details which were needed to fill out his record ("Well, well, I daresay that a couple of rabbits would account both for the blood and for the charred ashes. If you ever write an account, Watson, you can make rabbits serve your turn").[20] Johnson, as Boswell records, "from time to time . . . obligingly satisfied my inquiries, by communicating to me the incidents of his early years." Holmes's reticence concerning all his personal affairs forbade his similarly obliging Watson (if he had, how much fertile ground for speculation would we have missed!) but he did go so far as to recount to him, with quite frank pride, the histories of some of his earliest cases, notably those concerning the Musgrave Ritual and the "Gloria Scott."

But if he was denied much of the biographical information Boswell had received so freely, Watson made up for it by the uninhibited use of what he had himself observed; and thus his memoirs became one long triumphant demonstration of the Boswellian method. Though unkind critics may do for Watson what they have done for Boswell, and attribute his frankness more to ingenuousness than to genius, the fact remains that his portrait of Holmes is full-length and three-dimensional, and a speaking likeness. Censorship occurs only when Holmes's professional ethics or public policy require it; otherwise, Watson is the world's most honest biographer. He has no desire to withhold from us some of the less appealing of Holmes's shortcomings, such as his indulging in cocaine, his vanity, his brusqueness, his positive inhumanity in certain

[19] *The Copper Beeches.*   [20] *The Norwood Builder.*

respects. "He would not cut off his claws, nor make his tiger a cat, to please anybody." (The sentiments are *Boswell's*, not Watson's; they were uttered to Hannah More when she begged him to "mitigate" some of Johnson's asperities.)

Watson was equally candid regarding himself. Without materially injuring the story he might have deleted some of Holmes's unflattering references to his (Watson's) lack of intelligence. But no; conscientious artist that he is, he must provide his hero with a foil, even if that foil is sometimes shown in a rather uncomplimentary light, and furthermore happens to be John H. Watson himself.

I deem it a matter for everlasting regret that we have no way of finding out how people regarded Watson—people, I mean, like the clients who came to Baker Street to tell Holmes state secrets of the highest importance or to lay bare an extremely delicate *affaire du coeur*, and found Watson placidly sitting with Holmes; or the police officials who, when Holmes's hansom cab rattled up to the scene of a new outrage, were forced to greet the ubiquitous Watson as well as Holmes —and confess to Holmes in front of him that they were stumped again! Though young Inspector MacDonald, Holmes's favorite official detective,[21] may be forgiven for thinking that Jonathan Wild was a detective, it is unfortunate that the Scotland Yard men were so ignorant about literary matters; they might have derived comfort from looking up contemporary opinion on Boswell. "Who is this Scotch cur at Johnson's heels?" Goldsmith was asked. "He is not a cur," he replied. "You are too severe. He is only a burr. Tom Davies flung him at Johnson in sport, and he has the faculty of sticking." Substitute "Holmes" for "Johnson" and "Stamford" for "Tom Davies" and even Lestrade and Gregson would have understood, and grinned.

But if it is confessed that sometimes Watson was as much

[21] *The Valley of Fear.*

of a pest as Boswell, in justice to him we must recall that Holmes started the whole business by telling Watson to get his hat and come with him as he set out for Brixton Road.[22] It was Sherlock's fault as much as Watson's that it soon became the rule that everywhere that Holmes went Watson was sure to go. One reason was, as I have suggested, Holmes's secret desire for a wondering audience; and a more important one was that which Watson described in this passage, which, without the alteration of a single word, might just as well have been written by Boswell:

The relations between us in those latter days were peculiar. He was a man of habits, narrow and concentrated habits, and I was one of them. . . . I was a whetstone for his mind. I stimulated him. He liked to think aloud in my presence. His remarks could hardly be said to be made to me—many of them would have been as appropriately addressed to his bedstead—but none the less, having formed the habit, it had become in some way helpful that I should register and interject. If I irritated him by a certain methodical slowness in my mentality, that irritation served only to make his own flame-like intuitions and impressions flash up the more vividly and swiftly. Such was my humble role in our alliance.[23]

Watson was, as he said, "one of the most long-suffering of mortals," [24] but even Job might have quit Baker Street in despair. Watson was perfectly within his rights in beginning an observation by saying, "I am inclined to think—" and we can wholeheartedly sympathize with his annoyance when Holmes cut in impatiently, "I should do so." [25] And, even though Watson bungled things when he set out to solve the mystery of the disappearance of Lady Frances Carfax, he did the best he could with his limited intellectual equipment; he did not deserve Holmes's petulant words, "And a singularly consistent investigation you have made, my dear Watson. I

[22] *A Study in Scarlet.*   [23] *The Creeping Man.*   [24] *The Valley of Fear.*
[25] *Ibid.*

cannot at the moment recall any possible blunder which you have omitted. . . ." [26]

However, Holmes was too much of a gentleman to show his disgust with Watson very frequently. Johnsonian example could have suggested to him many nasty digs, if he had chosen to use them; for instance, when his strategy required that a certain person be kept safely out of the way while he did some rapid investigating (as in the affair of *The Dying Detective* and the *Adventure of Charles Augustus Milverton*) he might have observed to Watson, "Nay, Sir, we'll send you to him. If your presence doesn't drive a man out of his house, nothing will." But, to his credit, Holmes never was so discourteous. On the contrary, it was only his immediate gentleness that saved the situation after he had uncovered the disgrace of Watson's brother.[27] Had Holmes been less of a gentleman about it, Watson might have followed Boswell's example and refused to go near his mentor for a week—which might have taken the friendship into precarious straits indeed.

But Holmes's very real anxiety when the Chicago thug, Killer Evans, shot Watson in the Garrideb Museum, more than compensated for his occasional impatience:

"You're not hurt, Watson? For God's sake, say that you are not hurt!"

It was worth a wound—it was worth many wounds—to know the depth of loyalty and love which lay behind that cold mask. The clear, hard eyes were dimmed for a moment, and the firm lips were shaking. For the one and only time I caught a glimpse of a great heart as well as of a great brain. All my years of humble but single-minded service culminated in that moment of revelation.[28]

I appeal to every impartial reader whether this faithful detail of his frankness, complacency, and kindness does not refute the unjust opinion of the harshness of his general demeanour. His

---

[26] *The Disappearance of Lady Frances Carfax.*
[27] *The Sign of the Four.*   [28] *The Three Garridebs.*

occasional reproofs of folly, impudence, or impiety, and even the sudden sallies of his constitutional irritability of temper, which have been preserved for the poignancy of their wit, have produced that opinion among those who have not considered that such instances . . . were, in fact, scattered through a long series of years. . . ."[29]

Right; the last paragraph is Boswell, and not Watson; but, were it not for the sudden reversion into eighteenth-century style, could not the whole passage have been lifted intact from *The Three Garridebs?* "This faithful detail of his frankness, complacency, and kindness" happened to be Johnson's encouraging Boswell to travel abroad; but since Boswell failed to realize that Johnson's motives may not have been entirely unselfish, who are we to take offense at the Doctor's gentle deception? We can at least free Johnson of the suspicion of insincerity in his letters; in one of them he told Boswell, "Never, my dear Sir, do you take it into your head to think that I do not love you; you may settle yourself in full confidence both of my love and my esteem." And these, we may well believe, were Holmes's true sentiments as well. He would have been remarkably unappreciative had he failed to recognize the many sterling qualities of his longtime companion and biographer.

The scriptural dictum that we cannot serve two masters is not without its tragi-comic significance in the sagas of Boswell and Watson. For while Mrs. Watson sat at home and told patients the doctor wasn't in and she didn't know when he would be in—omitting to add that he was flying about London with Holmes, the well-known consulting detective, in pursuit of some clever criminal—her thoughts may conceivably have wandered to her sister in misery, the lonely lady who had sat at Auchinleck over a century before and heaped malediction upon the ugly man of letters who had lured her

[29] *Life of Samuel Johnson.*

husband from her. Mrs. Boswell was very outspoken about her feelings toward Dr. Johnson; her husband, whose passion for artistic completeness eclipsed the unpleasantness of writing about one's marital disaffection, quotes her as saying "in a little warmth" but (as he hastens to add) "with more point than justice," "I have seen many a bear led by a man; but I never before saw a man led by a bear."

Though Dr. Johnson wrote to Boswell, in 1775, that Mrs. Boswell "knows that she does not care what becomes of me, and for that she may be sure I think her very much to blame," he sent, as he always did, his compliments to the good lady. Holmes almost never wrote to Watson, and his curt telegrams were too short for any greetings to his disciple's wife; nevertheless we may surmise that Holmes knew that "she had not that high admiration of him which was felt by most of those who knew him" (phraseology by Boswell). What woman would have a high regard for the man who disrupted her well-ordered household by sending peremptory summonses such as "Come at once if convenient—if inconvenient come all the same" [30] and practically abducted her respectable husband from a vile opium den in Upper Swandam Lane, where he had gone on a charitable mission? [31] And even if Holmes did not have Dr. Johnson's obnoxious habit of letting tallow drip on his hostess' rugs, he still could not expect a very warm welcome when, hotly pursued by gentlemen with air-guns, he turned her respectable house into a place of refuge and insisted upon leaving *via* the back garden wall. Superficially, Mrs. Watson seemed favorable enough toward her husband's running off with Holmes; when the wire arrived summoning him to the Boscombe Valley she said, "I think that the change would do you good, and you are always so interested in Mr. Sherlock Holmes's cases." [32] But the bitingly sarcastic inflec-

[30] *The Creeping Man.*   [31] *The Man with the Twisted Lip.*
[32] *The Boscombe Valley Mystery.*

tion of her voice was lost only upon the excited Watson; never upon his readers. Thus we may commiserate with Mrs. Watson; driven to an early grave by her husband's neglect of her, she nevertheless may have the satisfaction of martyrdom. For without her acquiescence, however unwilling, we might never have heard of the Creeping Man, the Man with the Twisted Lip, and the Stock-Broker's Clerk. Her husband's stories are her monument, even as the *Life of Johnson* is, in a very true sense, Mrs. Boswell's.

The intolerance that characterized the two geniuses; their pride in being all intellect and no heart; their secret love of praise; their impatience, concealing their real love for their respective companions; their roles of more or less unwitting home-wreckers—all serve to suggest the spiritual affinity that existed between Sherlock Holmes and Dr. Johnson. (We might even suggest a sort of kinship between their respective tendencies toward melancholia.) But the subject upon which, of all others, Johnsonians and Sherlockians could spend endless hours of happy speculation, is their conversation. Once Watson and Boswell straightened out their masters' temperamental antipathies, what a prodigious flow of good talk would have resulted from their meeting! Dr. Johnson might have shied away from a learned discussion of the polyphonic motets of Lasso, and Holmes for his part might not have shown much interest in the digestive faculties of dogs, which Johnson once learnedly discussed with a country rector. (More in his line would have been the curious incident of the dog in the night time—see *Silver Blaze*.) But between these poles there is a vast expanse of information, and we may feel certain that the two great talkers would not miss much. From boxing to dancing (Johnson's knowledge of which once dazzled a dancing-master); from the letters of Gustave Flaubert to George Sand to the Erse grammar; from the Buddhism of Ceylon to the management of a farm; from the cause of the

A willowy Sherlock Holmes, by C. R. Macauley (from "The Return of Sherlock Holmes," New York, 1905, courtesy of Doubleday, Doran & Co.)

change in the obliquity of the ecliptic to Scottish law (a phase of Dr. Johnson's knowledge at which Sir Arthur Conan Doyle especially marvelled): back and forth the talk would go, with Watson perhaps adding a few comments of his own, for he was by no means an uneducated man, and Boswell scribbling furiously upon his tablets. Watson would recall Boswell's remark about Johnson, "He had accumulated a vast and various collection of learning and knowledge, which was so arranged in his mind, as to be ever in readiness to be brought forth," and wonder why he had never thought of quoting it.

The Baker Street apartments would have to be the scene of this epoch-making evening, for, though Holmes himself often "found it a very soothing atmosphere," the Diogenes Club would scarcely have proved an agreeable milieu for the expansive, clubbable Dr. Johnson. And if (as it was likely to do) the talk became too heated, the four of them could descend to the streets of the city and there again find spiritual communion; for they were among the most devoted Londoners of whom we have record.

They might walk first in the park, where Holmes and Watson were accustomed to stroll in the twilight. Dr. Johnson would ask, "Is not this very fine?" Boswell, "having no exquisite relish of the beauties of Nature, and being more delighted with 'the busy hum of men,'" would reply, "Yes, Sir; but not equal to Fleet Street." And Johnson, with an air of finality of which Holmes and Watson would heartily approve, would say, "You are right, Sir."

And so for Fleet Street they would head, and in Fleet Street we shall leave them: four of literature's most agreeable comrades, who may be depended upon, wherever they walk, to provide us with perpetually good company. My Holmesian addiction offers me fewer pleasanter moments than when I think of them, unsubstantial and yet as real as my next-door neighbor, still walking through the streets of their beloved city: Holmes and Johnson side by side, and their biographers following after them, listening "amused and enthralled" to their characteristic talk as they "strolled about together, watching the ever-changing kaleidoscope of life as it ebbs and flows through Fleet Street and the Strand."

SHERLOCK HOLMES IN PICTURES

By FREDERIC DORR STEELE

SHERLOCK HOLMES IS fifty years old. William Gillette is dead. Neither fact is quite credible.

This is written by the illustrator who, since *The Return of Sherlock Holmes* in 1903, has made pictures for nearly all the tales. Oddly enough, I do not care for "defective" stories, and never have had any desire to curl up with a good one. But thanks to my long association with the Emperor of Detectives, I have found myself looked upon as an expert in crime. My plight is a little like that of Mr. Reginald Birch, who drew pictures for *Little Lord Fauntleroy* in 1885 and has carried that golden-curled, velvet-suited incubus on the back of his neck ever since.

Let us consider the pictures of Sherlock, beginning with those drawn long before my time. You know my methods, Watson. We must have facts; it is a capital mistake to theorize before one has data.

Sidney Paget was not the earliest illustrator of Sherlock Holmes (the first was D. H. Friston, who illustrated *A Study in Scarlet* in 1887), but it was Paget who imposed his conception on the English mind. Beginning with the *Adventures* in 1891 in the *Strand Magazine*, he continued through a second series (*Memoirs*); then followed with *The Hound of the Baskervilles* and *The Return*. He died, prematurely, a few years later. Sir Arthur writes of "poor Sidney Paget," and of the younger brother who posed for him and made Sherlock handsomer than the author intended. Paget's pictures improved as he went along; if the earlier ones seem imperfect to our eyes, it is partly because of the crude woodcut reproduction. Scenes of gloom and terror were likely to appear faintly comic. Few American readers saw these English illustrations, and for some the first Sherlock was the plump and dapper blade portrayed by W. H. Hyde when a few of the tales were printed in *Harper's Weekly* in 1893. H. C. Edwards illustrated the last *Memoir*, *The Final Problem*, in *McClure's* for December.

For most Americans, the image of our hero was created by the actor William Gillette, who wrote the absurd and delightful melodrama entitled *Sherlock Holmes*, which reached the New York stage in November, 1899, ran two seasons in America and a season in London. Mr. Gillette was blessed by nature with the lean, sinewy figure and keen visage required, and his quiet but incisive histrionic method exactly fitted such a part as Sherlock. I can think of no more perfect realization of a fictional character on the stage.

In 1903, just ten years after Doyle had killed Sherlock, he brought him back to life. His series entitled *The Return of Sherlock Holmes* began publication at the end of that year, in the *Strand Magazine* with illustrations by Paget, and simultaneously in *Collier's Weekly* with pictures by myself. For the first story, *The Empty House*, I made six illustrations, and by a curious coincidence, Paget and I chose the same subjects in four instances. That date, 1903, corrects, of course, the faulty chronology of those who have vaguely supposed that my drawings preceded the play.

I did not need to be told to make my Sherlock look like Gillette. The thing was inevitable. I kept him in mind and even copied or adapted parts of a few of the stage photographs. At that time I never had seen the play, and it was not until 1929 that Mr. Gillette actually became my model in the flesh. Lured from retirement for a farewell tour by the artful George C. Tyler, cornered in the Biltmore by the hounds of publicity, he seated himself—with the air of one taking the

William Gillette, sketched from life by Frederic Dorr Steele
(by permission of the artist)

electric chair—and for the duration of three cigarettes talked to Mr. H. I. Brock of the *Times* and exhibited his famous profile for my first drawing of it from life.

My original model for Sherlock Holmes was an Englishman named Robert King, who posed as him throughout the thirteen tales of the *Return*. The drawings for the first story were made in Deerfield, Massachusetts, and Mr. King journeyed there to help me. He was a sensitive, fine fellow; his nose was not hawklike, but he had cavernous eyes—and he owned a frock coat. When later stories came along, about 1908, King, to my regret, had swum out of my ken, and I fell back on that standby of the studios, Frank B. Wilson. Irish by ancestry (his real name was Wall), he had gone on the stage as a youth and had been for some years actor and stage manager in the company of Sir Henry Irving. After a breakdown of health, he set his face resolutely toward a new job. He became a model, kept an amazing store of costumes and other equipment stowed away in odd places, and for thirty years or more was the most resourceful, faithful, and competent man in that stop-gap profession. About 1926, while the later stories were appearing in *Liberty*, two of Wilson's tall sons followed in their father's footsteps; but most of the Sherlocks in this series were drawn from the fine frame and crag-like head of a model called S. B. Doughty.

Mr. Vincent Starrett in *The Private Life of Sherlock Holmes* lists twelve Englishmen and six Americans who have illustrated the text, and even that list is incomplete. Mr. Edmund Pearson, the eminent criminalographer, wrote an admirable paper, *Sherlock Holmes Among the Illustrators*, for the *Bookman* of August, 1932. Speaking of Arthur I. Keller, one of the Americans, who had taken a fling at Sherlock in *The Valley of Fear*, he says it was he who "dealt the cruelest blow at Watson. From merely the innocent Johnny of Mr. Steele's drawings, Watson emerges in Mr. Keller's pictures as *boobus*

Britannicus." . . . Mr. Keller himself spoke some memorable words to me on the subject of models: "Oh yes, I probably used Wilson, but it didn't matter who it was. I only use models for construction anyway." The individuality in his figures was supplied from his own head; he never could have been accused of "type casting."

Readers of the early tales have remarked a rapid change in Sherlock. The thinking machine who rigidly excluded from his mental storehouse any knowledge not useful for his immediate purpose soon became a walking encyclopedia. But physically Sherlock needed no change or development; Dr. Doyle from the outset knew what his hero looked like. It is odd that the "great hawk's bill of a nose" so explicitly described was ignored by the English draughtsmen for many years. Not until the *Return* series was well under way did one see in Paget's noses a suggestion of aquilinity. Was it the Gillette influence? Such considerations bring up old questions: Do illustrators ever read the text? And the corollary: Should all illustrators die at dawn, and all books come out with their text undefiled? Shall we make exceptions in the rare instances in which author and artist are one, as in Thackeray, du Maurier, Pyle? What would Doyle's own pictures have been like? Did he like Paget best?

Here I can tell what Sir Arthur said to me on the one occasion when I met him. It was at a luncheon given for him in New York by Mark Sullivan, of *Collier's*, some time during the second term of Theodore Roosevelt. The President could not come, but his daughter Ethel and one or two Cabinet members and their wives were there. A weighty occasion. I was somewhat palpitant when my turn came to talk with the great man. Would he be kind to me? Would he commend my earnest efforts? I must be self-effacing, I thought; I will ask him about Paget first. "Young man," he began briskly, "do you know who did the best illustrations ever made for me? Cyrus Cuneo!" He began to tell me why; something interrupted; the interview ended. I had not needed to be self-effacing. Sir Arthur effaced me. I can make no explanation of his preference: Mr. Cuneo was notorious for committing the illustrator's deadliest sin, giving the plot away. If he had done the drawings for Watson's tales, I felt sure no cunningly hidden solution, no trick ending was safe. Later I found out that he had illustrated many of Doyle's other novels but never a Sherlock.

Evidences have come to me in the mail of a vast invisible army of Sherlock Holmes idolaters—bits of curious information, inquiries for the "old originals," now and then a request for "data to help me on a monograph I desire to write on Sherlock Holmes." Perhaps the most extraordinary of these communications came to me from Dr. Gray Chandler Briggs of St. Louis, a devoted collector of Sherlockiana, who wrote me that he had spent a summer vacation in London, mapped Baker Street with care, located the lodgings at the present No. 111 Baker Street, and submitted his findings to the author. He sent me the map, descriptions, and photographs, and they were published later in the Gillette souvenir program. His theory about the location of the house thus attracted much attention. It has been approved by Vincent Starrett, disapproved by H. W. Bell (author of an amazing Holmes-Watson chronology), and, we must add, blandly dismissed by Doyle himself. Whether we can accept the Briggs theory or not, it is a most ingenious addition to the lore of the subject. On a visit to London in May, 1931, I spent a pleasant evening following the ardent Doctor's footsteps, and can report that, save for a new arc light near the "kerb," the premises remained as he described them.

The matter of the original drawings also involves Dr. Briggs. He had seen one at the Louisiana Purchase Exposition in his own city in 1904, and were there any left, and could he get them? Artists are disorderly beings, but something must necessarily be done with studio accumulations. In my own case these were kept in a packing box, the object of frequent profane revilings. My fellow-craftsmen will agree, I am sure, that the joy of creation is exceeded only by the joy of destruction. Hence during the agony of moving, or cleaning, the box was dragged out and the less fit were slaughtered. So some years ago the number had been reduced to perhaps a score, and Dr. Briggs has them all.

The late Ralph Barton cheered one Christmas for me with what is now a valued souvenir. He had redrawn one of my cover designs of long ago, a profile of Sherlock in a dressing gown, with a bloody handprint on the wall. The hawklike beak was undisturbed but the chin had disappeared beneath a Santa Claus beard, complete with string.

"But how did you remember that design so clearly?" I wrote in my letter of thanks.

"Because," he replied, "it was pasted on the ceiling over my bed."

After three years I am still pleasantly embarrassed by the outrageous overpraise accorded my drawings by Mr. Starrett in *The Private Life of Sherlock Holmes.* "No happier association of author and artist can be imagined; one thinks of Tenniel and his Alice." You may take even giddier flights in the chapter called "The Evolution of a Profile:" "Sixty tales, in all, comprise the saga of Sherlock Holmes; and Steele has illustrated twenty-nine. While he yet lives and loves, and lifts his pencil, will he not do the other thirty-one?" Meantime my own favorite edition remains the one-volume *Complete Sherlock Holmes,* with no cuts—in either sense of the word.

In writing of stage Sherlocks, Mr. Pearson makes a shrewd guess: "The Steele pictures had in their turn an influence on the stage or upon the screen for it seems probable that the enormous number of properties assembled for the Baker

Arthur Wontner as Sherlock Holmes (from the film "The Missing Rembrandt")

Street scene in John Barrymore's film play (1922) originated in Mr. Steele's fascinating pictures of Holmes's rooms." I can testify to the accuracy of that chance shot. I happened to meet Jack Barrymore, just off the train from Hollywood. "There's a film I want you to see," he said. "Just finished it. 'Sherlock Holmes.' I dug up an old German named Von Seyffertitz for Moriarty. Had a lot of fun. Think you'll be interested."

"Indeed I will," I said, hoping the old drawings were remembered. "I used to make pictures of Sherlock."

His eyebrows twisted with the Barrymore grin. "Why, hell, we had all your old pictures out on the lot. You're more to blame than Gillette."

On a murky winter evening some years ago,[1] the Baker Street Irregulars, a little group of Sherlock devotees, met in a coffeehouse in the Forties for votive rites in honor of their patron saint. After some tramping in the slush I found the unmarked door and was ushered into a warm, smoky room. Long train of tables, Italian wines, savory odors. Just such a room as one might look for in Soho, perhaps. What were these strange words floating in the smoke? Gasogenes, Trichinopoly cigars, orange pips? . . . Christopher Morley greeted me kindly. He, it seemed, was a gasogene. No, he was *the* Gasogene. The other officers were the Tantalus and the Commissar, and let no true Sherlockian ask why. "That is your drink, right there by the Blue Carbuncle."

"Fine. It was all perfectly obvious from the first, my dear Watson."

I had been a little cold. If I could catch up in my drinking, would I understand a little better what they were talking about? If someone asked me for the papers, would I know enough to say they were on the sundial? If one muffed the answer to such a challenge, the next round was on him, I was

[1] December 7, 1934.

told. Surely this was a dangerous place. Another drink? Well, they all looked friendly enough. Increasingly so. But how did they all know so much? Could I remember Enoch J. Drebber's address? Another drink, perhaps? Well, why argue? One must not be quarrelsome. On my left sat the Gasogene, on my right Gene Tunney. No, I would not be quarrelsome. . . . Time for the first toast. "There are only three standard toasts, gentlemen, three obligatory toasts. We will rise for the first one, gentlemen. I give you THE Woman!" *The* Woman? Could it be Irene Adler? I was beginning to get the hang of it. Elementary. . . . Alexander Woollcott, who had insisted on coming in a hansom, still wore a hideous red fore-and-aft cap. . . . The second toast was Mrs. Hudson. The third, Dr. Watson's Second Wife. Time for a pipe. Pipes are occasionally of extraordinary interest, Watson. But where is Gillette? Afraid he's not coming; it's half past eight. Patience, my dear Watson. If I am not mistaken, I hear his step even now upon the stair.

A commotion at the entrance. Yes, it was he. We saw the tall, fragile figure, the pale, smiling face above the concave dress shirt. "Splendid, Mr. Gillette. We'd given you up. It was good of you to leave your other party to join us."

"Other party? Certainly not. I've been four hours on the way from Hadlyme, Connecticut, and I'm damned hungry."

After he had been fed, he told us that it was Charles Frohman who had suggested his play, that it had been concocted in a few weeks, and—even more incredible—that before that time he never had read a Sherlock Holmes story.

The unquenchable Woollcott reported this incident later in the *New Yorker*. A certain artist, he wrote, wept softly into his soufflé at the sight of his most famous model. Mr. Woollcott must stand corrected. I am sure it was not a soufflé we wept in, but a *compote Lestrade*.

Conan Doyle never quite forgave the reading public for

preferring "these lighter sketches," nor could he quite forgive his own Sherlock Holmes, who "may perhaps have stood a little in the way of my more serious literary work." But what man can control the lightning of his own fame? Today his brain child, so often disparaged by its father, unquestionably is known to more people living on this oblate spheroid than any other character in secular fiction. Why do these uncounted millions love the tales and, forsaking all others, return to them with deep satisfaction and a sense of personal attachment? In mere ingenuity of structure they are no better than those of the present-day artificers. Not all the tales observe the strict rules of the game—the game between writer and reader. In some, accident rather than deduction plays a part in the solution. Sometimes there is no solution at all. But what do these lapses weigh against the gift of the priceless Watson, against the wealth of color, atmosphere, and racy, humorous character? To read the tales is to take the perfect anodyne, to be carried back gently across fifty years to a dim, gaslit London, with the four-wheeler coming up out of the yellow fog, bearing our client—and a little problem which may present some points of interest.

THE CREATOR OF HOLMES IN THE FLESH

By Henry James Forman

A HIGH-SCHOOL TEACHER of chemistry, back in the nineties, little knew what he precipitated when, to stimulate his pupils, he read out a passage about a strange, gaunt Englishman who had just discovered "a precipitate for haemoglobin."

With many of those in that little school laboratory the phrase doubtless passed in one ear and out of the other:—it was just "teacher's stuff," the eternal effort of interesting the uninterested. In the case of one thin wide-eyed boy of fourteen or fifteen, however, the crepitating mysterious romantic syllables "a precipitate for haemoglobin" set up a train of reverberations through the hollows of that hungry anemic little brain that has not wholly died to this day.

"Galeotto fu lo libre e chi lo scrisse," wailed Francesca in Hell, so powerful had been the impression left upon her by the book she had been reading with Paolo when they fell into their sweet and fatal sin.

Similarly—"What is the title of that book," demanded the hungry boy, still quivering under the impact of the magic syllables.

"It is called *A Study in Scarlet*, and it is by A. Conan Doyle," smiled the chemistry teacher. "If you want to read it, I will lend you my copy. I think it will entertain you."

Entertain!—Simple soul that he was, that teacher! The boy read—he read and swallowed and gloated and drank and absorbed at every pore, and read again. For strange though it may appear, up to that time the boy (remember it was in the nineties) had never read any mystery or detective stories. Well! He made up for it from that moment on. A wild and turbulent passion seized him, a hunger, an appetite, a storm of desire. He grasped at this new field of knowledge, super-human wisdom rather, like those alchemists who were ever on the verge of discovering the philosopher's stone. Entertain! Here was knowledge, here was learning, here was the mystery of life and death and romance, excitement, thrill and vicarious danger, and all of it, all, in the keeping and to be had for the asking at the hands of A. Conan Doyle!

A new life began for that boy. In his humble one-track little mind had been the notion of becoming a doctor, a phy-sician. But from gods and demigods one can learn much. Having sought for every scrap of information about the au-thor, as well as his work, the boy learned that A. Conan Doyle was a physician who wrote "on the side." There then was the goal to aim at, obviously. What other unction can small mortals bring to gods and heroes than the flattery of imita-tion? As to imitating Doyle's work, one might as well imitate the *Odyssey* or *King Lear* or the works of G. A. Henty. There was nothing else to do but to imitate the life of A. Conan Doyle.

So that, at any rate, was determined, irrevocably. A doc-tor who wrote—and perhaps in the fulness of time and wis-dom and ripeness, the boy might, who could tell, write such things as *A Study in Scarlet*, with precipitates for haemo-globin, or *The Sign of the Four*, or indeed anything remotely resembling the quick and wise and deathless life of that mod-ern magician, Sherlock Holmes.

God, however, notoriously, disposes. In time, say a score or so of years later, that boy became an editor. And (you need not believe this if you suffer from haemoglobal skepti-cism) he found himself actually in treaty with A. Conan Doyle (the creator of Sherlock Holmes!), with the agent of Doyle, —in treaty for what? For the sacred acts, gesta, deeds and stories of Sherlock Holmes—buying them for money, mind you (at somewhere round a dollar a word) just as though they were an article of commerce! When a word costs a dollar it assumes an extraordinary sanctity, as all devout folk know. But that was not all. Who could suitably and fittingly illustrate such stories in the pages of that magazine? Only one high priest had the necessary amount of talent and reverence for the task—Frederic Dorr Steele. Steele had created the likeness of Sherlock for American readers. Steele might be in Timbuctoo or, indeed, farther. But no sooner did a Sherlock Holmes story come into that periodical's office than all the agencies of detection were set to work to find and summon Fred Steele—for here was high festival in preparation.

The boy grew older. When he went to London, as he often did, the hour of dusk, when otherwise unoccupied, might find him in Baker Street strolling past the spot where the mystery-laden rooms of Holmes and Watson ought to have been. The small shops of stationers and green-grocers appeared strangely, deceptively uninteresting. Surely there was more than met the eye in those quite commonplace doorways. For did not the wraith, the aura of Sherlock and of Watson, too, still haunt and overshadow them? In the purlieus of Baker Street hung about some seemingly unoccupied boys—could they be the ungrown-up remnants of that once glorious Gang, the Baker Street Irregulars? Two, in particular, upon one occasion, caught the eye; full-bodied, competent lads. Perhaps they were earlier incarnations of Alec Woollcott and Chris Morley? Who could tell?

Then one evening at a London Club, an early aircraft builder was going to speak of a new plane he had recently constructed. In the throng was one well-set-up solid man with a graying though still dark mustache.

"That," whispered a friend, "is Sir Arthur—you know—Conan Doyle."

First appearance of the Baker Street Irregulars (from drawing by Doyle's father)

This was not Dr. Watson nor yet Sherlock. The somewhat massive figure was that of a doer, a substantial British citizen of the type you see at Lord's cricket matches, in the grandstand at Epsom, or wherever the well-to-do healthy outdoor Britishers foregather. But in his eyes was something both speculative and inscrutable. It was in his eyes that Dr. Watson and Sherlock met.

Later I was introduced to the author of so much of my pleasure. The brief conversation was general and concerned aviation and the aviator. It was too much to hope that either Sherlock or Baker Street would be touched upon. But the apostolic succession had been consummated. The boy who had for so many years been able to enter a magic world of thrill and excitement by merely opening a book of Dr. Watson's deathless chronicles had at last shaken the hand that had created the incomparable, the imperial, the ineluctable Sherlock Holmes.

APPOINTMENT IN BAKER STREET

By Edgar W. Smith

I

THE MASTER ATTENDS

Mr. Sherlock Holmes no longer walks corporeal upon the earth. We can accept this assumption with a mournful finality —not because of any lurking disbelief in the reality of his existence, but because, on the internal evidence of the Watson saga alone, the sage of Baker Street would today have overstayed the limits set upon his mortal span by Holy Writ and the actuarial statisticians alike.

For Sherlock Holmes did live. He lived more really than legions who have trod the boards in flesh corruptible and corrupt and passed unnoticed to their graves. He lived—and lives today—in the world of ultimate reality which is the consciousness of all mankind; that world of the subjective which alone conveys immortality, and which can surely, by the same token, convey the lesser thing called life. As a vital force, as an inspiration to universal acceptance and acclaim, historical incident is no match for mythological fancy; the feeble figure of objectivity stands today, as it has always stood, abject and crestfallen in the presence of the subjective.

The fact that Holmes was conceived in the mind of a single genius, and born in the cold bed of the printed page, gives not the slightest denial to his reality. The test of any man's having lived lies at last in the imprint he has made upon the minds of the millions who knew and loved him well.

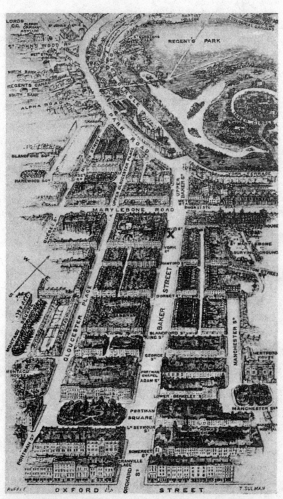

Bird's-eye view of Baker Street: X marks approximate
location of 221-B (from Fry's "London—Illustrated,"
1880)

It is not my task here to add even a modicum to the convincing evidence of Holmes's real existence. All that the world could ask in such testimony has been given with tenderness and charm by Vincent Starrett in his *Private Life of Sherlock Holmes*. Through another medium, in the days when he was with us, Mr. William Gillette afforded us a glimpse of the substance behind the shadow when, to our untiring delight, he brought the triumphant vision before our very eyes. And Mr. S. C. Roberts, in his immortal prolegomena to the study of Doctor Watson's life, has written a biography of Holmes's colleague the incisiveness and veracity of which not even Holmes himself would question.

These two have had their due—their renown is secure beyond cavil or dispute. But with them, through the pages of the saga, there moved a host of minor characters who strode heroically upon their ways, or slunk cringing before the whip of Holmes's righteous wrath. They came and went, most of them in one tale alone, but some, like the good Mrs. Hudson or the moronic Lestrade, recurrently. They toiled up the seventeen steps to the sanctum where Holmes attended them; or they waited, alive or dead, in the manor houses and cesspools of the kingdom while the great detective sought them out.

To me, Professor Moriarty is a more heinous and imminent criminal than the weakling Dillinger—I have never seen him in a newsreel lying riddled on a mortuary slab, but if I were given to nightmares it would be he, and not Dillinger, who would haunt them. Nor have I met, outside the immediate circle of my family and friends, a nobler, more forebearing lad than Arthur Holder, who, affronted by his father's vile suspicion and inspired by love for his betrayed cousin, stood ready in silence to take the rap for a deed he had never done. And the breathless views we are given of beauty in distress, of damsels pale but brave, clad enticingly in some fluffy substance with a touch of white at the throat and wrists—these I would not trade for the most brazen displays of naked flesh in the floor-shows of New York.

No—these minor *personæ* lived too, and still live; and I have tried in the pages that follow to recount them all, and to say some few words about each one to make them come again to the memory of all who knew them. They were those who had a rendezvous with love or death—or, more exciting still, an appointment in Baker Street. Or they were those who filled passing and modest rôles to give the scenes in which they moved a finer grace or a deeper terror. They were not of the stature of Sherlock Holmes himself, nor did they nearly approach that stature; but they were a part of him as he is a part of us, and they deserve a belated moment in the sun.

If my hand has slipped in the drawing of their portraits, or if any of the originals have escaped my view, it is because, in turning the treasured pages for the hundredth time, a nostalgic tear has dimmed the eyes that once saw them all so clearly, face to face. Or perhaps, on the nights I labored, the fog swirled so thickly against the panes of the house at 221B Baker Street, and a four-wheeler rumbled so loudly past the door, that I could not see or hear precisely what it was these callers did within.

But there is no fog thick enough to shut out the picture of the gaunt figure stretched in the chair by the fireplace, Persian slipper within easy reach and pipe aglow; there is no sound so loud as to drown the wail of the violin lulling the great mind to rest or inspiring it to more titanic effort.

A ring comes at the bell; a step is heard upon the stair. The drooping eyelids lift, and the nostrils quiver with the nascent thrill of the chase.

"Come, Watson, come! The game is afoot!"

2

THE APPOINTMENTS ARE KEPT

A

ABDULLAH KHAN: One of the Four.—*The Sign of the Four*

ABERGAVENNY, ——: Whose impending murder trial almost kept Holmes from joining Thorneycroft Huxtable in his search for the missing Lord Saltire.
> —*The Adventure of the Priory School*

ABERNETTY, ——: The family which gave its name to the case precipitated by the depth to which parsley had sunk into the butter on a hot day.
> —*The Adventure of the Six Napoleons*

ABRAHAMS, ——: Whose mortal terror served ostensibly to keep Holmes in London while Watson bungled afield.
> —*The Disappearance of Lady Frances Carfax*

ACHMET: The rajah's servant who masqueraded as a merchant, and from whom the Agra treasure was first despoiled.
> —*The Sign of the Four*

ACTON, ——: The old gentleman whose home was broken into by the law-suited Cunninghams.—*The Reigate Squires*

ADAIR, HILDA: Of 427 Park Lane; sister of the Honourable Ronald Adair.   —*The Adventure of the Empty House*

ADAIR, HONOURABLE RONALD: Whose murder in 1894 interested all London, dismayed the world of fashion—and brought Sherlock Holmes back to life.
> —*The Adventure of the Empty House*

ADAMS, ——: Who, Sherlock and Mycroft agreed, had done the job in the Manor House case, whatever that job may have been.   —*The Greek Interpreter*

ADDLETON, ——: Referred to obscurely as the principal in the tragedy of that name.
    —*The Adventure of the Golden Pince-Nez*

ADLER, IRENE: A New Jersey prima donna, whose beauty and wit made thrones totter; the daintiest thing under a bonnet, with a face that a man might die for. To Holmes, she was always *the* woman.   —*A Scandal in Bohemia*
    —*A Case of Identity*
    —*His Last Bow*

AGAR, DR. MOORE: The Harley Street specialist who sent Holmes packing off to Cornwall for a complete rest, which was rudely interrupted.—*The Adventure of the Devil's Foot*

——, AGATHA: The housemaid in the Milverton establishment to whom Holmes, alias Escott, became affianced—with ulterior motives.
    —*The Adventure of Charles Augustus Milverton*

AINSTREE, DR.: Greatest living authority on tropical diseases, whom Watson wanted to call in for Holmes's sake.
    —*The Adventure of the Dying Detective*

AKBAR, DOST: One of the Four, and worthy of his sinister name.   —*The Sign of the Four*

ALDRIDGE, ——: Lestrade referred to him as having been of help in the bogus laundry affair.
    —*The Adventure of the Cardboard Box*

——, ALEXIS: A Russian pinko whose innocence the Nihilist Anna sought to prove, to the sorrow of young Willoughby Smith.   —*The Adventure of the Golden Pince-Nez*

ALGAR, ——: Holmes's friend on the Liverpool force, who helped him in the case of the severed ears.
—*The Adventure of the Cardboard Box*

——, ALICE: Maid to Mrs. Francis H. Moulton, née Doran.
—*The Adventure of the Noble Bachelor*

ALISON, ——: At whose rooms Holmes had fought three rounds with McMurdo on the occasion of McMurdo's benefit.
—*The Sign of the Four*

ALLAN BROTHERS: The principal land agents at Esher, of whom Holmes made useful inquiries.
—*The Adventure of Wisteria Lodge*

ALLARDYCE, ——: The butcher in whose shop Holmes speared a dead pig to prove a point.
—*The Adventure of Black Peter*

ALLEN, MRS.: Buxom and cheerful housekeeper at the Manor House of Birlstone.
—*The Valley of Fear*

ALTAMONT, ——: Alias of Holmes as the slangy Irish-American who double crossed his employer Von Bork for the glory of England.
—*His Last Bow*

AMBERLEY, JOSIAH: The chess-player who, having killed his wife and her suspected lover by asphyxiation, was foolhardy enough to call in Holmes to investigate their disappearance.
—*The Adventure of the Retired Colourman*

AMBERLEY, MRS. JOSIAH: Many years her husband's junior, she trifled with a young and handsome doctor to her sorrow.
—*The Adventure of the Retired Colourman*

AMES, ——: Butler at the Manor House of Birlstone, who conspired at the shamming of his master's death.
—*The Valley of Fear*

ANDERSON, ——: The ginger-moustached village constable who first worked on the case of Fitzroy McPherson.
                    —*The Adventure of the Lion's Mane*

ANDERSON, ——: Soldier in the Boer War who fell with Baldy Simpson while Godfrey Emsworth escaped to a leper home.   —*The Adventure of the Blanched Soldier*

ANDERSON, ——: Of North Carolina, who gave his name to certain murders there which Holmes cited.
                    —*The Hound of the Baskervilles*

ANDREWS, ——: One of the imported gangsters at Vermissa, who was frankfaced and cheerful of aspect.
                    —*The Valley of Fear*

ANGEL, HOSMER: The Lothario whom Mary Sutherland met at the gasfitters' ball, and who turned out to be her own covetous stepfather.   —*A Case of Identity*

——, ANNA: The Russian woman who dropped her glasses when she came to clear the name of her fellow-refugee, and who killed a harmless secretary into the bargain.
                    —*The Adventure of the Golden Pince-Nez*

ANSTRUTHER, DR.: One of the physicians who blessedly took Watson's practice when occasion demanded, and thereby freed him for the chase. —*The Boscombe Valley Mystery*

——, ANTHONY: Probably originally Antonio, the Costa Rican man-servant at Merripit House who cared for the hound in Stapleton's absence.
                    —*The Hound of the Baskervilles*

APPLEDORE, SIR CHARLES: An otherwise undescribed gentleman whose daughter Edith married the Duke of Holdernesse.   —*The Adventure of the Priory School*

APPLEDORE, LADY EDITH: Who did her part by marrying the

Duke of Holdernesse and bringing little Lord Saltire to the world.   —*The Adventure of the Priory School*

ARMITAGE, JAMES: Who later became Justice of the Peace Trevor, which see.   —*The "Gloria Scott"*

ARMITAGE, PERCY: Second son of Mr. Armitage, of Crane Water near Reading; fiancé of Helen Stoner.
—*The Adventure of the Speckled Band*

ARMSTRONG, DR. LESLIE: A thinker of European reputation, who shielded Godfrey Staunton and his clandestine bride.
—*The Adventure of the Missing Three-Quarter*

ATKINSON, ——: The brothers who gave their names to the singular tragedy occurring at Trincomalee in Ceylon; an episode unfortunately unrecorded.
—*A Scandal in Bohemia*

AVELING, ——: The mathematical master at the Priory School, who knew the make of bicycle Heidegger rode.
—*The Adventure of the Priory School*

B

BACKWATER, LORD: Owner of the large training establishment of Capleton. He raced Desborough against Silver Blaze, and later told Lord St. Simon of his trust in Holmes's abilities.   —*The Adventure of the Noble Bachelor*
—*Silver Blaze*

BAIN, SANDY: A jockey in the employ of the esteemed Sir Robert Norberton.
—*The Adventure of Shoscombe Old Place*

BAKER, HENRY: The shabby-genteel buyer of the priceless and evasive goose: his lost head-gear put Holmes upon the track of the fabulous gem.
—*The Adventure of the Blue Carbuncle*

BAKER, MRS. HENRY: Mr. Baker's estranged wife, for whom the goose was an intended peace-offering.
—The Adventure of the Blue Carbuncle

BALDWIN, TED: Boss of the Scowrers, who escaped Birdy Edwards in Vermissa Valley but had his face blown off by John Douglas in Birlstone.   *—The Valley of Fear*

BALMORAL, DUCHESS OF: Present at the bigamous marriage of her second son, but innocent of its consequences.
—The Adventure of the Noble Bachelor

BALMORAL, DUKE OF: His art treasures gone, he reconciled himself to his son's marriage with an American parvenue, and unquestionably bewailed its frustration. He also raced Iris against Silver Blaze.
—The Adventure of the Noble Bachelor
—Silver Blaze

BALMORAL, LORD: Who, with Godfrey Milner, lost £420 at whist to Colonel Moran and the Honourable Ronald Adair.
—The Adventure of the Empty House

BANNISTER, ——: Servant of Mr. Soames at St. Luke's, who shielded the lad he had dandled on his knee as a baby.
—The Adventure of the Three Students

BARCLAY, COLONEL JAMES: Of the Royal Mallows. The sight of his betrayed comrade and unsuccessful rival brought on apoplexy.   *—The Crooked Man*

BARCLAY, MRS. JAMES: Née Nancy Devoy, queenly daughter of a colour-sergeant. She called her husband a David, and watched him stricken to his death. *—The Crooked Man*

BARDLE, ——: Inspector of the Sussex Constabulary, who had official charge of the case involving the strange death of Fitzroy McPherson.
—The Adventure of the Lion's Mane

BARELLI, AUGUSTO: Father of Emilia Lucca, whose emigration from Posilippo brought adventure and tragedy in its wake.   —*The Adventure of the Red Circle*

BARKER, CECIL JAMES: Faithful friend of John Douglas and his wife, who conspired at the substitution of Ted Baldwin's body for that of his host.   —*The Valley of Fear*

BARKER, ——: The rising private detective who was Holmes's "hated rival" on the Surrey shore.
                    —*The Adventure of the Retired Colourman*

BARNES, JOSIAH: Landlord of the Green Dragon, to whom Sir Robert Norberton gave Lady Beatrice Falder's spaniel.
                    —*The Adventure of Shoscombe Old Place*

BARNICOT, DR. ——: Who lost a Napoleon both from his home and from his surgery—neither of which was the important one.
                    —*The Adventure of the Six Napoleons*

BARRETT, P. C.: Who, passing along Godolphin Street at a quarter to twelve, observed that the door of No. 16 was ajar.
                    —*The Adventure of the Second Stain*

BARRYMORE, MRS. ELIZA: Née Selden, wife of John Barrymore, and housekeeper of Baskerville Hall. Her bestial brother was a refugee in the Grimpen Mire.
                    —*The Hound of the Baskervilles*

BARRYMORE, JOHN: Butler at Baskerville Hall, who walked of nights and flashed signals to the desolate moor.
                    —*The Hound of the Baskervilles*

BARTON, DR. HILL: Alias of Watson in his call on Baron Gruner with a choice bit of Ming pottery about which he knew nothing.   —*The Adventure of the Illustrious Client*

BARTON, ——: An inspector of Scotland Yard. His calibre is difficult to determine.—*The Man With the Twisted Lip*

BASIL, CAPTAIN: One of Holmes's working aliases.
—*The Adventure of Black Peter*

BASKERVILLE, BERYL: Née Garcia, alias Vandeleur and Stapleton, which see.   —*The Hound of the Baskervilles*

BASKERVILLE, SIR CHARLES: Circa 1830; who was lured to the moor gate by a lady's letter, and died of horror at the sight of a hound out of hell.   —*The Hound of the Baskervilles*

BASKERVILLE, ELIZABETH: Daughter of the 1700 Hugo, from whom her brothers Rodger and John were admonished to conceal the legend.   —*The Hound of the Baskervilles*

BASKERVILLE, SIR HENRY: Nephew of Sir Charles, who fell heir to the curse of the Baskervilles, and was saved from a terrible fate by five shots from Holmes's pistol.
—*The Hound of the Baskervilles*

BASKERVILLE, HUGO: Circa 1600. The infamous ancestor who stole a fair maiden and had his throat chewed out by the legendary hound.   —*The Hound of the Baskervilles*

BASKERVILLE, HUGO: Circa 1700. The author of the family manuscript which James Mortimer introduced to Holmes's notice.   —*The Hound of the Baskervilles*

BASKERVILLE, JOHN: Son of the 1700 Hugo, who received, with his brother Rodger, the stirring tale of the original hound from the hand of his father.
—*The Hound of the Baskervilles*

BASKERVILLE, JOHN: Son of Rodger Baskerville, who changed his name to Vandeleur and then to Stapleton, which see.
—*The Hound of the Baskervilles*

BASKERVILLE, REAR ADMIRAL: Circa 1725, who served under Rodney in the West Indies, and whose portrait adorned the walls of the Hall. Possibly one of the sons of the 1700 Hugo. *—The Hound of the Baskervilles*

BASKERVILLE, RODGER: Son of the 1700 Hugo, to whom, with his brother John, the account of the legend was indited. *—The Hound of the Baskervilles*

BASKERVILLE, RODGER: Circa 1840. Youngest brother, deceased, of Sir Charles, and father of John Baskerville, alias Vandeleur, alias Stapleton. *—The Hound of the Baskervilles*

BASKERVILLE, SIR WILLIAM: Circa 1770, who was chairman of the committees of the House of Commons under Pitt. *—The Hound of the Baskervilles*

BASKERVILLE, ——: Circa 1835. Second brother of Sir Charles, and father of Sir Henry. *—The Hound of the Baskervilles*

BATES, MARLOW: An employee of Neil Gibson, who confided to Holmes that the Gold King was a villain. *—The Problem of Thor Bridge*

BAXTER, EDITH: Maid at the Capleton racing establishment. *—Silver Blaze*

BAYNES, INSPECTOR: Of the Surrey Constabulary. He matched Holmes's deductions step by step, and Holmes complimented him on his instinct and intuition. *—The Adventure of Wisteria Lodge*

BECHER, DR.: Alias Mr. Ferguson. Owner of the house in Eyford, where the cadaverous Lysander Stark collaborated in the production of spurious coin. *—The Adventure of the Engineer's Thumb*

BEDDINGTON, ——: The notorious robber, partner of Arthur Pinner. He bashed in the head of the nameless watchman of Mawson & Williams's. —*The Stockbroker's Clerk*

BEDDOES, ——: Né Evans. He mutinied with the rest on the prison ship, but was hunted down and imposed upon by the scoundrel Hudson. —*The "Gloria Scott"*

BEECHER, HENRY WARD: 1813–1887. The great American abolitionist and divine, whose unframed portrait adorned Watson's bookshelf and inspired his thoughts.
—*The Adventure of the Cardboard Box*

BELLAMY, MAUD: The beauty of the neighborhood, who loved the unfortunate Fitzroy McPherson even though he was far above her humble station.
—*The Adventure of the Lion's Mane*

BELLAMY, TOM: Maud Bellamy's flame-bearded father, owner of the boats and bathing cots at Fulworth.
—*The Adventure of the Lion's Mane*

BELLAMY, WILLIAM: Son of Tom Bellamy and brother of Maud, who helped his father at his work.
—*The Adventure of the Lion's Mane*

BELLINGER, LORD: Twice premier of Britain, whose patrician calm steadied the Right Honourable Trelawney Hope in the hour of his great distress.
—*The Adventure of the Second Stain*

BELMINSTER, DUKE OF: Father of Lady Hilda Trelawney Hope, otherwise undistinguished.
—*The Adventure of the Second Stain*

BENDER, ——: Who died of thirst in the desert.
—*A Study in Scarlet*

BENNETT, TREVOR: Professional assistant to the simian Professor Presbury, and in love with his very human daughter.
—*The Adventure of the Creeping Man*

——, BEPPO: A man whose lower face projected like the muzzle of a baboon. He hid the pearl of the Borgias in a plaster bust.   —*The Adventure of the Six Napoleons*

BERNSTONE, MRS.: Bartholomew Sholto's old housekeeper. Her advent coincides with the moment when love came to Watson and Miss Morstan.   —*The Sign of the Four*

BERTILLON, ALPHONSE: 1853–1914. The French savant whom Holmes enthusiastically admired; inventor of the system of measurements that has since made him world-famous.
—*The Naval Treaty*
—*The Hound of the Baskervilles*

BEVINGTON, ——: Proprietor of a pawnshop in Westminster Road, where Annie Fraser's presence put Holmes on the trail.   —*The Disappearance of Lady Frances Carfax*

BIDDLE, ——: One of the Worthingdon bank robbers. It was probably he who disguised himself as a Russian nobleman.
—*The Resident Patient*

——, BILLY: Page boy at 221–B Baker Street—perhaps the same as those nameless in other tales.
—*The Valley of Fear*
—*The Adventure of the Mazarin Stone*
—*The Problem of Thor Bridge*

BIRD, SIMON: One of the victims of the Ancient Order of Freemen in Vermissa Valley.   —*The Valley of Fear*

BLACKWATER, EARL OF: Dr. Huxtable was proud that so noble a man had sent his son to the Priory School.
—*The Adventure of the Priory School*

BLAKER, FOREMAN: Who was due to get it, full and proper, from the Scowrers.   —*The Valley of Fear*

BLESSINGTON, ——: Hide-out name of Sutton, the bank robber who turned state's evidence and thereby saved his neck for something less than fifteen years.—*The Resident Patient*

BLOUNT, ——: One of the students at Harold Stackhurst's school who found the dead Airedale on the beach.
          —*The Adventure of the Lion's Mane*

BOCCACCIO, GIOVANNI: 1313–1375. A pocket edition of the *Decameron* was found on the murdered Drebber's person.
          —*A Study in Scarlet*

BOONE, HUGH: The lodger in the opium den; a crippled wretch of hideous aspect. Off duty, he was the highly respectable Neville St. Clair.
          —*The Man With the Twisted Lip*

BOSWELL, JAMES: 1740–1795. The prototype of John H. Watson. "I am lost without my Boswell."
          —*A Scandal in Bohemia*

BOUGUEREAU, ADOLPHE WILLIAM: 1825–1905. Thaddeus Sholto favored him as one of the modern French school.
          —*The Sign of the Four*

BRACKENSTALL, SIR EUSTACE: One of the richest men in Kent —and one of the vilest. He fell before the onslaught of honest Jack Croker.
          —*The Adventure of the Abbey Grange*

BRACKENSTALL, LADY: Née Mary Fraser. She lied to shield the slayer of her brutal husband, and, black eye or not, she was no ordinary looker.
          —*The Adventure of the Abbey Grange*

BRACKWELL, LADY EVA: It was Mr. Milverton's determination to blackmail her that led Holmes to undertake a burglary.
—*The Adventure of Charles Augustus Milverton*

BRADLEY, ——: The tobacco merchant from whom Holmes bought his strongest shag, a pound at a time.
—*The Hound of the Baskervilles*

BRADSTREET, ——: An inspector, B Division, attached to the Bow Street Station. Later attached to Scotland Yard.
—*The Man With the Twisted Lip*
—*The Adventure of the Blue Carbuncle*
—*The Adventure of the Engineer's Thumb*

BRECKINRIDGE, ——: A horsey looking individual who wholesaled geese and waxed irascible when they were discussed.
—*The Adventure of the Blue Carbuncle*

BREWER, SAM: The well-known Curzon Street money-lender, who was horsewhipped by Sir Robert Norberton but still held him in his clutches.
—*The Adventure of Shoscombe Old Place*

BRICKFALL & AMBERLEY: The firm of paint makers in which Josiah Amberley had been junior partner.
—*The Adventure of the Retired Colourman*

BRIGGS, MATILDA: For whom was named the ship associated with the case of the giant rat of Sumatra—for which the world is now ready, but which it will never know.
—*The Adventure of the Sussex Vampire*

BROOKS, ——: One of the estimated fifty men who had good reason for taking Holmes's life.
—*The Adventure of the Bruce-Partington Plans*

BROWN, LIEUTENANT BROMLEY: Officer in command of the native troops in the Andamans, and a messmate of Major Sholto and Captain Morstan.   —*The Sign of the Four*

BROWN, JOSIAH: Who bought one of the six Napoleons, and in the burglary of whose house the rascal Beppo was trapped.   —*The Adventure of the Six Napoleons*

BROWN, SAM: One of Athelney Jones's men who bewailed the loss of reward that went with loss of the treasure.
—*The Sign of the Four*

BROWN, SILAS: Lord Backwater's manager at Capleton, into whose ear Holmes whispered a pregnant word.
—*Silver Blaze*

BROWNER, JAMES: Steward on the *May Day*, who murdered his wife and her lover, and sent an ear from each of them to his sister-in-law.
—*The Adventure of the Cardboard Box*

BROWNER, MRS. JAMES: Née Mary Cushing, a sweet girl who was driven from her husband's arms by a Jezebel.
—*The Adventure of the Cardboard Box*

BRUCE-PARTINGTON, ——: Designer of the revolutionary submarine, the plans of which were stolen by a dastardly traitor.
—*The Adventure of the Bruce-Partington Plans*

BRUNTON, RICHARD: Reginald Musgrave's polyglot butler; a Don Juan who died with the ancestral treasure within his grasp.   —*The Musgrave Ritual*

BURNET, MISS: Alias of Signora Durando, governess at High Gable and confederate within the house of Aloysius Garcia.
—*The Adventure of Wisteria Lodge*

BURNWELL, SIR GEORGE: A bad lot who stole, at one and the same time, the love of Alexander Holder's niece and a corner of the beryl coronet.—*The Adventure of the Beryl Coronet*

C

CAIRNS, PATRICK: A harpooner who swore he had not murdered Peter Carey, but who rejoiced that he had killed him.
—*The Adventure of Black Peter*

CALHOUN, CAPTAIN JAMES: Of the bark *Lone Star*, from Savannah, Georgia, and, with his two mates, avenger of the honor of the Ku Klux Klan. Drowned at sea.
—*The Five Orange Pips*

CANTLEMERE, LORD: An excellent and loyal person, who doubted Holmes's powers but found the precious stone astoundingly back in his pocket.
—*The Adventure of the Mazarin Stone*

CAPUS, HUGO DE: Who built a fortalice in the center of Birlstone at the time of the first crusade. —*The Valley of Fear*

CARÈRE, MLLE.: Referred to as one who was thought murdered, but who turned up alive in New York.
—*The Hound of the Baskervilles*

CAREY, CAPTAIN PETER: A strict Puritan and intermittent drunkard, who was stuck to the wall of his cabin like a butterfly on a panel.   —*The Adventure of Black Peter*

CAREY, MRS. PETER: Wife of Black Peter, and undoubtedly several degrees higher in the moral plane.
—*The Adventure of Black Peter*

CAREY, MISS: Daughter of Black Peter, who rejoiced aloud that her father had died.   —*The Adventure of Black Peter*

CARFAX, LADY FRANCES: Who was saved by Holmes from the horrible experience of burial alive in the same coffin with a withered corpse.
—*The Disappearance of Lady Frances Carfax*

CARLO, ——: The mastiff at the Copper Beeches, whose teeth met in the throat of Jephro Rucastle.
—*The Adventure of the Copper Beeches*

CARLO, ——: The spaniel of the Fergusons, on which the diabolical Jacky tried out his poison.
—*The Adventure of the Sussex Vampire*

CARLYLE, THOMAS: 1795–1881. When Watson quoted him, Holmes asked naïvely who he was and what he had done.
—*A Study in Scarlet*

CARNAWAY, JAMES: Killed in action in the Lodge's attempted slaying of Chester Wilcox.   —*The Valley of Fear*

CARNAWAY, MRS. JAMES: Jim Carnaway's widow, who drew a pension from the Ancient Order of Freemen for her husband's death.   —*The Valley of Fear*

CARRUTHERS, COLONEL: Holmes mentioned having locked him up; probably not the Robert Carruthers who wooed Violet Smith so violently.
—*The Adventure of Wisteria Lodge*

CARRUTHERS, MISS: Ten-year-old daughter of Bob Carruthers, to whom Violet Smith gave music lessons.
—*The Adventure of the Solitary Cyclist*

CARRUTHERS, ROBERT: The plotter against Violet Smith, who fell in love with his prey and almost saw her married in a woodland glade.   —*The Adventure of the Solitary Cyclist*

CARTER, ——: Treasurer of Vermissa Lodge, who was in at Birdy Edwards's final showdown.   —*The Valley of Fear*

CARTWRIGHT, ——: A lad employed by the district messenger office, who served Holmes faithfully and well, both in London and on the moor.—*The Hound of the Baskervilles*

CARTWRIGHT, ——: One of the five bank-robbers, who was hanged for the murder of Tobin, the caretaker.
—The Resident Patient

CASTALOTTE, TITO: Bowery patron of Gennaro Lucca, whose good offices could not keep the young Italian from the toils of Black Gorgiano and the Red Circle.
—The Adventure of the Red Circle

CAUNTER, ——: Lord Saltire's roommate at the Priory School, who heard no sound on the night of the disappearance.
—The Adventure of the Priory School

CHANDOS, SIR CHARLES: For whom Ames, the butler, worked for ten years before coming with the Douglases.
—The Valley of Fear

CHARLES I: 1600–1649. King of England, who, during the Civil War, lay concealed in the Manor House at Birlstone for several days.
—A Study in Scarlet
—The Valley of Fear
—The Musgrave Ritual

CHARLES II: 1630–1685. King of England, who had Sir Ralph Musgrave as a right-hand man.
—The Musgrave Ritual

CHARPENTIER, ALICE: Daughter of Madame Charpentier, and sister of Arthur, who lives for her aphorism, "No good can ever come of falsehood, mother."   *—A Study in Scarlet*

CHARPENTIER, ARTHUR: The innocent sub-lieutenant in Her Majesty's navy, apprehended by Gregson for the murder of Enoch Drebber.   *—A Study in Scarlet*

CHARPENTIER, MADAME: At whose house in Torquay Terrace, in Camberwell, the fugitive Mormons paid their last board.   *—A Study in Scarlet*

CHEESEMAN, ——: Who built the house in Sussex, centuries before, where the Fergusons had their goings-on.
—*The Adventure of the Sussex Vampire*

CHOWDAR, LAL: A former servant of the Sholtos, who helped the innocent Thaddeus dispose of Captain Morstan's body.
—*The Sign of the Four*

CLARENDON, LORD: 1609–1674. British historian commended in the Baskerville manuscript for his treatment of the Great Rebellion.   —*The Hound of the Baskervilles*

CLAY, JOHN: The third or fourth smartest man in London. Alias Vincent Spaulding, which see.
—*The Red-Headed League*

CLAYTON, JOHN: The cab-driver who conducted the be-whiskered shadower of Sir Henry Baskerville and Mr. Mortimer through the streets of London.
—*The Hound of the Baskervilles*

COBB, JOHN: Charles McCarthy's groom.
—*The Boscombe Valley Mystery*

COLONNA, PRINCE OF: From whose bedroom in the Dacre Hotel the famous pearl of the Borgias was stolen.
—*The Adventure of the Six Napoleons*

COLONNA, PRINCESS OF: Whose maid, Lucretia Venucci, was suspected in the theft of the pearl.
—*The Adventure of the Six Napoleons*

CONK-SINGLETON: Possibly a single name parted in the middle, possibly two entities—identified simply as a forgery case Holmes was anxious to tackle.
—*The Adventure of the Six Napoleons*

COOK, P. C.: The police constable who heard John Openshaw's body splash in the Thames.—*The Five Orange Pips*

CORAM, PROFESSOR: Alias of the refugee Nihilist, called Sergius, who was a chain-smoker of cigarettes and a harborer of his embittered wife Anna.
—*The Adventure of the Golden Pince-Nez*

CORMAC, TIGER: One of those chosen to do in Andrew Rae, and quite a fellow in the eyes of his brother Scowrers.
—*The Valley of Fear*

CORNELIUS, ——: Alias of Jonas Oldacre, which see.
—*The Adventure of the Norwood Builder*

COROT, JEAN-BAPTISTE CAMILLE: 1796–1875. A landscape by the great painter hung on Thaddeus Sholto's wall.
—*The Sign of the Four*

COVENTRY, SERGEANT: Of the local police, who stood by while Holmes solved the suicide of Mrs. Gibson.
—*The Problem of Thor Bridge*

COWPER, ——: A Mormon, who reluctantly told Jefferson Hope of Lucy Ferrier's marriage to Enoch Drebber.
—*A Study in Scarlet*

Cox & Co.: The bankers to whose custody was entrusted Watson's tin dispatch box containing the mourned cases which the eye of man shall never see.
—*The Problem of Thor Bridge*

COXON, ——: Of Coxon and Woodhouse's, who gave Hall Pycroft a ripping good testimonial when the firm went smash.
—*The Stockbroker's Clerk*

CRABBE, ——: The old man at Stylestown, who was shot by the Scowrers.
—*The Valley of Fear*

CROKER, JACK: First officer of the *Rock of Gibraltar*, who slew the wife-beating Sir Eustace Brackenstall and was acquitted by Dr. Watson as the one-man voice of God.
—*The Adventure of the Abbey Grange*

CROSBY, ——: The banker, whose terrible death is linked, in Watson's notes, with reference to the repulsive story of the red leech.   —*The Adventure of the Golden Pince-Nez*

CROWDER, WILLIAM: Game-keeper at the Boscombe Valley estate, who saw McCarthy *père* and McCarthy *fils* pass by, and feared the worst.   —*The Boscombe Valley Mystery*

CUBITT, HILTON: A simple Norfolk squire, who held his family honor highly and died uncomplaining in its defense.
—*The Adventure of the Dancing Men*

CUBITT, MRS. HILTON: Née Elsie Patrick, of Chicago. Her husband saw terror in her eyes, and came to Holmes with the tale of the dancing men.
—*The Adventure of the Dancing Men*

CUMMINGS, JOYCE: The rising barrister who was entrusted with the defense of the innocent Grace Dunbar.
—*The Problem of Thor Bridge*

CUNNINGHAM, ALEC: Son of the J. P., who lured the spying coachman William to his death by taking Annie Morrison's name in vain.   —*The Reigate Squires*

CUNNINGHAM, ——: The senior Cunningham, Justice of the Peace at Reigate in Surrey, but a murderer withal.
—*The Reigate Squires*

CUSACK, CATHERINE: Maid to the Countess of Morcar, and James Ryder's inside accomplice.
—*The Adventure of the Blue Carbuncle*

CUSHING, SARAH: A hellion and a home-wrecker, whose lust for Jim Browner drove Mary Browner, née Cushing, to the arms of Jim's best friend.
—*The Adventure of the Cardboard Box*

CUSHING, SUSAN: Maiden lady of 50, who was the mistaken recipient of a box containing her sister's ear and that of her sister's lover.   —*The Adventure of the Cardboard Box*

D

D'ALBERT, COUNTESS: It was in the guise of a maid in her service that a mysterious noblewoman, who rid the earth of Milverton, found entry to his house.
—*The Adventure of Charles Augustus Milverton*

DAMERY, COLONEL SIR JAMES: Who came to Holmes in behalf of a High Personage to break up the fiançailles of Violet de Merville and Baron Gruner.
—*The Adventure of the Illustrious Client*

DARBYSHIRE, WILLIAM: Alias John Straker, which see.
—*Silver Blaze*

DARBYSHIRE, MRS. WILLIAM: Mistress of the double-living John Straker. Her expensive tastes in dresses gave Holmes an important clue.   —*Silver Blaze*

DARWIN, CHARLES ROBERT: 1809–1882. Propounder of the world-shaking doctrine of natural selection, whose theory that music preceded speech was taken by Holmes for granted.   —*A Study in Scarlet*

DAVENPORT, J.: Who knew Sophy Kratides, and answered an advertisement appearing in all the papers asking of her whereabouts.   —*The Greek Interpreter*

DAWSON, ——: A groom at the Capleton racing establishment.
—*Silver Blaze*

DAWSON, ——: Of Dawson and Neligan, West Country Bankers.   —*The Adventure of Black Peter*

DAWSON, ——: Who did the book-work and the managing at Abel White's plantation in India.—*The Sign of the Four*

DeCroy, Philippe: Printer at Liége of *De Jure inter Gentes*.
—*A Study in Scarlet*

de Merville, General: Of Khyber fame, whose daughter Violet was in danger of marriage to the unspeakable Baron Gruner.   —*The Adventure of the Illustrious Client*

de Merville, Violet: A lovely, innocent girl, saved by Holmes from the clutches of a fiendish would-be husband.
—*The Adventure of the Illustrious Client*

Dennis, Sally: The fictitious sailor's wife said by Mrs. Sawyer to have lost her wedding ring.   —*A Study in Scarlet*

DeQuincey, Thomas: 1785–1859. Author of *The Confessions of an English Opium-Eater*, which lead Isa Whitney astray.   —*The Man With the Twisted Lip*

De Reszke, Jean; De Reszke, Edouard: Holmes heard the famous brothers were singing in *Les Huguenots*, and was moved to attend them.   —*The Hound of the Baskervilles*

Desmond, James: An elderly clergyman in Westmoreland, distant cousin of the Baskervilles, and utterly innocent of a part in the horror.   —*The Hound of the Baskervilles*

Devine, Marie: Maid of Lady Frances Carfax, who took Jules Vibart as her lover.
—*The Disappearance of Lady Frances Carfax*

Devine, ——: Sculptor of the original of the bust of Napoleon I from which the plaster casts were reproduced.
—*The Adventure of the Six Napoleons*

Devoy, Nancy: Beauteous daughter of a colour-sergeant, who became Mrs. James Barclay, which see.
—*The Crooked Man*

DIXIE, STEVE: Huge negro, of the Spencer John gang, who had the temerity to threaten Holmes in his own sanctum.
—*The Adventure of The Three Gables*

DIXON, JEREMY: Of Trinity College, who owned Pompey, and thereby contributed to the solution of Godfrey Staunton's disappearance.
—*The Adventure of the Missing Three-Quarter*

DIXON, MRS. ——: Housekeeper for the Carruthers at Chiltern Grange.   —*The Adventure of the Solitary Cyclist*

DOBNEY, SUSAN: Old governess of Lady Carfax, addicted to a mob-cap and reminiscences.
—*The Disappearance of Lady Frances Carfax*

DODD, JAMES M.: The big, fresh, sunburned, upstanding Briton who besought Holmes to help him find his friend and comrade-in-arms Godfrey Emsworth.
—*The Adventure of the Blanched Soldier*

——, DOLORES: Peruvian maid to Mrs. Robert Ferguson, of Cheeseman's, Lamberley.
—*The Adventure of the Sussex Vampire*

DOLSKY, ——: Involved in a poisoning case in Odessa, as recalled by Holmes.   —*A Study in Scarlet*

DORAK, A.: The Bohemian agent in London who forwarded the monkey serum to Professor Presbury.
—*The Adventure of the Creeping Man*

DORAN, ALOYSIUS: California millionaire, whose daughter Hatty married a lord before going back to her husband.
—*The Adventure of the Noble Bachelor*

DORAN, HATTY: Mrs. Francis Hay Moulton, which see.
—*The Adventure of the Noble Bachelor*

DORKING, COLONEL: Whose engagement to the Honourable Miss Miles was disrupted by Mr. Milverton's blackmail.
—*The Adventure of Charles Augustus Milverton*

DOUGLAS, JOHN: The latter-day Birdy Edwards, alias John McMurdo. He outwitted his American avengers in Birlstone, but Moriarty got him at last in mid-ocean.
—*The Valley of Fear*

DOUGLAS, MRS. JOHN: Her carefree laughter shocked Watson as the body of her supposed husband lay murdered in the manor house at Birlstone.   —*The Valley of Fear*

DOVERCOURT, EARL OF: Fiancé of Lady Eva Brackwell, whose potential marital joy was endangered by the blackmailing machinations of Mr. Milverton.
—*The Adventure of Charles Augustus Milverton*

DOWNING, P. C.: Whose finger, in the line of duty, was bitten nearly off by the huge mulatto.
—*The Adventure of Wisteria Lodge*

DOWSON, BARON: Who said of Holmes, before he was hanged, that what the law had gained the stage had lost.
—*The Adventure of the Mazarin Stone*

DREBBER, ELDER: Father of Enoch Drebber; one of the four principal elders of the Mormon Church.
—*A Study in Scarlet*

DREBBER, ENOCH J.: Of Cleveland, Ohio, U. S. A., and erstwhile of Salt Lake City; widower of Lucy Drebber, née Ferrier. He was found dead in the house in Lauriston Gardens.   —*A Study in Scarlet*

DUBUQUE, MONSIEUR: Of the Paris police, who wasted his energy, according to Holmes, on unrecorded side-issues in the adventure of the Second Stain.   —*The Naval Treaty*

DUNBAR, GRACE: Governess at Thor Place, whose rivalry for the love of Neil Gibson led to a suicide masked as murder.
—*The Problem of Thor Bridge*

DUNDAS, ——: A teetotaller who had the interesting post-prandial habit of hurling his false teeth at his wife; hence the separation case bearing his name. —*A Case of Identity*

DUNN, JOSIAH H.: Manager of the Crow Hill mine, who was shot in the belly by the Scowrers.   —*The Valley of Fear*

DUPIN, C. AUGUSTE: A very inferior fellow.
—*A Study in Scarlet*

DURANDO, SIGNOR VICTOR: Erstwhile San Pedro minister in London. A nobler man never lived upon earth.
—*The Adventure of Wisteria Lodge*

DURANDO, SIGNORA VICTOR: Who became Miss Burnet, governess of the children of the Central American tyrant she hated.   —*The Adventure of Wisteria Lodge*

E

ECCLES, JOHN SCOTT: Conservative, churchman, good citizen, orthodox, conventional—and a stooge in a drama of Central American vengeance.
—*The Adventure of Wisteria Lodge*

EDMUNDS, ——: Of the Berkshire constabulary, who had worked on the killing of the bestial Ronder.
—*The Adventure of the Veiled Lodger*

EDWARDS, BIRDY: The Pinkerton operative, who became John McMurdo in Vermissa and John Douglas in Birlstone.
—*The Valley of Fear*

EDWARDS, MRS. BIRDY: Née Ettie Shafter, which see.
—*The Valley of Fear*

EGAN, ——: Who, with one Lander, claimed the head-money for the doing in of Mr. Crabbe.   —*The Valley of Fear*

——, ELISE: The German girl who risked the wrath of Lysander Stark to save Victor Hatherley from the horrors of a hydraulic death.
                    —*The Adventure of the Engineer's Thumb*

ELMAN, J. C., M.A.: Vicar who had the living of Mossmoor cum Little Purlington, and whose name Holmes forged to a telegram.   —*The Adventure of the Retired Colourman*

ELRIGE, ——: Who does not appear, but who presumably owned the farm bearing his name where Abe Slaney stayed.
                    —*The Adventure of the Dancing Men*

EMSWORTH, COLONEL, V. C.: The old campaigner who thought he was shielding a leper, and who kicked his son's crony out of the house.
                    —*The Adventure of the Blanched Soldier*

EMSWORTH, GODFREY: Who lay down in the bed of a leper and came out, for all his fears, with nothing worse than ichthyosis.   —*The Adventure of the Blanched Soldier*

EMSWORTH, MRS.: Wife of the colonel and mother of Godfrey, who fainted from the joyous shock of the news Sir James Saunders brought.
                    —*The Adventure of the Blanched Soldier*

ERNEST, DR. RAY: The friend and neighbor of the Amberleys, who played chess with Josiah and the fool with his wife, and died by asphyxiation.
                    —*The Adventure of the Retired Colourman*

ESCOTT, ——: Holmes's alias as a rising young plumber who wooed a housemaid to get the lay of the Milverton establishment.—*The Adventure of Charles Augustus Milverton*

ETHEREGE, MRS.: A friend of Mary Sutherland's whose husband Holmes had found "so easy" when the police had given him up for dead.   —*A Case of Identity*

EVANS, CARRIE: Impudent-faced maid to Lady Beatrice Falder, who was married to one Norlett.
                    —*The Adventure of Shoscombe Old Place*

EVANS, "KILLER": American gangster who posed as John Garrideb, which see.
                    —*The Adventure of the Three Garridebs*

EVANS, ——: A mine policeman, who was shot in the line of duty by the Scowrers.   —*The Valley of Fear*

EVANS, ——: Who became Mr. Beddoes of Hampshire, which see.   —*The "Gloria Scott"*

F

FABER, JOHANN: Pencil manufacturer, whose name on one of his wares gave Holmes a clue in his pursuit of a cheating student.   —*The Adventure of the Three Students*

FAIRBAIRN, ALEC: The good friend who stole Jim Browner's wife, and died with her by Jim's hand in a haze at sea.
                    —*The Adventure of the Cardboard Box*

FALDER, LADY BEATRICE: Widowed sister of Sir Robert Norberton, who passed away of the dropsy and was buried in secret in the family crypt.
                    —*The Adventure of Shoscombe Old Place*

FALDER, SIR JAMES: Deceased husband of Lady Beatrice Falder, from whom she inherited.
                    —*The Adventure of Shoscombe Old Place*

FARINTOSH, MRS.: Who recommended Holmes to Helen Stoner. He had helped her in the hour of her sore need— a case concerned with an opal tiara.
                    —*The Adventure of the Speckled Band*

FARQUHAR, OLD MR.: The doctor afflicted with St. Vitus's dance, from whom Watson bought his connection in the Paddington district.   —*The Stockbroker's Clerk*

FERGUSON, JOHN: Little Jacky, a cripple physically and mentally, whose hatred of his baby stepbrother led him to do unspeakable things.—*The Adventure of the Sussex Vampire*

FERGUSON, ROBERT: An old footballer, whose wife risked suspicion as a vampire to spare him the pain of his son's perfidy.   —*The Adventure of the Sussex Vampire*

FERGUSON, MRS. ROBERT: A noble Peruvian, who sucked poison from her baby as fast as her stepson pumped it in, and held her tongue in proud and devoted silence.
      —*The Adventure of the Sussex Vampire*

FERGUSON, ——: The innocent babe whose life was threatened by his stepbrother and saved again and again by his mother.   —*The Adventure of the Sussex Vampire*

FERGUSON, ——: Secretary to Neil Gibson of Thor Place.
      —*The Problem of Thor Bridge*

FERGUSON, ——: A retired sea captain who was the previous occupant of the Maberleys' house.
      —*The Adventure of The Three Gables*

FERGUSON, ——: Alias of Dr. Becher, which see.
      —*The Adventure of the Engineer's Thumb*

FERRIER, DR., ——: Tadpole Phelps's physician, who took charge of the fit he threw in the railway station.
      —*The Naval Treaty*

FERRIER, JOHN: Who brought the orphan Lucy to safety and Mormonism, but whose own orthodoxy was marred by a tenacious celibacy.   —*A Study in Scarlet*

FERRIER, LUCY: The beauteous foundling of the desert, whose death, as Mrs. Drebber, sent Jefferson Hope upon his quest for "Rache."   —*A Study in Scarlet*

FFOLLIOTT, SIR GEORGE: Of Oxshott Towers; one of the neighbors of Aloysius Garcia checked up by Holmes.
       —*The Adventure of Wisteria Lodge*

FISHER, PENROSE: One of London's leading medical specialists, whose services Watson suggested for a case of the black Formosa corruption.
       —*The Adventure of the Dying Detective*

FLOWERS, LORD: Who had correspondence with the Right Honourable Trelawney Hope.
       —*The Adventure of the Second Stain*

FORBES, ——: A detective of Scotland Yard, small and foxy, who was put in his place by Holmes.—*The Naval Treaty*

FORDHAM, DR.: Who attended Justice Trevor in his last hours.   —*The "Gloria Scott"*

FORDHAM, ——: The Horsham lawyer; consulted by the Openshaws when tragedy beckoned.
       —*The Five Orange Pips*

FORRESTER, MRS. CECIL: For whom Miss Morstan worked as governess, and for whom Holmes once rendered an unrecorded service in a little domestic complication.
       —*The Sign of the Four*

FORRESTER, ——: A local inspector who stood by and marveled while Holmes solved the mystery of the coachman's murder.   —*The Reigate Squires*

FORTESCUE, ——: Donor of the valuable Fortescue Scholarship, which inspired the theft of the examination papers at St. Luke's.   —*The Adventure of the Three Students*

FOURNAYE, MME. HENRI: The mad creole beauty who shared Eduardo Lucas's illicit life in Paris until she rose up to kill him.   —*The Adventure of the Second Stain*

FOWLER, ——: Fiancé of Alice Rucastle, who lurked in the road and made off with her through the roof.
    —*The Adventure of the Copper Beeches*

FRANKLAND, ——: Of Lafter Hall. An expert in litigation and lawsuits, an amateur astronomer, and one of the few neighbors of the Baskervilles.
    —*The Hound of the Baskervilles*

FRANZ JOSEPH I: 1830–1916. Emperor of Austria-Hungary, from whose Schoenbrunn cellars came the Imperial Tokay which warmed the hearts of Holmes and Watson in Von Bork's parlor.   —*His Last Bow*

FRASER, ANNIE: Consort of Holy Peters, who aided and abetted his nefarious schemes. Alias Mrs. Shlessinger, which see.   —*The Disappearance of Lady Frances Carfax*

FRASER, MARY: Of Adelaide, Australia, who became Lady Brackenstall, which see.
    —*The Adventure of the Abbey Grange*

FRASER, ——: A consumptive tutor, on whose coat-tails John Baskerville started his ill-fated school under the name of Vandeleur.   —*The Hound of the Baskervilles*

FREEBODY, MAJOR: An old friend of Joseph Openshaw's; commander of one of the forts upon Portsdown Hill.
    —*The Five Orange Pips*

G

GABORIAU, EMILE: 1833–1873. Holmes called his creature Lecoq a miserable bungler despite his energy.
    —*A Study in Scarlet*

GARCIA, ALOYSIUS: Who was found on Oxshott Common with his head smashed to pulp as a consequence of his loyal effort to rid the world of a human tiger.
—The Adventure of Wisteria Lodge

GARCIA, BERYL: Who became successively Baskerville, Vandeleur and Stapleton, which see.
—The Hound of the Baskervilles

GARRIDEB, ALEXANDER HAMILTON: The fictitious millionaire who supposedly bequeathed his fortune to three others who might bear his name.
—The Adventure of the Three Garridebs

GARRIDEB, HOWARD: Not a man, but a name in the paper to make Killer Evans's plot complete.
—The Adventure of the Three Garridebs

GARRIDEB, JOHN: Alias of Killer Evans of Moorville, Kansas, U.S.A., who invented an American millionaire to get at Rodger Prescott's forgery apparatus.
—The Adventure of the Three Garridebs

GARRIDEB, NATHAN: The true Garrideb, squatting innocently over Rodger Prescott's money-making machinery, to get at which the whole fantastic tale was concocted.
—The Adventure of the Three Garridebs

GELDER & Co.: The manufacturers of plaster busts in Stepney, whose German manager cooperated with Holmes to the best of his ability.
—The Adventure of the Six Napoleons

GEORGE II: 1683-1760. King of England, whose visit to the Manor House of Birlstone was a matter of record.
—The Valley of Fear

GIBSON, J. NEIL: The Gold King and former United States senator, who besought Holmes to clear his sweetheart of the accusation of his wife's murder.

—*The Problem of Thor Bridge*

GIBSON, MRS. J. NEIL: Née Maria Pinto of Brazil, who schemed to drag her rival with her to the grave.

—*The Problem of Thor Bridge*

GILCHRIST, SIR JABEZ: Father of young Gilchrist; who had ruined himself on the turf.

—*The Adventure of the Three Students*

GILCHRIST, ——: Scholar and long-jumper, who yielded to temptation but had already repented ere his cheating was discovered.   —*The Adventure of the Three Students*

GOLDINI, ——: Restaurateur in Gloucester Road, Kensington, whither Holmes summoned Watson to dine.

—*The Adventure of the Bruce-Partington Plans*

GORDON, GENERAL CHARLES GEORGE: "Chinese" Gordon, whose portrait, duly framed, hung upon the wall of the Baker Street sanctum.

—*The Adventure of the Cardboard Box*

GORGIANO, GIUSEPPE: Black Gorgiano of the Red Circle, whose path of sin in New York led to violent death in lodgings on Great Orme Street.

—*The Adventure of the Red Circle*

GOROT, CHARLES: A clerk in the Foreign Office, and a loyal Briton despite his Gallic name.   —*The Naval Treaty*

GOWER, ——: One of the gang designated to perform assault and battery on the body of James Stanger.

—*The Valley of Fear*

GRAFENSTEIN, COUNT VON UND ZU: Uncle of Von Bork, saved by Holmes from the murderous intentions of the Nihilist Klopman. *—His Last Bow*

GRAHAM & McFARLANE: Of 426 Gresham Buildings, E.C., the legal firm of which John Hector McFarlane was junior partner. *—The Adventure of the Norwood Builder*

GREEN, HONOURABLE PHILIP: Devoted admirer of Lady Frances Carfax, who aided intelligently in the battle to find and save her.*—The Disappearance of Lady Frances Carfax*

GREGORY, ——: An inspector who was rapidly making his name in the English detective service. It was to him that Holmes cited the curious incident of the dog in the night-time. *—Silver Blaze*

GREGSON, TOBIAS: An inspector of Scotland Yard: Energetic, gallant, and, within his limitations, a capable officer.
—A Study in Scarlet
—The Sign of the Four
—The Greek Interpreter
—The Adventure of Wisteria Lodge
—The Adventure of the Red Circle

GREUZE, JEAN BAPTISTE: 1725–1805. Whose picture, *La Jeune Fille à l'Agneau*, hung on the walls of Professor Moriarty's study, and thereby attested to unearned affluence. *—The Valley of Fear*

GREYMINSTER, DUKE OF: Who was, according to Holmes, involved in the matter of the Abbey School. The reference is probably to the Duke of Holdernesse, who was involved in the matter of the Priory School.
—The Adventure of the Blanched Soldier

GRIGGS, JIMMY: Clown in the Ronder circus, who helped save Eugenia Ronder's life, but not her face, from the assault of a bloodthirsty lion.
—*The Adventure of the Veiled Lodger*

GRUNER, BARON ADELBERT: The Austrian murderer whose marriage designs on Violet de Merville were frustrated by his lust-diary and a bottle of vitriol.
—*The Adventure of the Illustrious Client*

H

HAINES-JOHNSON, ——: A bogus house agent, who offered to rent the Maberley's establishment, fully furnished, at a suspiciously handsome price.
—*The Adventure of The Three Gables*

HALES, WILLIAM: Of the Stake Royal mine, who was put on the spot by the Scowrers.   —*The Valley of Fear*

HARDEN, JOHN VINCENT: The tobacco millionaire, in whose problem Holmes was immersed when Violet Smith came upon the scene.   —*The Adventure of the Solitary Cyclist*

HARDING, ——: Of the firm of Harding Brothers, who sold three of the six busts, including the fateful one acquired by Mr. Sandeman of Reading.
—*The Adventure of the Six Napoleons*

HARDY, SIR CHARLES: Some of his correspondence was in the pilfered dispatch box of the Right Honourable Trelawney Hope.   —*The Adventure of the Second Stain*

HARDY, SIR JOHN: One of the Honourable Ronald Adair's whist cronies at the Bagatelle Club.
—*The Adventure of the Empty House*

HARDY, ——: Foreman of the plumbing firm left by Mary Sutherland's late father.   —*A Case of Identity*

HARE, SIR JOHN: 1844–1921. Well-known English actor, whose histrionic abilities compared favorably with those of Sherlock Holmes.   —*A Scandal in Bohemia*

HARGRAVE, ——: The name under which was rented the bicycle ridden by Ted Baldwin to, but not back from, the Manor House.   —*The Valley of Fear*

HARGREAVE, WILSON: Of the New York Police Bureau; Holmes's friend, and user more than once of his knowledge.
    —*The Adventure of the Dancing Men*

HARKER, HORACE: Of the Central Press Syndicate, who had a murder on his own doorstep and thereby missed the scoop he might have had.—*The Adventure of the Six Napoleons*

HAROLD, MRS.: Who left Count Sylvius the Blymer estate, which was promptly gambled away.
    —*The Adventure of the Mazarin Stone*

HARRAWAY, ——: A vulture-faced old gray-beard, member in good standing of Vermissa Lodge, Ancient Order of Freemen.   —*The Valley of Fear*

HARRINGBY, LORD: Of the Dingle, near Esher, who was one of those checked up on by Holmes in the killing of Aloysius Garcia.   —*The Adventure of Wisteria Lodge*

HARRIS, ——: Of Bermondsey; the name by which Hall Pycroft introduced Holmes to Arthur Pinner.
    —*The Stockbroker's Clerk*

HARRISON, ANNIE: Tadpole Phelps's fiancée, who was innocent of her brother's scheme to betray his country's secrets.
    —*The Naval Treaty*

HARRISON, JOSEPH: Prospective brother-in-law of Tadpole Phelps: a fact which did not deter him in his act of perfidy to friend and King.   —*The Naval Treaty*

HARVEY, ———: One of the lads working under John Mason at the Shoscombe training establishment.
—*The Adventure of Shoscombe Old Place*

HATHERLEY, VICTOR: The engineer who left his thumb upon the window-sill of a house in Eyford near Reading.
—*The Adventure of the Engineer's Thumb*

HAYES, REUBEN: Innkeeper of the Fighting Cock, and the ruffian who murdered the bicycling Heidegger.
—*The Adventure of the Priory School*

HAYES, MRS. REUBEN: A kindly woman, to whose custody and care Lord Saltire was confided.
—*The Adventure of the Priory School*

HAYLING, JEREMIAH: The hydraulic engineer who lost his life in Eyford, where Victor Hatherley lost only his thumb.
—*The Adventure of the Engineer's Thumb*

HAYTER, COLONEL ———: Of Reigate, in Surrey. Watson's fellow campaigner in Afghanistan and a fine old soldier.
—*The Reigate Squires*

HAYWARD, ———: One of the plunderers of the Worthingdon Bank who took vengeance on the stool-pigeon Sutton, alias Blessington.   —*The Resident Patient*

HEBRON, JOHN: An Afro-American—but a nobler man never walked the earth. High yellow, but his offspring was a throw-back.   —*The Yellow Face*

HEBRON, LUCY: Black as the ace of spades behind her mask, she was Mrs. Munro's darling just the same.
—*The Yellow Face*

HEIDEGGER, ———: The heroic German master, whose head was bashed in and whose bicycle was smeared and slobbered with blood.   —*The Adventure of the Priory School*

HENDERSON, ——: Of High Gable, near Esher; alias of Don Murillo, which see. *—The Adventure of Wisteria Lodge*

HENDERSON, MISS: Aged 13; daughter of Don Juan Murillo.
—The Adventure of Wisteria Lodge

HENDERSON, MISS: Aged 11; daughter of Don Juan Murillo.
—The Adventure of Wisteria Lodge

HIGGINS, ——: Treasurer of Merton County Lodge 249, Ancient Order of Freemen. *—The Valley of Fear*

HILL, ——: Inspector of police, who was familiar with the haunts of the Italian quarter in London.
—The Adventure of the Six Napoleons

HOBBS, FAIRDALE: A former lodger of Mrs. Warren's, for whom Holmes had once solved a simple case.
—The Adventure of the Red Circle

HOBY, SIR EDWARD: Cited by Justice Trevor as having been attacked by poachers. *—The "Gloria Scott"*

HOLDER, ALEXANDER: Of the banking firm of Holder & Stevenson of Threadneedle Street. He lent £50,000 on a priceless coronet to a man bearing one of the highest, noblest, most exalted names in England.
—The Adventure of the Beryl Coronet

HOLDER, ARTHUR: To his father, Alexander Holder, he had been a grievous disappointment. But Holmes thought him a noble lad, and proved him such.
—The Adventure of the Beryl Coronet

HOLDER, JOHN: A regimental mate of Jonathan Small's, who pulled him, but not his leg, out of the Ganges.
—The Sign of the Four

HOLDER, MARY: Niece of Alexander Holder, and the sunbeam in his house. But she conspired despicably with the ignoble Sir George Burnwell.
—The Adventure of the Beryl Coronet

HOLDERNESSE, DUKE OF: The late cabinet minister who harbored a bastard as his secretary, and packed his legitimate son off to school. *—The Adventure of the Priory School*

HOLDERNESSE, DUCHESS OF: Née Edith Appledore; estranged wife of the Duke, and resident in the South of France.
—The Adventure of the Priory School

HOLDHURST, LORD: Uncle of Tadpole Phelps, and a great Conservative politician—a nobleman who was in truth noble. *—The Naval Treaty*

HOLLIS, ———: A spy in the German service who went a bit woozy before his final downfall. *—His Last Bow*

HOLLOWAY and STEELE: House-agents in the Edgware Road, who handled Nathan Garrideb's premises.
—The Three Garridebs

HOLMES, MYCROFT: Brother of Sherlock; seven years older, many stone heavier, but lacking the energy to capitalize his superior talents. *—The Greek Interpreter*
—The Final Problem
—The Adventure of the Empty House
—The Adventure of the Bruce-Partington Plans

HOLMES, SHERLOCK

HONES, JOHNNY: A pioneer who never reached the Western land he sought. *—A Study in Scarlet*

HOPE, LADY HILDA TRELAWNEY: Who purloined a state document under duress, and witnessed a bloody murder.
—The Adventure of the Second Stain

HOPE, JEFFERSON: Murderer of Enoch Drebber and Joseph Stangerson, who rode the long trail from Utah to Lauriston Gardens and cheated the gallows with a bursted aneurism.
—*A Study in Scarlet*

HOPE, RIGHT HONOURABLE TRELAWNEY: (Possibly Trelawney-Hope) Secretary for European Affairs, who lost a letter from a hot-headed potentate, but found it again in his own dispatch box.
—*The Adventure of the Second Stain*

HOPKINS, EZEKIAH: The mythical millionaire of Lebanon, Penn., U. S. A., whose bequest provided lucrative scholarships in the League of the Red-Headed Men.
—*The Red-Headed League*

HOPKINS, STANLEY: A young police inspector, for whose future Holmes had high hopes, but who occasionally disappointed him badly with his bungling.
—*The Adventure of Black Peter*
—*The Adventure of the Golden Pince-Nez*
—*The Adventure of the Missing Three-Quarter*
—*The Adventure of the Abbey Grange*

HORNER, JOHN: A plumber, falsely accused of having stolen the Countess of Morcar's priceless gem.
—*The Adventure of the Blue Carbuncle*

HORSOM, DR.: Called in by Holy Peters to attest the death of Rose Spender, intended coffin-companion of Lady Frances Carfax.   —*The Disappearance of Lady Frances Carfax*

HOWELLS, RACHEL: Second house-maid of the Musgraves, jilted into a case of brain fever by the gifted butler Brunton.
—*The Musgrave Ritual*

HUDSON, MORSE: An art dealer in Kennington Road whose possession of three of the six Napoleons caused him no more than passing perplexity and consternation.
—The Adventure of the Six Napoleons

HUDSON, MRS.: The worthy landlady of 221-B Baker Street.
—The Sign of the Four
—The Adventure of the Blue Carbuncle
—The Adventure of the Speckled Band
—The Naval Treaty
—The Adventure of the Empty House
—The Adventure of Black Peter
—The Adventure of the Second Stain
—The Valley of Fear
—The Adventure of Wisteria Lodge
—The Adventure of the Dying Detective
—The Adventure of the Mazarin Stone

HUDSON, ——: Seaman, gardener, butler. Rescued from the sea, he blackmailed his saviors.   *—The "Gloria Scott"*

HUDSON, ——: Mentioned in the enigmatical K.K.K. fragments.   *—The Five Orange Pips*

HUNT, ——: One of the Vermissa mine police, done to death by the Ancient Order of Freemen.   *—The Valley of Fear*

HUNTER, NED: The stable lad on guard at the stables when Silver Blaze was stolen.   *—Silver Blaze*

HUNTER, VIOLET: Freckled of face and long of tresses, she was paid handsomely to act as stand-in for Alice Rucastle.
—The Adventure of the Copper Beeches

HURET, ——: Referred to as the Boulevard assassin, for whose capture Holmes won the Légion d'Honneur.
—The Adventure of the Golden Pince-Nez

HUXTABLE, THORNEYCROFT, M.A., Ph.D., etc.: Who conducted the most exclusive preparatory school in all England, and fainted upon the bear-skin hearthrug in Baker Street.   —*The Adventure of the Priory School*

HYAM, ——: A Vermissan who was murdered among so many others by the spawn of the Ancient Order of Freemen.   —*The Valley of Fear*

HYAMS, ——: Jonas Oldacre's tailor, who obligingly stamped his name on the trousers-buttons he supplied.
                —*The Adventure of the Norwood Builder*

HYNES, HYNES, J. P.: A neighbor of Aloysius Garcia near Esher, who had nothing to do with the case.
                —*The Adventure of Wisteria Lodge*

I

IONIDES, ——: A cigarette manufacturer of Alexandria, who supplied Professor Coram at the rate of a thousand fortnightly.   —*The Adventure of the Golden Prince-Nez*

ISONOMY: The famous and very real ancestor of Silver Blaze.
                —*Silver Blaze*

J

JACKSON, DR.: A physician who occasionally took over Watson's practice when Holmes was on a scent.
                —*The Crooked Man*

JACOBS, ——: Butler to the Trelawney Hopes.
                —*The Adventure of the Second Stain*

JAMES, BILLY: One of the victims of the Ancient Order of Freemen.   —*The Valley of Fear*

JAMES, JACK: An American in the German spy service who, despite his citizenship, was doing time in an English gaol.
                —*His Last Bow*

JAMES I: 1566–1625. King of England, in the fifth year of whose reign the Manor House of Birlstone was erected.
—*The Valley of Fear*

——, JAMES: Son of the village postmaster and grocer, who delivered a telegram to Baskerville Hall.
—*The Hound of the Baskervilles*

JENKINS, ——: Two brothers killed one after the other by the emissaries of the Scowrers.   —*The Valley of Fear*

JOHN, SPENCER: Head of the gang retained by Isadora Klein to recover the manuscript that would have ruined her.
—*The Adventure of The Three Gables*

——, JOHN: A pompous butler in the employ of the irascible Dr. Armstrong.
—*The Adventure of the Missing Three-Quarter*

JOHNSON, SHINWELL: Porky Shinwell, the reformed criminal who became Holmes's ally in the underworld of London.
—*The Adventure of the Illustrious Client*

JOHNSON, SIDNEY: Senior clerk and draughtsman at the Admiralty, who had a key to the safe where the plans were kept.   —*The Adventure of the Bruce-Partington Plans*

JOHNSON, THEOPHILUS: Who, with his family, was registered below Sir Henry Baskerville at the Northumberland Hotel.
—*The Hound of the Baskervilles*

JOHNSON, ——: One of the Oxford fliers, whose prowess the Cambridge team, and especially Cyril Overton, deeply feared.   —*The Adventure of the Missing Three-Quarter*

JOHNSTON, ——: One of the four principal elders of the Mormon Church.   —*A Study in Scarlet*

JONES, ATHELNEY: An inspector of Scotland Yard.
—*The Sign of the Four*

JONES, BILLY: A victim of the killing wrath of the Scowrers of Vermissa.   —*The Valley of Fear*

JONES, PETER: An official police agent of Scotland Yard. Vis-à-vis Athelney, perhaps confusion—or perhaps nepotism.   —*The Red-Headed League*

——, JOSE: Servant to Don Juan Murillo, who fled with him from San Pedro to England, and from England to Spain.
—*The Adventure of Wisteria Lodge*

K

KEMBALL, HEBER C.*: One of the four principal elders of the Mormon Church.   —*A Study in Scarlet*

KEMP, WILSON: An old man who giggled, but who came of the foulest antecedents.   —*The Greek Interpreter*

KENT, ——: The surgeon who administered in secret to Godfrey Emsworth in his hide-away on the grounds of Tuxbury Old Hall.—*The Adventure of the Blanched Soldier*

KESWICK, ——: The respectable paperhanger who lived, instead of Mrs. Sawyer, at 13 Duncan Street in Houndsditch.
—*A Study in Scarlet*

KHALIFA, THE: Abdullah et Taaisha. 1846–1899. Holmes, during his exile, visited him at Khartoum, and the report he made was of great interest to the Foreign Office.
—*The Adventure of the Empty House*

KING, MRS.: Cook at Riding Thorpe Manor, who, with the housemaid, discovered the tragedy in the study.
—*The Adventure of the Dancing Men*

KIRWAN, WILLIAM: Coachman at the Cunningham's, who was silenced in death for fear of the things he knew.
—*The Reigate Squires*

* Historically, Heber C. Kimball.

KIRWAN, MRS.: Mother of William; very old and very deaf.
                              —*The Reigate Squires*

KLEIN, ISADORA: Erstwhile mistress of Douglas Maberley, who would have turned heaven and earth to recover a manuscript that revealed her as she was.
                    —*The Adventure of The Three Gables*

KLEIN, ———: The aged German sugar king, who left his widow the richest as well as the loveliest of her kind upon earth.   —*The Adventure of The Three Gables*

KLOPMAN, ———: Nihilist from whose attack Holmes had once been instrumental in saving Count Von und Zu Grafenstein.   —*His Last Bow*

KNELLER, SIR GODFREY: 1648–1723. The portrait painter whose work Holmes thought he identified on the walls of Baskerville Hall.   —*The Hound of the Baskervilles*

KNOX, JACK: One of the owners in Vermissa Valley who had so far been spared the attention of the Scowrers.
                              —*The Valley of Fear*

KRATIDES, PAUL: Who came from Athens to London on a mission of rescue in behalf of his sister, and who nearly paid with his life.   —*The Greek Interpreter*

KRATIDES, SOPHY: Sister of Paul Kratides, who avenged her abduction at last by a double stabbing on a train in Hungary.   —*The Greek Interpreter*

L

LANCASTER, JAMES: A harpooner who applied unsuccessfully for a berth in Holmes's fictitious Arctic expedition.
                    —*The Adventure of Black Peter*

LANDER, ——: One of the two who claimed the head money for the shooting of Mr. Crabbe at Stylestown.
—*The Valley of Fear*

LANNER, ——: A smart-looking inspector, whose actions completely belied appearances.   —*The Resident Patient*

LARBEY, MRS.: One of the female victims of the unholy wrath of the Scowrers.   —*The Valley of Fear*

LA ROTHIERE, LOUIS: The theft of the potentate's letter, according to Holmes, could have been the job only of him or Lucas or Oberstein. He was suspected also in the submarine case.   —*The Adventure of the Second Stain*
—*The Adventure of the Bruce-Partington Plans*

LATIMER, HAROLD: Who wielded a mesmeric influence over Sophy Kratides, but who paid at last with his life for his treachery.   —*The Greek Interpreter*

LAWLER, ——: Gunman imported from a nearby Lodge to do dirty work in Vermissa. He resembled an itinerant preacher.   —*The Valley of Fear*

LE BRUN, ——: The French police agent whose official interest in Baron Gruner made him a cripple for life.
—*The Adventure of the Illustrious Client*

LEFEVRE, ——: A murderer of Montpellier, France, whom the Sherlock Holmes test for blood-stains would have convicted.   —*A Study in Scarlet*

LEONARDO: The acrobat and strong man in Ronder's circus who clawed his patron to death with nails and left his sweetheart at the mercy of Sahara King.
—*The Adventure of the Veiled Lodger*

LESTRADE, G.: Inspector of Scotland Yard, who on one occasion at least undertook private cases.

> —*A Study in Scarlet*
> —*The Sign of the Four*
> —*The Boscombe Valley Mystery*
> —*The Adventure of the Noble Bachelor*
> —*The Adventure of the Empty House*
> —*The Adventure of the Norwood Builder*
> —*The Adventure of Charles Augustus Milverton*
> —*The Adventure of the Six Napoleons*
> —*The Adventure of the Second Stain*
> —*The Hound of the Baskervilles*
> —*The Adventure of the Cardboard Box*
> —*The Adventure of the Bruce-Partington Plans*
> —*The Disappearance of Lady Frances Carfax*
> —*The Adventure of the Three Garridebs*

LESURIER, MADAME: A fashionable milliner of Bond Street, patronized by the spurious Darbyshires.   —*Silver Blaze*

LETURIER, ——: Principal in a murder case in Montpellier involving the forcible administration of poison.
> —*A Study in Scarlet*

LEVERSTOKE, LORD: He chose the Priory School for the education of his son, to Mr. Huxtable's great satisfaction.
> —*The Adventure of the Priory School*

LEVERTON, ——: American Pinkerton operative, hero of the Long Island cave mystery, who was on the hunt for Black Gorgiano in London.   —*The Adventure of the Red Circle*

LE VILLARD, FRANCOIS: Of the French detective service; who translated Holmes's monographs for the edification of his own countrymen.   —*The Sign of the Four*

LEWIS, SIR GEORGE: Who had had negotiations with Sir James Damery over the Hammerford will case.
—*The Adventure of the Illustrious Client*

LEXINGTON, MRS.: Jonas Oldacre's housekeeper, who connived in his disappearance and specious murder.
—*The Adventure of the Norwood Builder*

LINCOLN, ABRAHAM: 1809–1865. The great Emancipator whom Neil Gibson resembled—except that he was keyed to base uses instead of high ones.
—*The Problem of Thor Bridge*

LOMAX, ——: Assistant at the London Library, who lent his friend Watson a volume on ceramics to prepare him for the encounter with Baron Gruner.
—*The Adventure of the Illustrious Client*

LOMOND, DUKE OF: Who might almost have been Isadora Klein's son, but whom she was going to marry.
—*The Adventure of The Three Gables*

LOPEZ, ——: The henchman of the Tiger of San Pedro, who became Lucas, his secretary, at High Gables near Esher.
—*The Adventure of Wisteria Lodge*

LOWENSTEIN, H.: The Bohemian who concocted the monkey serum with which Professor Presbury inspired himself.
—*The Adventure of the Creeping Man*

LUCAS, EDUARDO: International spy, who bludgeoned Lady Hope into theft from her husband, and was murdered by his demented mistress.
—*The Adventure of the Second Stain*

LUCAS, ——: Friend and secretary of the fugitive Don Murillo, who was known as Lopez in the better days.
—*The Adventure of Wisteria Lodge*

LUCCA, EMILIA: Wife of Gennaro. She danced for joy when her lustful suitor was found sprawled in death in the house on Great Orme Street.
> —*The Adventure of the Red Circle*

LUCCA, GENNARO: The honest Italian who hid himself in Mrs. Warren's lodgings and killed Black Gorgiano as he came to rout him out. —*The Adventure of the Red Circle*

LYNCH, VICTOR: The forger, catalogued in Holmes's index under "V". —*The Adventure of the Sussex Vampire*

LYONS, ——: Husband of Laura Lyons, née Frankland; a blackguard and a deserter. —*The Hound of the Baskervilles*

LYONS, MRS. LAURA: Daughter of Mr. Frankland. Her love for the villainous Stapleton let her lure Sir Charles Baskerville to his death at the moor gate.
> —*The Hound of the Baskervilles*

M

MABERLEY, DOUGLAS: A strapping lad, untimely deceased, who had written a novel in which his former mistress Isadora Klein was shown in her true colors.
> —*The Adventure of The Three Gables*

MABERLEY, MARY: Of The Three Gables, Harrow Weald, who was innocently in possession of a much-sought-after manuscript from her dead son's hand.
> —*The Adventure of The Three Gables*

MABERLEY, MORTIMER: Deceased husband of Mary Maberley and father of Douglas Maberley.
> —*The Adventure of The Three Gables*

MACDONALD, ALEC: Inspector of Scotland Yard, who later was to distinguish himself on the force, but who gummed things up badly at Birlstone. —*The Valley of Fear*

MacKINNON, ——: A smart young police inspector who worked on the case of the missing Mrs. Amberley.
—*The Adventure of the Retired Colourman*

MacNAMARA, MRS.: Widow in whose abode McMurdo took up quarters when he left the Shafters, and within whose walls the round-up was engineered. —*The Valley of Fear*

MACPHAIL, ——: Coachman at the Presburys', who slept over the stable and witnessed strange goings-on at night.
—*The Adventure of the Creeping Man*

MacPHERSON, P. C.: Threatened by Lestrade with Queer Street for having admitted a woman to the death chamber in Godolphin Street. —*The Adventure of the Second Stain*

MANDERS, ——: A member of Vermissa Lodge, who ran with the pack.   —*The Valley of Fear*

MANSEL, ——: One of the gang sent after James Stanger, which left the doughty old editor bloody but unbowed.
—*The Valley of Fear*

MARCINI, ——: Restaurateur who catered at least once to Holmes and Watson.   —*The Hound of the Baskervilles*

MARKER, MRS. ——: Professor Coram's sad-faced and elderly housekeeper, who knew not the kind she was serving.
—*The Adventure of the Golden Pince-Nez*

——, MARTHA: Housekeeper for the spy Von Bork, who aided Holmes faithfully in his triumphant counter-espionage.   —*His Last Bow*

MARTIN, LIEUTENANT: Of the "Gloria Scott", who remained loyal to his sorrow.   —*The "Gloria Scott"*

MARTIN, ——: Inspector of the Norfolk Constabulary, who had a wholesome respect for Holmes's methods.
—*The Adventure of the Dancing Men*

MARVIN, CAPTAIN TEDDY: Of the mine police, and erstwhile of the Chicago Central, who collaborated with Edwards-McMurdo in the capture of the Scowrers.

—*The Valley of Fear*

MARX & Co.: Tailors of High Holborn; outfitters of Aloysius Garcia.   —*The Adventure of Wisteria Lodge*

——, MARY: Maid at the Maberleys in Harrow Weald.
—*The Adventure of The Three Gables*

——, MARY: Maid at the Openshaws in Sussex, near Horsham.
—*The Five Orange Pips*

——, MARY JANE: The servant girl of the Watsons, who was summarily dismissed for reasons unspecified.

—*A Scandal in Bohemia*

MASON, JOHN: Head trainer at Shoscombe Old Place, who brought the mysterious doings at his master's establishment to Holmes's notice.

—*The Adventure of Shoscombe Old Place*

MASON, MRS.: Faithful nurse at the Fergusons, who shared her mistress's secret of young Jacky's shame.

—*The Adventure of the Sussex Vampire*

MASON, ——: Plate-layer on the Underground, who discovered Cadogan West's body outside Aldgate Station.
—*The Adventure of the Bruce-Partington Plans*

MASON, ——: A criminal of Bradford, cited by Holmes as having escaped the gallows because no definitive test for bloodstains existed.   —*A Study in Scarlet*

MATHEWS, ——: Holmes's note-book listed him as the man who had knocked out his tooth in the waiting-room at Charing Cross.   —*The Adventure of the Empty House*

MAUDSLEY, ——: James Ryder's friend, who had served in Pentonville, and whose advice the unfortunate Ryder followed. —*The Adventure of the Blue Carbuncle*

MAUPERTUIS, BARON: Whose colossal schemes Watson thought too recent, and too intimately concerned with politics and finance, to risk recounting. —*The Reigate Squires*

MAWSON, ——: Of Mawson & Williams's, whose office was the scene of an unsuccessful robbery and a successful homicide. —*The Stockbroker's Clerk*

MAYNOOTH, COUNTESS OF: Mother of the Honourable Ronald Adair. She was operated upon for cataract.
—*The Adventure of the Empty House*

MAYNOOTH, EARL OF: Governor of one of the Australian colonies and father of the Honourable Ronald Adair.
—*The Adventure of the Empty House*

McCARTHY, CHARLES: A devil incarnate, who was murdered by the Boscombe Pool after an altercation with his son.
—*The Boscombe Valley Mystery*

McCARTHY, JAMES: The irresponsible son of a villainous father, who married a barmaid before he was 18. Of the barmaid's age: no record.
—*The Boscombe Valley Mystery*

McCAULEY, ——: A victim of the pips.
—*The Five Orange Pips*

McFARLANE, JOHN HECTOR: Condemned for the murder of Jonas Oldacre, he would have provided that living scoundrel with horrid revenge.
—*The Adventure of the Norwood Builder*

McFARLANE, MRS. ——: Mother of John Hector McFarlane, upon whom Jonas Oldacre sought to wreak a cruel and unusual punishment.
—The Adventure of the Norwood Builder

McGINTY, JOHN: Bodymaster of Vermissa Lodge of the Ancient Order of Freemen. A villainous giant, black of beard and of heart.   *—The Valley of Fear*

McGREGOR, MRS.: Lost on the trail to the West, where only John and Lucy Ferrier survived.   *—A Study in Scarlet*

McLAREN, MILES: Wayward, dissipated but brilliant—and innocent of the theft of the examination papers.
—The Adventure of the Three Students

McMURDO, JOHN: Alias of Birdy Edwards in the days of his sleuthing in Vermissa Valley. He later became John Douglas of Birlstone.   *—The Valley of Fear*

McMURDO, ——: Henchman of the Sholtos; a retired pugilist who had great respect for Holmes's cross-hit under the jaw.
—The Sign of the Four

McPHERSON, FITZROY: Who met a horrible death in the clutches of *Cyanea capillata* within a stone's-throw of Holmes's bee-farm on the Sussex Downs.
—The Adventure of the Lion's Mane

MEEK, SIR JASPER: Specialist suggested by Watson for treatment of Holmes's malingered case of Tapanuli fever.
—The Adventure of the Dying Detective

MELAS, ——: Whose linguistic ability carried him into dangerous fields, but who was saved at last from the brazier.
—The Greek Interpreter

MELVILLE, ——: *Chez* whom John Scott Eccles first met Aloysius Garcia.   *—The Adventure of Wisteria Lodge*

MENDELSSOHN-BARTHOLDY, JAKOB LUDWIG FELIX: 1809–1847. German composer, whose *Lieder* Holmes delighted in playing on his violin.   —*A Study in Scarlet*

MENZIES, ——: The Scotch mine engineer at Crow Hill, who was wantonly done to death by the Scowrers.
—*The Valley of Fear*

MERCER, ——: Holmes's latterly acquired general utility man, who looked after his routine business.
—*The Adventure of the Creeping Man*

MERCER, ——: Second mate of the "Gloria Scott", who shared the fate of the other honest men.   —*The "Gloria Scott"*

MERIVALE, ——: Holmes's friend at the Yard, with whom he occasionally consulted.
—*The Adventure of Shoscombe Old Place*

MERRIDEW, ——: Of abominable memory—but why, Holmes's index of biographies did not reveal.
—*The Adventure of the Empty House*

MERRILOW, MRS.: The landlady of South Brixton who summoned Holmes to attend the once-beautiful Eugenia Ronder in her seclusion.   —*The Adventure of the Veiled Lodger*

MERROW, LORD: Whose correspondence was among the other papers in the Right Honourable Trelawney Hope's dispatch box.   —*The Adventure of the Second Stain*

MERRYWEATHER, ——: Chairman of directors of the City and Suburban Bank, the raid upon whose Coburg (or City) Branch he helped frustrate.   —*The Red-Headed League*

MERTON, SAM: Boxer and bodyguard of Count Sylvius, who was as strong as an ox and just about as smart.
—*The Adventure of the Mazarin Stone*

MEUNIER, MONS. OSCAR: The sculptor of Grenoble, who did the waxen bust of Holmes which lured Colonel Sebastian Moran to confusion.—*The Adventure of the Empty House*

MEYER, ADOLPH: An international spy who was among Holmes's suspects in the theft of the submarine papers.
—*The Adventure of the Bruce-Partington Plans*

MEYERS, ———: The Toronto bootmaker whose mark identified the medium through which the hound had been put upon the scent.   —*The Hound of the Baskervilles*

———, MICHAEL: Stable hand at the Fergusons in Cheeseman's.
—*The Adventure of the Sussex Vampire*

MILES, THE HONOURABLE MISS: The *Morning Post* announced one day that her engagement to Colonel Dorking had been broken.
—*The Adventure of Charles Augustus Milverton*

MILLAR, FLORA: The girl in Lord St. Simon's life, whose intervention at his wedding was superfluous.
—*The Adventure of the Noble Bachelor*

MILMAN, ———: One of the owners' group in Vermissa Valley who was slain by the Scowrers.   —*The Valley of Fear*

MILNER, GODFREY: Who lost £420 at whist in a single evening at the Bagatelle.—*The Adventure of the Empty House*

MILVERTON, CHARLES AUGUSTUS: The worst man in London, with a smiling face and a heart of marble. Holmes and Watson were witness to his welcome murder by a lovely and noble lady.—*The Adventure of Charles Augustus Milverton*

MITTON, JOHN: Valet to Eduardo Lucas, arrested for his murder but freed on his alibi.
—*The Adventure of the Second Stain*

Holmes and Colonel Moran (illustration by Steele for "The Empty House" by permission of the artist)

MOFFAT, ——: With Biddle and Hayward he escaped the toils of the law, but probably drowned when the *Norah Creina* went down.   —*The Resident Patient*

MONTALVA, MARQUESS OF: The name under which Don Juan Murillo died by violence in Madrid.
                 —*The Adventure of Wisteria Lodge*

MONTGOMERY, ——: Inspector of the Shadwell police, who did nothing much in the case of the pickled ears.
                 —*The Adventure of the Cardboard Box*

MONTPENSIER, MME.: Referred to as having been charged with the murder of her step-daughter, who was later found safe.   —*The Hound of the Baskervilles*

MOORHOUSE, ——: A first reserve on the Cambridge team, who was not good enough to make Godfrey Staunton's absence palatable.   —*The Adventure of the Missing Three-Quarter*

MORAN, SIR AUGUSTUS C. B.: Father of Sebastian. His son disgraced an honored name.
                 —*The Adventure of the Empty House*

MORAN, COLONEL SEBASTIAN: He had the career of an honorable soldier, but he became, after Moriarty's death, the most cunning and dangerous criminal in all London.
                 —*The Adventure of the Empty House*
                 —*The Valley of Fear*
                 —*His Last Bow*
                 —*The Adventure of the Illustrious Client*

MORAN, PATIENCE: Daughter of the lodge-keeper at Boscombe Valley, who picked flowers while Charles and James McCarthy raised their voices.
                 —*The Boscombe Valley Mystery*

MORAN, ——: Lodge-keeper at the Boscombe Valley estate, whose indicated quizzing by Holmes is unrecorded.
—*The Boscombe Valley Mystery*

MORCAR, COUNTESS OF: Owner of the blue carbuncle, stolen from her rooms in the Hotel Cosmopolitan by a tyro whom Holmes forgave.   —*The Adventure of the Blue Carbuncle*

MORECROFT, ——: Alias of Killer Evans, which see.
—*The Three Garridebs*

MORGAN, ——: A poisoner listed in Holmes's index of biographies.   —*The Adventure of the Empty House*

MORIARTY, PROFESSOR JAMES: "The Napoleon of crime, Watson!"   —*The Final Problem*
—*The Adventure of the Empty House*
—*The Adventure of the Norwood Builder*
—*The Adventure of the Missing Three-Quarter*
—*The Valley of Fear*
—*His Last Bow*
—*The Adventure of the Illustrious Client*

(Note: I find the Professor's first name mentioned only once: in *The Adventure of the Empty House*, where it is clearly given as "James." Mr. Vincent Starrett's authority for "Robert" I cannot place.)*

---

* In *The Private Life of Sherlock Holmes* I have called the professor Robert; yet, as Mr. Smith points out, he is very clearly given as James in *The Adventure of the Empty House*. The fact is, there is a curious problem involved in the nomenclature of the brothers Moriarty; for there were two of them. The professor's name was certainly James in *The Empty House*, toward the end of which episode Holmes remarks that "Professor James Moriarty . . . had one of the great brains of the century." In *The Final Problem*, however, Watson sets forth that his hand has been forced . . . "by the recent letters in which Colonel James Moriarty defends the memory of his brother." We have, then, the unique problem of the Moriarty brothers, James and James, both clearly of record. Now when was the Doctor—who is authority for both Jameses—right? When he wrote that line in *The Final Problem* or when he quoted Holmes in *The Empty House*? It may be argued that Watson, at the time of the earlier episode, was dis-

MORIARTY, COLONEL JAMES: Brother of him whose presence boded not danger, but destruction. His efforts to defend the Professor's memory led Watson to reveal the whole horrid truth.
—*The Final Problem*
—*The Valley of Fear*

MORLAND, SIR JOHN: The barratrous Mr. Frankland said he had him for trespass because he shot in his own warren.
—*The Hound of the Baskervilles*

MORPHY, ALICE: Whose reluctance to join May to December doubtless led Professor Presbury to seek simian rejuvenation.
—*The Adventure of the Creeping Man*

MORPHY, PROFESSOR: Professor Presbury's colleague, whose daughter he aspired to marry.
—*The Adventure of the Creeping Man*

traught; writing, as he was, of his friend's death (as he supposed) in Switzerland: yet at such a time would he not have been particularly careful? And it is to be remembered that he was distraught also at the time of *The Adventure of the Empty House:* he had just received his friend back from the dead! Which occasion would be more likely to plunge him into error —death or resurrection? Or were there really two brothers Moriarty, each of them named James?

In scientific, if sporting, spirit I went to the only other source-authority who had written about the professor, Mr. William Gillette, who I knew had consulted the detective's amanuensis, at least, before writing his Sherlockian play. And there, sure enough, in the dramatis personæ, was the professor's name; it was clearly revealed as Robert. In the circumstances, I have assumed that Watson erred, in his emotional presentation of *The Empty House,* and for a moment confused the professor with his brother. I do not insist on this explanation, for indeed there is considerable mystery about this whole business of the brothers. In *The Valley of Fear* we are told by Holmes—via Watson, of course—that the professor's brother was a station-master in the West of England; yet in *The Final Problem* he is a colonel. He may have been both, to be sure; but somehow it seems unlikely. Is it not even possible that there was a third brother—whose name perhaps also was James? Two brothers named James would appear a trifle silly; but if there were three one might suppose some sort of sinister pattern in the phenomenon. It is all very confusing, at any rate, and until Miss Dorothy Sayers shall attempt the solution I am content to look with suspicion on *all* the brothers Moriarty.

V. S.

MORRIS, BROTHER: Of Vermissa Lodge, who repented his association with the Scowrers and wept in John McMurdo's bosom.
—The Valley of Fear

MORRIS, WILLIAM: Alias of Duncan Ross, who opened a very temporary office at 7 Pope's Court, Fleet Street.
—The Red-Headed League

MORRISON, ANNIE: She does not appear, but her name in a note was the bait that lured William Kirwan to his death.
—The Reigate Squires

MORRISON, MORRISON, AND DODD: The lawyers who referred the vampire case to Holmes, as being out of their province.
—The Adventure of the Sussex Vampire

MORRISON, MISS ——: Next door neighbor of the Barclays; an ethereal slip of a girl who witnessed Mrs. Barclay's meeting with Henry Wood.
—The Crooked Man

MORSTAN, CAPTAIN ARTHUR: Father of Mary Morstan; senior captain of his Indian regiment, who came back to London and limbo.
—The Sign of the Four

MORSTAN, MISS MARY: Blonde, small, dainty, and well-gloved. She became Dr. Watson's first wife, and almost undid the work that young Stamford had done.*—The Sign of the Four*

MORTIMER, JAMES, M.R.C.S.: The Baskerville physician and friend, who brought the hound to Holmes's notice. He also coveted Holmes's dolicocephalic skull.
—The Hound of the Baskervilles

MORTIMER, ——: Gardener at the Yoxley Old Place establishment of the spurious Professor Coram.
—The Adventure of the Golden Pince-Nez

MORTON, CYRIL: Fiancé of Violet Smith, who became senior partner of Morton & Kennedy, the famous Westminster electricians.   *—The Adventure of the Solitary Cyclist*

MORTON, ——: Inspector of Scotland Yard, who collaborated in the capture of the nefarious Culverton Smith.
—The Adventure of the Dying Detective

MORTON, ——: An Oxford flier who was feared by the Cambridge team with Staunton out.
—The Adventure of the Missing Three-Quarter

MORTON & WAYLIGHT: Of Tottenham Court Road, where the knocked-about Mr. Warren was timekeeper.
—The Adventure of the Red Circle

MOSER, MONS.: Well-known manager of the National Hotel at Lausanne, who helped Watson along the trail.
—The Disappearance of Lady Frances Carfax

MOULTON, FRANCIS HAY: Who escaped from the Apaches, and snatched his bride almost from the altar of fashionable St. George's in Hanover Square.
—The Adventure of the Noble Bachelor

MOULTON, MRS. FRANCIS HAY: Née Hatty Doran. Saved by her rediscovered marital status from becoming Lady Robert St. Simon.—*The Adventure of the Noble Bachelor*

MOUNT-JAMES, LORD: Uncle of Godfrey Staunton; one of the richest men in England, and so full of gout he could chalk a billiard-cue with his knuckles.
—The Adventure of the Missing Three-Quarter

MUIRHEAD, ——: Of the firm of Ferguson and Muirhead, in which Bob Ferguson was senior partner.
—The Adventure of the Sussex Vampire

MULLER, ——: Notorious criminal who escaped justice because no Sherlock Holmes test for blood-stains existed.
—A Study in Scarlet

MUNRO, GRANT: His pipe told Holmes all about him in advance—except as to the mystery of the face in the window. His wife called him "Jack."   —*The Yellow Face*

MUNRO, MRS. GRANT: Effie, erstwhile wife of John Hebron, of Atlanta, Georgia. She was torn between love of her child and love of her husband.   —*The Yellow Face*

MUNRO, COLONEL SPENCE: Violet Hunter's former employer. His departure for Halifax, in Nova Scotia, led Miss Hunter into high adventure.

—*The Adventure of the Copper Beeches*

MURCHER, HARRY: Constable Rance's confrère, who gossiped with him on a street-corner while Enoch Drebber lay murdered.   —*A Study in Scarlet*

MURDOCH, IAN: Mathematical coach at the Stackhurst establishment, who was suspected in the death of Fitzroy McPherson until he, too, was lashed by the mane.

—*The Adventure of the Lion's Mane*

MURDOCH, JAMES: Who was "mutilated" by the Scowrers, in what horrible fashion we can only surmise.

—*The Valley of Fear*

MURGER, HENRI: 1822–1861. Author of *La Vie de Bohème*, which Watson skimmed over a pipe.   —*A Study in Scarlet*

MURILLO, DON JUAN: The Tiger of San Pedro, alias Henderson, who fled his Central American despotism to be hunted down in Esher and Madrid.

—*The Adventure of the Norwood Builder*
—*The Adventure of Wisteria Lodge*

MURPHY, MAJOR: One of Colonel Barclay's fellow officers in the Mallows, who gave Holmes most of the facts in the Colonel's demise.   —*The Crooked Man*

MURPHY, ——: A gipsy horse-dealer who heard cries on the moor while in his cups.   —*The Hound of the Baskervilles*

MURRAY, ——: Watson's orderly at the battle of Maiwand, whose bravery stood the good doctor well and conferred infinite blessing on the readers of the chronicles which Watson lived to write.   —*A Study in Scarlet*

MURRAY, ——: Who played a rubber of whist at the Bagatelle in company with the Honourable Ronald Adair.
—*The Adventure of the Empty House*

MUSGRAVE, SIR RALPH: Ancestor of Reginald Musgrave; a prominent Cavalier and right-hand man of Charles the Second.   —*The Musgrave Ritual*

MUSGRAVE, REGINALD: Who went to college with Holmes, and for whom the ancestral crown was retrieved. The case was Holmes's third.   —*The Musgrave Ritual*

N

NAPOLEON I: 1769–1821. Né Buonaparte, a cast of whose bust by Devine served as the hiding place for the stolen pearl of the Borgias.—*The Adventure of the Six Napoleons*

NEALE, ——: "Outfitter, Vermissa, U. S. A.". An overcoat bearing that impossible tab was fished out of the moat at Birlstone.   —*The Valley of Fear*

NEILL, GENERAL: A British officer during the Indian Mutiny, to whom Henry Wood was sent on the mission which betrayed him.   —*The Crooked Man*

NELIGAN, JOHN HOPLEY: His presence in Peter Carey's cabin led Inspector Hopkins—but not Holmes—to suspect him of murder.   —*The Adventure of Black Peter*

NELIGAN, ——: Father of John Hopley Neligan, who was rescued from the sea, and turned back into it again, by Black Peter.   —*The Adventure of Black Peter*

NERUDA, NORMAN: A violiniste whose attack and bowing excited the admiration of her fellow virtuoso.
    —*A Study in Scarlet*

NEWTON, HEATH: Owner of The Negro, which raced against Silver Blaze.   —*Silver Blaze*

NICHOLSON, ——: Head of the family of that name which was wiped out by the Scowrers.   —*The Valley of Fear*

NORBERTON, SIR ROBERT: An improvident soul, who concealed the death of his sister for legal reasons on which he duly cashed in when the Derby was run.
    —*The Adventure of Shoscombe Old Place*

NORLETT, ——: An actor who posed as Lady Beatrice Falder while that good woman lay rotting in the family crypt.
    —*The Adventure of Shoscombe Old Place*

NORLETT, MRS.: Née Carrie Evans, maid to Lady Beatrice Falder and party to the plot to delay knowledge of her mistress's death.—*The Adventure of Shoscombe Old Place*

NORTON, GODFREY: Of the Inner Temple. Irene Adler's impetuously achieved husband.   —*A Scandal in Bohemia*

O

OAKSHOTT, SIR LESLIE: Who attended Holmes for lacerations received at the hands of the minions of Baron Gruner.
    —*The Adventure of the Illustrious Client*

OAKSHOTT, MRS. MAGGIE: James Ryder's sister, who supplied the wholesaler Breckinridge with town-bred geese.
    —*The Adventure of the Blue Carbuncle*

OBERSTEIN, HUGO: Innocent of the theft of the diplomatic document, but guilty in the case of the submarine plans.
—The Adventure of the Second Stain
—The Adventure of the Bruce-Partington Plans

OLDACRE, JONAS: He once turned a cat loose in an aviary; but his cruelty took even more vicious forms than this.
—The Adventure of the Norwood Builder

OLDMORE, MRS.: Holmes checked her name on the register of the Northumberland Hotel where Sir Henry Baskerville was staying.   *—The Hound of the Baskervilles*

OPENSHAW, COLONEL ELIAS: Tracked by the Ku Klux Klan to his hide-out in Horsham, and found dead, on May 2, 1883, face downward in a little green-scummed pool.
—The Five Orange Pips

OPENSHAW, JOHN: The client who came to Holmes two days too late, and who paid for the delay with his life.
—The Five Orange Pips

OPENSHAW, JOSEPH: Father of John, and another victim of the Ku Klux Klan—with a shattered skull in a chalk-pit.
—The Five Orange Pips

ORMSTEIN, WILHELM GOTTSREICH SIGISMOND VON: Alias Count von Kramm. Grand Duke of Cassel-Felstein, and hereditary King of Bohemia. His mask did not disguise him from Holmes's keen eye.   *—A Scandal in Bohemia*
—His Last Bow

OVERTON, CYRIL: The sixteen-stone Cantabrigian, who came to Holmes to report the loss of the indispensable Godfrey Staunton.   *—The Adventure of the Missing Three-Quarter*

P

PALMER, WILLIAM: A doctor cited by Holmes as having gone very wrong indeed. (He was executed in 1856 for the murder of a friend by poison).   —*The Speckled Band*

PARAMORE, ——: Doomed by the K.K.K.
                              —*The Five Orange Pips*

PARKER, (REVEREND) ——: Vicar of the parish at Riding Thorpe, at whose favorite boarding-house in Russell Square Hilton Cubitt met Elsie Patrick.
                    —*The Adventure of the Dancing Men*

PARKER, ——: Arthur Pinner told Hall Pycroft he had spoken well of Pycroft's capacities.   —*The Stockbroker's Clerk*

PARKER, ——: One of the Moriarty-Moran gang; a garroter by trade, but by avocation a sweet singer on the Jew's harp.
                    —*The Adventure of the Empty House*

PARR, LUCY: Second waiting-maid at the Holder's, of whom Alexander's suspicions were groundless.
                    —*The Adventure of the Beryl Coronet*

PATERSON, GRICE: (Perhaps Grice-Paterson) Who, with his wife or son, had singular but unrecorded adventures in the island of Uffa.   —*The Five Orange Pips*

PATRICK, ELSIE: Daughter of a gangster, who became the respectable Mrs. Hilton Cubitt, which see.
                    —*The Adventure of the Dancing Men*

PATRICK, ——: Father of Mrs. Hilton Cubitt, and boss of the Joint, in Chicago, U. S. A.
                    —*The Adventure of the Dancing Men*

PATTERSON, INSPECTOR: Referred to in Holmes's farewell note from the Reichenbach Falls as the officer ready to close in on the Moriarty gang.   —*The Final Problem*

PATTINS, HUGH: His application for a job as harpooner was rejected because he was not the man Holmes was after.
—The Adventure of Black Peter

PEACE, CHARLES: The famous English criminal, who was, incidentally, a violin virtuoso.
—The Adventure of the Illustrious Client

PERKINS, ——: Whose death outside the Holborn bar Holmes held as a club over the black head of Steve Dixie.
—The Adventure of The Three Gables

PERKINS, ——: A groom at Baskerville Hall.
—The Hound of the Baskervilles

PERSANO, ISADORE: The epic character who was found stark staring mad with a matchbox and a strange worm before him.   *—The Problem of Thor Bridge*

——, PETER: The groom at Chiltern Grange, who was hurt defending the honor of his mistress.
—The Adventure of the Solitary Cyclist

PETERS, HENRY: Holy Peters, one of the most unscrupulous rascals Australia ever evolved. Alias Reverend Dr. Shlessinger.   *—The Disappearance of Lady Frances Carfax*

PETERSON, ——: The commissionaire, who picked up the goose containing the Countess of Morcar's carbuncle.
—The Adventure of the Blue Carbuncle

PHELPS, PERCY: The famous Tadpole, given to fainting fits, screams and brain fever, who kept unconscious vigil over the document of which he had been robbed.
—The Naval Treaty

PHILLIMORE, JAMES: He it was who stepped back into his house to get an umbrella and disappeared forever.
—The Problem of Thor Bridge

PIERROT: The name used by Hugo Oberstein in his agony-column messages to Colonel Walters.

—*The Bruce-Partington Plans*

PIKE, LANGDALE: Holmes's mentor and human book of reference upon all matters of social scandal.

—*The Adventure of The Three Gables*

PINKERTON, ALLAN: 1819–1884. The noted organizer of a private detective service, by which Birdy Edwards and Leverton were employed.   —*The Valley of Fear*
—*The Red Circle*

PINKERTON, BRUCE: Donor of the prize and medal for a monograph on nervous lesions, won by Dr. Trevelyan.

—*The Resident Patient*

PINNER, ARTHUR: Alias Harry Pinner. He doubled in Birmingham to clear the way for Beddington's assault on the vaults of Mawson & Williams's.—*The Stockbroker's Clerk*

PINTO, JONAS: The story of whose murder in Chicago by John McMurdo built up the bad reputation McMurdo cultivated.   —*The Valley of Fear*

PINTO, MARIA: Who became Mrs. J. Neil Gibson, which see.
—*The Problem of Thor Bridge*

POE, EDGAR ALLAN: 1809–1849. Creator of Dupin, whom Holmes regarded as a very inferior fellow.

—*A Study in Scarlet*

POLLOCK, P. C.: The constable who assisted in the arrest of Beddington.   —*The Stockbroker's Clerk*

POMPEY: Pride of the local drag-hounds, who could follow aniseed from here to John o' Groat's.

—*The Adventure of the Missing Three-Quarter*

PORLOCK, FRED: Signer of the warning Holmes received of bad doings at Birlstone—according to Holmes a nom-deplume and a mere identification mark.—*The Valley of Fear*

PORTER, MRS.: Old cook and housekeeper for the family Tregennis, upon whose house an awful blight descended.
—*The Adventure of the Devil's Foot*

POTT, EVANS: A sly little gray-haired rat of a man; official of the County Delegate of the Ancient Order of Freemen.
—*The Valley of Fear*

PRENDERGAST, JACK: Six and a half feet of viciousness, whose hidden treasure financed the mutiny.—*The "Gloria Scott"*

PRENDERGAST, MAJOR: Quoted by John Openshaw as having been saved by Holmes in the Tankerville Club scandal.
—*The Five Orange Pips*

PRESBURY, EDITH: Daughter of Professor Presbury, and enamored of his assistant Trevor Bennett whom she called Jack.   —*The Adventure of the Creeping Man*

PRESBURY, PROFESSOR: The Camford physiologist, who, seeking youth and vigor from the serum of the black-faced langur, climbed trees and walked on his knuckles.
—*The Adventure of the Creeping Man*

PRESCOTT, RODGER: Counterfeiter slain in Chicago by Killer Evans, and whose house and plant in London Evans sought out.   —*The Adventure of the Three Garridebs*

PRICE, ——: Of Birmingham; the fleeting alias of Dr. Watson in his encounter with Arthur Pinner.
—*The Stockbroker's Clerk*

PRINGLE, MRS.: Elderly housekeeper for the spying and double-dealing Eduardo Lucas.
—*The Adventure of the Second Stain*

PRITCHARD, EDWARD WILLIAM: A Glasgow practitioner who was hanged for poisoning his wife and mother-in-law, in 1865. Cited by Holmes.   —*The Speckled Band*

PROSPER, FRANCIS: A wooden-legged greengrocer, with whom Lucy Parr was walking out in full innocence of the treasure her master was harboring.
                    —*The Adventure of the Beryl Coronet*

PYCROFT, HALL: A cockney clerk who was lured to Birmingham that his name and reputation might be used in vain for criminal purposes.   —*The Stockbroker's Clerk*

R

RAE, ANDREW: Of Rae & Sturmash, coal owners, on whom the Lodge decided a job was to be done.
                    —*The Valley of Fear*

——, RALPH: Butler at Tuxbury Old Hall, who carried food to his young master with gloves to protect him from the leprosy he feared.—*The Adventure of the Blanched Soldier*

RANCE, JOHN: The constable who found Enoch Drebber's body, and who, Holmes predicted, would never rise in the force.   —*A Study in Scarlet*

RANDALLS, THE THREE: The Kentish burglars, *père* and *fils*, whose arrest in New York exculpated them from complicity in the killing at the Abbey Grange.
                    —*The Adventure of the Abbey Grange*

RAO, LAL: The Sholtos' Indian butler; Jonathan Small's confederate within the walls of Pondicherry Lodge.
                    —*The Sign of the Four*

RAS, DAULAT: The Indian student, one of the three suspected in the theft of Mr. Soame's precious examination paper.
                    —*The Adventure of the Three Students*

READE, WINWOOD: Author of *The Martyrdom of Man*, recommended by Holmes as one of the most remarkable books ever penned. —*The Sign of the Four*

REILLY, ——: The mouthpiece of Vermissa Lodge, who kept the boys' noses clean. —*The Valley of Fear*

REYNOLDS, SIR JOSHUA: 1723–1792. The famous English artist whose portrait of a gentleman with a wig hung on the walls of Baskerville Hall.—*The Hound of the Baskervilles*

RICHARDS, DR.: His call to Tredannick Wartha disclosed a dead woman and two crazy men. —*The Adventure of the Devil's Foot*

RICHTER, JOHANN PAUL FRIEDRICH: 1763–1825. *Dit* Jean Paul, whose aphorism anent man's greatness Holmes quoted. —*The Sign of the Four*

RICOLETTI, ——: Possessor of a club foot and an abominable wife, about whose adventures we'd fain know more but never shall. —*The Musgrave Ritual*

ROBERTS, LORD: 1832–1914. Held by Holmes to be one whom a new subaltern would be delighted in meeting. —*The Adventure of the Blanched Soldier*

ROBINSON, JOHN: The name first given by James Ryder when Holmes accosted him. —*The Adventure of the Blue Carbuncle*

RONDER,——: Bestial, boar-faced proprietor of a wild beast show whom his wife and Leonardo the strong-man conspired to kill. —*The Adventure of the Veiled Lodger*

RONDER, MRS. EUGENIA: The daughter of the sawdust who was horribly mutilated by Sahara King but who, at Holmes's urging, kept the courage to live on. —*The Adventure of the Veiled Lodger*

Rosa, Salvator: 1615–1673. Italian painter, one of whose works (probably) graced Thaddeus Sholto's collection.
—*The Sign of the Four*

Ross, Colonel: Owner of Silver Blaze, who stood by and saw him win unknowing.   —*Silver Blaze*

Ross, Duncan: Alias William Morris, alias "Archie"; the red-headed stooge who set Jabez White to copying out of the Encyclopedia Britannica.   —*The Red-Headed League*

Ross and Mangles: The dog dealers in Fulham Road, where Stapleton bought the great hound he smeared with phosphorus.   —*The Hound of the Baskervilles*

Roundhay, Reverend Mr.: Vicar of the parish at Tredannick Wollas, who harbored a murderer beneath his roof.
—*The Adventure of the Devil's Foot*

Roy: Professor Presbury's wolfhound, which attacked him again and again because he smelt like an ape.
—*The Adventure of the Creeping Man*

Roylott, Dr. Grimesby: Who beat his butler to death in India, consorted with gipsies in England, and died at last in the toils of the speckled band.
—*The Adventure of the Speckled Band*

Roylott, Mrs.: Deceased mother of Helen and Julia Stoner; who had taken as her second husband, in India, the infamous Dr. Roylott.   —*The Adventure of the Speckled Band*

Rucastle, Alice: Supposedly resident in Philadelphia, but actually confined to quarters in The Copper Beeches.
—*The Adventure of The Copper Beeches*

Rucastle, Master Edward: Aged six, but precociously wise in the ways of torture and mayhem.
—*The Adventure of The Copper Beeches*

RUCASTLE, JEPHRO: Proprietor of The Copper Beeches, who insisted that Violet Hunter cut off her hair, and sit where and when he pleased.
—*The Adventure of The Copper Beeches*

RUCASTLE, MRS. JEPHRO: A nonentity, according to Violet Hunter, but very partial to her own child.
—*The Adventure of The Copper Beeches*

RUFTON, EARL OF: Of whose family the gullible Lady Frances Carfax was the sole survivor.
—*The Disappearance of Lady Frances Carfax*

RULLI, SIGNOR: The name under which death came, in Madrid, to Lopez, alias Lucas, secretary to the Tiger of San Pedro.
—*The Adventure of Wisteria Lodge*

RUSSELL, CLARK: Author of the "fine sea stories" so described by Watson.
—*The Five Orange Pips*

RYDER, JAMES: Alias John Robinson. Upper attendant at the Hotel Cosmopolitan, whose larceny Holmes forgave.
—*The Adventure of the Blue Carbuncle*

S

SAHARA KING: The great North African lion which mangled Mrs. Eugenia Ronder to a state of enforced seclusion for life.
—*The Adventure of the Veiled Lodger*

ST. CLAIR, NEVILLE: The Dr. Jekyll of Hugh Boone's Hyde: he found begging profitable, but so lacking in respectability that he was driven to a double existence.
—*The Man With the Twisted Lip*

ST. CLAIR, MRS. NEVILLE: She it was who wore some sort of light *mousseline de soie*, with a touch of fluffy pink chiffon at her neck and wrists.
—*The Man With the Twisted Lip*

ST. SIMON, LADY CLARA: Present at the bigamous wedding of her priggish brother.

—The Adventure of the Noble Bachelor

ST. SIMON, LORD EUSTACE: Present at the St. Simon-Doran nuptials, which failed, fortunately, to take.

—The Noble Bachelor

ST. SIMON, LORD ROBERT WALSINGHAM DE VERE: Second son of the Duke of Balmoral, whose sorrow at the deprival of his wife was less than his shame at having wed a married woman.   *—The Adventure of the Noble Bachelor*

SALTIRE, LORD: Arthur, legitimate son of the Duke of Holdernesse, aged ten, whose bastardly half-brother schemed to put him out of the way in his own favor.

—The Adventure of the Priory School

SAMSON, ——: Of New Orleans, Louisiana, U. S. A., who escaped conviction for murder because the Sherlock Holmes test had not yet been discovered.   *—A Study in Scarlet*

SANDEFORD, ——: Who sold the sixth and pregnant bust of Napoleon I to Holmes for the sum of ten pounds, without recourse.   *—The Adventure of the Six Napoleons*

SANDERS, IKEY: Who refused to cut the Mazarin stone for Count Sylvius, and who peached.

—The Adventure of the Mazarin Stone

SANGER, ——: A showman in competition on the tank circuit with Ronder and Wombwell.

—The Adventure of the Veiled Lodger

SAUNDERS, SIR JAMES: The eminent specialist who brought great good news to the Emsworths in the matter of young Godfrey.   *—The Adventure of the Blanched Soldier*

SAUNDERS, MRS.: Caretaker for Nathan Garrideb, who admitted Holmes in his absence, to Killer Evans's sorrow.
                    —*The Adventure of the Three Garridebs*

SAUNDERS, ——: Housemaid at Riding Thorpe Manor, who helped sound the alarm when Hilton Cubitt was shot.
                    —*The Adventure of the Dancing Men*

SAVAGE, VICTOR: Nephew of Culverton Smith, and victim of a horrible germ-murder.
                    —*The Adventure of the Dying Detective*

SAWYER, MRS.: Of 13, Duncan Street, Houndsditch—a weary way from Baker Street. An impostor, she was *soi-disant* the mother of Sally Dennis, whose wedding ring she claimed.
                    —*A Study in Scarlet*

SAXE-MENINGEN, CLOTILDE LOTHMAN VON: Second daughter of the King of Scandinavia, and fiancée of the King of Bohemia.   —*A Scandal in Bohemia*

SCANLAN, MICHAEL: Of Lodge 341, Vermissa Valley, Ancient Order of Freemen, who was one of the least heinous of a bad lot.   —*The Valley of Fear*

SCOTT, JAMES H.: Bodymaster of Lodge 29, Chicago, of the Ancient Order of Freemen.   —*The Valley of Fear*

SELDEN, ——: The Notting Hill Murderer, a fugitive from Princetown, killed on the moor. To his sister Mrs. Barrymore he was still the curly-headed boy she had nursed.
                    —*The Hound of the Baskervilles*

SHAFTER, ETTIE: A lovely violet growing upon the black slag-heaps of the mines, who married the gallant Pinkerton Birdy Edwards, alias McMurdo.   —*The Valley of Fear*

SHAFTER, JACOB: The kindly Swedish boarding-house keeper with whom John McMurdo first lodged in Vermissa Valley.
                    —*The Valley of Fear*

SHERMAN, "OLD": The owner of Toby; a bird-stuffer who lived in Pinchin Lane by the water's edge in Lambeth.
—The Sign of the Four

SHLESSINGER, REVEREND DR.: Alias of Holy Peters; who abducted Lady Frances Carfax and almost buried her alive.
—The Disappearance of Lady Frances Carfax

SHLESSINGER, MRS.: Alias of Annie Fraser, who posed as Holy Peter's wife and toiled with him in the workshop of crime.
—The Disappearance of Lady Frances Carfax

SHOLTO, BARTHOLOMEW: Of Pondicherry Lodge, where he was foully and grinningly murdered.—*The Sign of the Four*

SHOLTO, MAJOR JOHN: Late of the 34th Bombay Infantry, who died on April 28, 1882.   *—The Sign of the Four*

SHOLTO, THADDEUS: Twin brother of the departed Bartholomew, who twitched and smoked the *hookah*.
—The Sign of the Four

SHOSCOMBE PRINCE: Sir Robert Norberton's colt, which won the Derby and saved Shoscombe Old Place.
—The Adventure of Shoscombe Old Place

SIGERSON, ——: The Norwegian alias assumed by Holmes during his remarkable explorations in Tibet.
—The Adventure of the Empty House

SILVER BLAZE: He resented the indignity to his equine person, and retaliated by killing his trainer.   *—Silver Blaze*

SIMPSON, BALDY: Who was slain in the skirmishing after the battle of Buffelsspruit.
—The Adventure of the Blanched Soldier

SIMPSON, FITZROY: Arrested for John Straker's murder in the course of doing a bit of innocent touting.   *—Silver Blaze*

SIMPSON, ——: Restaurateur in the Strand, in whose establishment Holmes longed to dine after he had fasted.
—The Adventure of the Dying Detective
—The Adventure of the Illustrious Client

SIMPSON, ——: Of the Baker Street Irregulars, who stuck to Henry Wood like a leech.   *—The Crooked Man*

SINCLAIR, ADMIRAL: In whose house at Barclay Square Sir James Walter was visiting on the evening the plans were stolen.   *—The Adventure of the Bruce-Partington Plans*

SINGH, MAHOMET: One of the Four.—*The Sign of the Four*

SINGLEFORD, LORD: Owner of Rasper, which raced against Silver Blaze.   *—Silver Blaze*

SLANEY, ABE: The most dangerous crook in Chicago, who carried his gun-play to the peaceful fastnesses of East Anglia.   *—The Adventure of the Dancing Men*

SLATER, ——: A stonemason, who first noticed that there were goings-on in Black Peter's cabin.
—The Adventure of Black Peter

SLOANE, SIR HANS: 1650–1753. The collector and physician. Nathan Garrideb expressed the pious hope that he might be the Hans Sloane of his age.
—The Adventure of the Three Garridebs

SMALL, JONATHAN: One of the Four; the peg-legged, unwilling instigator of Bartholomew Sholto's murder.
—The Sign of the Four

SMITH, CULVERTON: Black-hearted murderer of Victor Savage. This similar attempt against Holmes led to his being caught with the goods.
—The Adventure of the Dying Detective

SMITH, JACK: Son of Mordecai; a likely urchin who preferred two shillin' to one.   *—The Sign of the Four*

SMITH, JAMES: Deceased father of Violet Smith, and erstwhile orchestra conductor at the old Imperial Theatre.
—The Adventure of the Solitary Cyclist

SMITH, JIM: Son of Mordecai; who was in with him at the death of the Andaman Islander aboard the "Aurora."
—The Sign of the Four

SMITH, JOSEPH, JR.: 1805–1844. Founder of the Church of Jesus Christ of Latter-Day Saints, whose followers sought a haven in the desert, and found Lucy Ferrier.
—A Study in Scarlet

SMITH, MORDECAI: A boatman; owner of the "Aurora," which lost the mad race down the Thames.
—The Sign of the Four

SMITH, MRS. MORDECAI: Wife of Mordecai; whose naïveté and susceptibility put Holmes at last on Jonathan Small's trail.   *—The Sign of the Four*

SMITH, RALPH: Uncle of Violet Smith; whose impending demise, intestate, was the signal for a plot against his heiress.
—The Adventure of the Solitary Cyclist

SMITH, VIOLET: A beautiful woman, tall, graceful and queenly. Even her would-be abductors loved her, and one subjected her to a mock marriage under duress.
—The Adventure of the Solitary Cyclist

SMITH, WILLOUGHBY: The unfortunate secretary at Yoxley Old Place who was stabbed in the neck repelling his employer's wife.   *—The Adventure of the Golden Pince-Nez*

SMITH-MORTIMER, ——: Referred to in comment on the succession case of that name.
—The Adventure of the Golden Pince-Nez

SOAMES, SIR CATHCART: Who recognized the eminence of the Priory School by confiding his son to its ministrations.
—*The Adventure of the Priory School*

SOAMES, HILTON: Tutor and lecturer at the College of St. Luke's, who feared scandal and disgrace if the theft of the examination papers were not solved.
—*The Adventure of the Three Students*

SOMERTON, DR.: The surgeon of Hope Town, in the Andamans, whence Jonathan Small escaped.
—*The Sign of the Four*

SPAULDING, VINCENT: Alias John Clay. As pawnbroker's assistant he nearly despoiled the Coburg Branch of the City and Suburban Bank.   —*The Red-Headed League*

SPENDER, ROSE: Victim of senility, on top of whose dead body in a coffin the live body of Lady Frances Carfax was laid.
—*The Disappearance of Lady Frances Carfax*

STACKHURST, HAROLD: Who kept a coaching establishment not far from Holmes's apiaries on the Sussex Downs.
—*The Adventure of the Lion's Mane*

STAMFORD, ARCHIE: The forger referred to by Holmes as having been captured near Farnham, on the borders of Surrey.   —*The Adventure of the Solitary Cyclist*

STAMFORD, "YOUNG": Watson's friend, and the *trait d'union* in the ineluctable menage.   —*A Study in Scarlet*

STANGER, JAMES: The decrepit editor of the *Herald*, whose crusade for law and order in Vermissa Valley got him beaten up.   —*The Valley of Fear*

STANGERSON, BROTHER: Father of Joseph Stangerson; one of the four principal elders of the Mormon Church.
—*A Study in Scarlet*

STANGERSON, JOSEPH: A rejected suitor of Lucy Ferrier's; cohort of Enoch Drebber; stabbed to death by Jefferson Hope *chez* Madame Charpentier.   *—A Study in Scarlet*

STAPHONSE, ——: The name of the family blown to kingdomcome by the Ancient Order of Freemen.
—The Valley of Fear

STAPLES, ——: Solemn butler in the employ of the loathsome Culverton Smith.
—The Adventure of the Dying Detective

STAPLETON, BERYL: Née Garcia; a Costa Rican beauty who married the infamous Baskerville-Stapleton, posed as his sister, and won in the end the love of a nobler scion of the family.   *—The Hound of the Baskervilles*

STAPLETON, JOHN: Né Baskerville, alias Vandeleur. He chased butterflies by day and unleashed the hell-hound by night—and died at last in the toils of the great Grimpen Mire.   *—The Hound of the Baskervilles*

STARK, COLONEL LYSANDER: Alias "Fritz," who manufactured half-crowns in Eyford, and sacrificed hydraulic engineers to the preservation of his secret.
—The Adventure of the Engineer's Thumb

STARR, DR. LYSANDER: Of Topeka, Kansas. A figment of Holmes's fertile imagination.
—The Adventure of the Three Garridebs

STAUNTON, ARTHUR H.: Noted in Holmes's listings as a rising young forger.
—The Adventure of the Missing Three-Quarter

STAUNTON, GODFREY: His devotion to his dying wife cost Cambridge the game with Oxford.
—The Adventure of the Missing Three-Quarter

STAUNTON, MRS. GODFREY: Only a landlady's daughter, but as good as she was beautiful and as intelligent as she was good. —*The Adventure of the Missing Three-Quarter*

STAUNTON, HENRY: Holmes's records showed that he helped to hang him.
—*The Adventure of the Missing Three-Quarter*

STEILER, PETER, SR.: Keeper of the Englischer Hof at Meiringen, whence Holmes and Moriarty went to their immortal duel. —*The Final Problem*

STEINER, ——: German spy in the service of Von Bork, betrayed by Holmes into capture. —*His Last Bow*

STENDAL, ——: Murdered in the plural by the Scowrers.
—*The Valley of Fear*

STEPHENS, ——: Butler at Shoscombe Old Place, employed by Sir Robert Norberton.
—*The Adventure of Shoscombe Old Place*

STERNDALE, DR. LEON: Intrepid lion-hunter and explorer, who loved Brenda Tregennis and gave her brother a dose of his own medicine.—*The Adventure of the Devil's Foot*

STEVENS, BERT: A mild-mannered Sunday-school young man, but, by Holmes's definition, a terrible murderer.
—*The Adventure of the Norwood Builder*

STEVENSON, ——: The Cambridge three-quarter who couldn't drop from the twenty-five line.
—*The Adventure of the Missing Three-Quarter*

STEWART, JANE: Housemaid at the Barclays'. The only quarrelsome word she heard was "David."—*The Crooked Man*

STEWART, MRS.: Of Lauder. Holmes was sure that Colonel Moran had killed her years ago, but nothing could ever be proven. —*The Adventure of the Empty House*

STIMSON & CO.: Morticians of Kennington Road, who were set to perform a double burial in a single coffin.
—*The Disappearance of Lady Frances Carfax*

STOCKDALE, BARNEY: One of the John gang, and Steve Dixie's immediate superior, who worked with Isadora Klein.
—*The Adventure of The Three Gables*

STOCKDALE, SUSAN: The harridan wife of Barney Stockdale, employed in the household of the widow Maberley.
—*The Adventure of The Three Gables*

STONE, REVEREND JOSHUA: Of Nether Walsling, near Esher, who was quickly excluded from the orbit of Holmes's suspicions.   —*The Adventure of Wisteria Lodge*

STONER, HELEN: Stepdaughter of Dr. Roylott of Stoke Moran, who let Sherlock Holmes, instead of death, into her bed-chamber.   —*The Adventure of the Speckled Band*

STONER, JULIA: Twin sister of Helen Stoner; who died white-haired at the age of thirty, a victim of step-infanticide.
—*The Adventure of the Speckled Band*

STONER, MAJOR-GENERAL: Of the Bengal Artillery. Deceased father of Helen and Julia Stoner; whose widow married Dr. Roylott.   —*The Adventure of the Speckled Band*

STOPER, MISS ——: Manager of Westaway's agency, where Violet Hunter found employment.
—*The Adventure of the Copper Beeches*

STRAKER, JOHN: Alias William Darbyshire. Retired jockey, trainer of Silver Blaze, and scoundrel. Found with his head shattered in a depression on the moor.   —*Silver Blaze*

STRAKER, MRS. JOHN: Haggard, thin and eager. Her husband left her in the middle of the night, never to return.
—*Silver Blaze*

STRAUBENZEE, ——: Who had a workshop in the Minories where he made an airgun for the dangerous Count Sylvius.
—The Adventure of the Mazarin Stone

STRAUSS, HERMAN: Who wasn't yet due to be put on the spot by the Scowrers.
—The Valley of Fear

SUDBURY, ——: One of the students at the Stackhurst establishment who found the dead dog on the beach.
—The Adventure of the Lion's Mane

SUMNER, ——: The shipping agent of Ratcliff Highway who sent three harpooners to Holmes, one of them the right man.
—The Adventure of Black Peter

SUTHERLAND, MISS MARY: Who presented Holmes with a very simple problem: she was wooed by her stepfather in disguise, but Holmes would not snatch her delusion from her.
—The Adventure of the Copper Beeches
—The Red-Headed League
—A Case of Identity

SUTRO, ——: The Maberley lawyer, who gave good advice but little protection.—*The Adventure of The Three Gables*

SUTTON, ——: One of the five who robbed the Worthingdon Bank. See Blessington.
—The Resident Patient

SWAIN, JOHN: In the fragmentary document shown Holmes by John Openshaw, he, together with one McCauley and one Paramore, are mentioned as having had the pips set on them.
—The Five Orange Pips

SWINDON, ARCHIE: The coal owner who sold out his business under duress applied by the Ancient Order of Freemen.
—The Valley of Fear

SYLVIUS, COUNT NEGRETTO: A deep-dyed criminal who once mistook a dummy for Holmes and later mistook Holmes for the dummy.
—The Adventure of the Mazarin Stone

T

TANGEY, ——: Commissionaire at the Foreign Office, and erstwhile of the Coldstream Guards. His only crime was his somnolence.   —*The Naval Treaty*

TANGEY, MRS. ——: Wife of the commissionaire. She drank, but was otherwise innocent.   —*The Naval Treaty*

TANGEY, MISS ——: Eldest daughter of the Tangeys, who opened the door to her mother and did little else.
—*The Naval Treaty*

TARLTON, SUSAN: Maid at the Coram establishment, who blocked the escape of her employer's wife.
—*The Adventure of the Golden Pince-Nez*

TAVERNIER, ——: The French modeller who made a wax-work figure of Holmes which outdid the best of Madame Tussaud.   —*The Adventure of the Mazarin Stone*

TEDDY: Henry Wood's pet mongoose, or ichneumon.
—*The Crooked Man*

THURSTON, ——: The only man with whom Watson ever played billiards, but whose option on South African mining stock Holmes deduced he would not share.
—*The Adventure of the Dancing Men*

TOBIN, ——: Caretaker of the Worthingdon Bank, who was murdered back in 1875.   —*The Resident Patient*

TOBY: The mongrel whose nose was keen enough to follow a trail of creosote through the tortuous streets of London.
—*The Sign of the Four*

TOLLER, ——: Who smelt perpetually of drink, and sobered up too late to save Jephro Rucastle's throat from a mangling.
—*The Adventure of The Copper Beeches*

TOLLER, MRS. ——: If young Mr. Fowler had not crossed her palm with silver, Alice Rucastle could not have eloped through the roof.—*The Adventure of The Copper Beeches*

TONGA: The Andaman Island blow-gun expert; henchman of Jonathan Small and murderer of Bartholomew Sholto.
—*The Sign of the Four*

TOSCA, CARDINAL: Whose sudden death was investigated by Holmes at the express desire of His Holiness the Pope.
—*The Adventure of Black Peter*

TREGELLIS, JANET: Welsh and excitable, who trapped her treacherous confederate in a vault of death.
—*The Musgrave Ritual*

TREGENNIS, BRENDA: Beloved of Dr. Leon Sterndale, she died in agony and delirium while two of her brothers went mad at the hand of a third.—*The Adventure of the Devil's Foot*

TREGENNIS, GEORGE: The fumes of the noxious root his brother burned drove him stark, staring crazy.
—*The Adventure of the Devil's Foot*

TREGENNIS, MORTIMER: The retired tin-miner who murdered his sister and drove two brothers mad with *radix pedis diaboli*.   —*The Adventure of the Devil's Foot*

TREGENNIS, OWEN: Who raved and gibbered with his brother George when the devil's foot was burned.
—*The Adventure of the Devil's Foot*

TREPOFF, ——: Whose murder, in an unrecorded case, caused Holmes to be summoned to Odessa.
—*A Scandal in Bohemia*

TREVELYAN, DR. PERCY: A pale, taper-faced man, in whose keeping a turncoat criminal was privately judged and hanged.   —*The Resident Patient*

TREVOR, VICTOR: Holmes's college chum, who unwittingly gave him his first case.   —*The "Gloria Scott"*

TREVOR, ——: Né James Armitage. Justice of the Peace of Donnithorpe, struck dead with horror at sight of a slip of paper.   —*The "Gloria Scott"*

TURNER, ALICE: Daughter of John Turner—one of the most lovely young women Watson had ever been privileged to see.   —*The Boscombe Valley Mystery*

TURNER, JOHN: The diabetic Australian who struck down Charles McCarthy as he would a foul and venomous beast.   —*The Boscombe Valley Mystery*

TURNER, MRS.: The apocryphal landlady of 221-B Baker Street; alter ego of Mrs. Hudson in the month of March, 1888.   —*A Scandal in Bohemia*

TUSON, SERGEANT: Of the City police, who arrested Beddington after a struggle.   —*The Stockbroker's Clerk*

TUSSAUD, MME. MARIE: 1760–1850. Famous wax-works exhibitor whose creatures were held up as criteria.   —*The Adventure of the Mazarin Stone*

U

UNDERWOOD, JOHN, AND SONS: The hatters of Camberwell Road, patronized by Enoch Drebber in his last hours.   —*A Study in Scarlet*

UPWOOD, COLONEL: Referred to by Holmes as having conducted himself atrociously in the famous card scandal of the Nonpareil Club.   —*The Hound of the Baskervilles*

V

VAMBERRY, ——: The wine merchant, whose case was never detailed by Watson, despite the records of it which existed.   —*The Musgrave Ritual*

VANDELEUR, BERYL: Alias the Beryl Baskerville, alias Stapleton, which see.   —*The Hound of the Baskervilles*

VANDELEUR, JOHN: The schoolmaster alias of John Baskerville, alias Stapleton, which see.
                        —*The Hound of the Baskervilles*

VANDERBILT, ——: Perhaps of the American clan, who had adventures with a yeggman of a nature unrecorded.
                —*The Adventure of the Sussex Vampire*

VAN JANSEN, ——: Of Utrecht, Holland; who died in 1834, according to Holmes, in circumstances similar to those attending the death of Enoch Drebber.—*A Study in Scarlet*

VAN SEDDAR, ——: Dutch confederate of Count Sylvius, who had designs on playing with the Mazarin Stone back home.
                —*The Adventure of the Mazarin Stone*

VAN SHORST, ——: One of the legion of upright capitalists done in by the Scowrers.   —*The Valley of Fear*

VENNER & MATHESON: The well-known firm of Greenwich, where Victor Hatherley had been apprenticed.
                —*The Adventure of the Engineer's Thumb*

VENUCCI, LUCRETIA: Maid to the Princess of Colonna, who was under suspicion in the theft of the pearl of the Borgias.
                —*The Adventure of the Six Napoleons*

VENUCCI, PIETRO: Murdered for the part he played—whatever it was—in the disappearance of the pearl of the Borgias.
                —*The Adventure of the Six Napoleons*

VERNER, DR. ——: A distant relation of Holmes who bought out Watson's practice with Holmes's connivance, that Baker Street might once more have two lodgers.
                —*The Adventure of the Norwood Builder*

VERNET, EMILE JEAN HORACE: 1789–1863. Eminent French painter, great-uncle of Sherlock Holmes, from whom he and Mycroft inherited their artistic talents.
—*The Greek Interpreter*

VIBART, JULES: Lover of the maid Marie Devine in Lausanne.
—*The Disappearance of Lady Frances Carfax*

VIGOR, ——: Probably, but not certainly, a man: catalogued in Holmes's index as the Hammersmith wonder.
—*The Adventure of the Sussex Vampire*

VITTORIA: The circus belle, who found a place unspecified in Holmes's index.—*The Adventure of the Sussex Vampire*

VON BISCHOFF, ——: Of Frankfort, Germany; a murderer whose crime would not have gone unpunished had the Sherlock Holmes test for bloodstains been known.
—*A Study in Scarlet*

VON BORK, ——: The German master-spy in whose service Holmes, alias Altamont, labored mightily albeit to a different purpose.   —*His Last Bow*

VON HERDER, ——: The blind German mechanic who built the air-gun fired by Colonel Moran at Holmes's shadow.
—*The Adventure of the Empty House*

VON HERLING, BARON: Henchman of Von Bork, and chief secretary of the German Legation in London.
—*His Last Bow*

VON KRAMM, COUNT: Intended alias of the King of Bohemia, which Holmes quickly pierced. —*A Scandal in Bohemia*

W

WAINEWRIGHT, THOMAS GRIFFITHS: An English criminal, cited by Holmes as having been also no mean artist.
—*The Adventure of the Illustrious Client*

WALDBAUM, FRITZ VON: The well-known specialist of Dantzig, reported to have gone astray in the case of the Second Stain.   —*The Naval Treaty*

WALDRON, ——: The name in which Rodger Prescott held the premises in London later occupied by Nathan Garrideb.
—*The Adventure of the Three Garridebs*

WALTER, SIR JAMES: Famous government expert, guardian of the submarine plans, whose despair at their loss brought on his death.—*The Adventure of the Bruce-Partington Plans*

WALTER, COLONEL VALENTINE: Younger brother of Sir James, who betrayed family and country to line his traitorous purse.—*The Adventure of the Bruce-Partington Plans*

WALTERS, P. C.: Who was on guard at Wisteria Lodge when the gigantic mulatto's face appeared at the window.
—*The Adventure of Wisteria Lodge*

WARBURTON, COLONEL: The nature and consequences of his madness are unrecorded.
—*The Adventure of the Engineer's Thumb*

WARDLAW, COLONEL: Owner of Pugilist, which raced against Silver Blaze.   —*Silver Blaze*

WARNER, JOHN: Late gardener at High Gable, who gave Holmes information of great value.
—*The Adventure of Wisteria Lodge*

WARREN, MRS.: The landlady (not of 221 B Baker Street) whose suspicions of a cloistered lodger led to the death of Black Gorgiano.   —*The Adventure of the Red Circle*

WARREN, ——: Who was occasionally knocked about by his wife's lodgers, and who was once taken for a rough ride.
—*The Adventure of the Red Circle*

WARRENDER, MINNIE: Whose whole life history Holmes had recorded in his note-book as part of his attack on Count Sylvius. —*The Adventure of the Mazarin Stone*

WATSON, JAMES, M.D.: Dr. Watson's apocryphal alter-ego —the "James" whom Mrs. John Watson offered to send off to bed. —*The Man With the Twisted Lip*

WATSON, JOHN H., M.D.

WATSON, MRS. JOHN H.: Née Mary Morstan, which see.
—*The Boscombe Valley Mystery*
—*The Five Orange Pips*
—*The Stockbroker's Clerk*
—*The Final Problem*
—*The Adventure of the Empty House*

WATSON, MRS. JOHN H.: The mysterious second wife of the good doctor. Mr. S. C. Roberts advances the speculation that she was Violet de Merville.

WATSON, H., SR.: Father of the two Watson boys, whose fifty-guinea watch descended through the elder to the more deserving John. —*The Sign of the Four*

WATSON, H., JR.: Prodigal brother of John H. Watson, M.D., whose character Holmes described accurately from observation of the fifty-guinea watch. —*The Sign of the Four*

WEST, ARTHUR CADOGAN: (Possibly Cadogan West, Arthur). The faithful clerk found dead on the Underground, a victim of his patriotic zeal. —*The Bruce-Partington Plans*

WEST, MRS.: Mother of Arthur Cadogan West, who was too dazed to be of any use. —*The Bruce-Partington Plans*

WESTAWAY, ——: For whom the well-known agency for governesses in the West End was named.
—*The Copper Beeches*

WESTBURY, VIOLET: Fiancée of Arthur Cadogan West, who left her in the fog on a quest which spelled his doom.
—*The Adventure of the Bruce-Partington Plans*

WESTHOUSE & MARBANK: The great claret importers of Fenchurch Street; employers of Mr. Windibank.
—*A Case of Identity*

WESTPHAIL, MISS HONORIA: At whose home Julia Stoner met a half-pay major of Marines and thereby paved the way for her death.   —*The Adventure of the Speckled Band*

WHITAKER, JOSEPH: 1820–1895. Publisher of the Almanack which enabled Holmes to decipher the message sent him by the mysterious Porlock.   —*The Valley of Fear*

WHITE, ABEL: An indigo planter, for whom Jonathan Small once rode range in India.   —*The Sign of the Four*

WHITE, MASON, ——: (Probably not Mason, White). The local police-officer at Birlstone, and a very live man indeed.
—*The Valley of Fear*

WHITNEY, ELIAS, D.D.: Principal of the Theological College of St. George's; brother of the drug-besotted Isa.
—*The Man With the Twisted Lip*

WHITNEY, ISA: Taking both de Quincey and laudanum too seriously, his misfortune brought Watson to a den where his path crossed fortuitously with that of Holmes.
—*The Man With the Twisted Lip*

WHITNEY, KATE: At whose behest Watson sallied forth to find Isa, and met Holmes.—*The Man With the Twisted Lip*

WHITTINGTON, LADY ALICIA: Present at the spurious wedding in St. George's, Hanover Square.
—*The Adventure of the Noble Bachelor*

WHYTE, WILLIAM: Who had written the inscription "Gulielmi Whyte" in an old book in Holmes's possession.
—*A Study in Scarlet*

WIGGINS, ——: Chief of the Baker Street Irregulars, of "insignificant and unsavoury person" but a mighty staff to lean upon.
—*A Study in Scarlet*
—*The Sign of the Four*

WILCOX, CHESTER: Chief foreman of the Iron Dyke Company. Jim Carnaway was shot the first time the Lodge tried to put the finger on him.   —*The Valley of Fear*

WILD, JONATHAN: A master criminal who flourished 1750 or thereabouts—the very prototype of Moriarty.
—*The Valley of Fear*

WILDER, JAMES: Illegitimate offspring of the Duke of Holdernesse, nourished as his secretary, who resembled his sainted mother in his face and his pretty ways, but who was a scoundrel nevertheless.
—*The Adventure of the Priory School*

WILHELM II: 1859– . Emperor of Germany, in whose service Von Bork and Von Herling labored in vain, thanks to Sherlock I.   —*His Last Bow*

WILLABY, ARTHUR: One of two brothers, the other nameless, selected for the beating up of the old and helpless James Stanger.   —*The Valley of Fear*

WILLIAMS, CHARLIE: One of the many victims of the terror at Vermissa.   —*The Valley of Fear*

WILLIAMS, JAMES BAKER: Of Forton Old Hall, near Esher, who had nothing to do with the killing of Aloysius Garcia.
—*The Adventure of Wisteria Lodge*

WILLIAMS, ——: Thaddeus Sholto's "man," who met Holmes, Watson and Miss Morstan at the third pillar outside the Lyceum.   —*The Sign of the Four*

WILLIAMSON, ——: The unfrocked parson of Charlington Hall, who did his blackguard best to marry Violet Smith to Jack Woodley.   —*The Adventure of the Solitary Cyclist*

WILLOWS, DR.: John Turner's physician. Foreseeing the end, he ordered the wealthy invalid to bed.
—*The Boscombe Valley Mystery*

WILSON, BARTHOLOMEW: Ruler of the District diocese of the Ancient Order of Freemen in which Chicago Lodge 29 lay.
—*The Valley of Fear*

WILSON, JABEZ: The pawnbroker whose chagrin at the dissolution of the League of the Red-Headed Men brought disaster to the fourth—or third—smartest man in London.
—*The Red-Headed League*

WILSON, SERGEANT: Of the Sussex Constabulary, who assisted the able White Mason in the Birlstone tragedy.
—*The Valley of Fear*

WILSON, STEVE: Reputed alias of Birdy Edwards, as cited by John McMurdo.   —*The Valley of Fear*

WILSON, ——: One of the members of Vermissa Lodge who volunteered to "handle the job" on Andrew Rae.
—*The Valley of Fear*

WILSON, ——: The notorious canary-trainer, whose arrest removed a plague spot from the East End of London.
—*The Adventure of Black Peter*

WILSON, ——: Constable at Yoxley Old Place, who assisted in the investigation of young Willoughby Smith's death.
—*The Adventure of the Golden Pince-Nez*

WILSON, ——: Manager of a district messenger office, whose good name—and perhaps his life—Holmes had once saved.
—*The Hound of the Baskervilles*

WILSON, ——: The spurious chaplain of the prison ship, whose tracts were pistols, powder and slugs.
—*The "Gloria Scott"*

WINDIBANK, JAMES: Mary Sutherland's stepfather, a traveler in wines, who connived at the disappearance of the mythical Hosmer Angel and fled from Holmes's righteous wrath and hunting crop.   —*A Case of Identity*

WINDIGATE, ——: Host of the Alpha Inn, near the Museum, whose institution of a goose club brought Holmes a new case.   —*The Adventure of the Blue Carbuncle*

WINDLE, J. W.: Division master, Merton County Lodge 249, Ancient Order of Freemen.   —*The Valley of Fear*

WINTER, JAMES: An alias of Killer Evans, alias John Garrideb.
—*The Adventure of the Three Garridebs*

WINTER, KITTY: Flame-like young woman of the underworld and ally of Shinwell Johnson, who avenged herself on Baron Gruner with a bottle of vitriol.
—*The Adventure of the Illustrious Client*

WOMBWELL, ——: English showman, whose exhibitions were rivaled by those of the porcine Ronder.
—*The Adventure of the Veiled Lodger*

WOOD, CORPORAL HENRY: Favorite of Nancy Devoy in India. His betrayal by Sergeant Barclay was later avenged when the sight of his face induced a stroke.—*The Crooked Man*

WOOD, J. G.: The famous observer whose book, *Out of Doors*, was quoted by Holmes in proving the real murderer of Fitzroy McPherson.—*The Adventure of the Lion's Mane*

Wood, Dr. ——: General practitioner of Birlstone; a brisk and capable fellow. —*The Valley of Fear*

Woodhouse, ——: Cited by Holmes as one of the fifty men who might justifiably seek his death.
—*The Adventure of the Bruce-Partington Plans*

Woodley, Edith: Of Carstairs. Her engagement to the Honourable Ronald Adair had been broken off by mutual consent and without regrets.
—*The Adventure of the Empty House*

Woodley, John: Roaring Jack Woodley—an odious person who brought the law of the African bush to the English countryside in the course of his designs on Violet Smith.
—*The Adventure of the Solitary Cyclist*

Wright, Theresa: Maid to Lady Brackenstall, who conspired with her mistress to shield the killer of Sir Eustace.
—*The Adventure of the Abbey Grange*

Y

Youghal, ——: Of the Criminal Investigation Department of Scotland Yard. —*The Adventure of the Mazarin Stone*

Young, Brigham: 1801–1877. Heir to the mantle of Joseph Smith, who led the Ferriers to false safety in the Chosen Valley. —*A Study in Scarlet*

Z

Zamba, Signor: Partner of Tito Castalotte in the fruit business in New York, whence Gennaro Lucca was torn by the machinations of the Red Circle.
—*The Adventure of the Red Circle*

Zeppelin, Count Ferdinand von: 1838–1917. Baron von Herling expressed the pious hope that, thanks to him, the heavens might not be peaceful. —*His Last Bow*

3

THE CHASE IS DONE

These, then, are the faces I saw as I peered through the windows in Baker Street and strained to catch the words that were spoken within. I have tried to mark them down, each and every one; to name them over with the glamorous names they bore, and to stir the reader's memory with some few words about the things they did and were.

Many of those who kept their appointments with the master were with him in the room in solid fact; others, like shadows, came and went in the ordered pages of the *index sontium*, or entered the scene from fields afar in the inner thoughts of Holmes and Watson as their fates were pondered. The Elder Drebber, for all his reality, was never closer to the actual fogs of London than the point from which he set forth on his holy trek to the Chosen Valley; but I saw Thorneycroft Huxtable with my own eyes as he staggered against the table, and I heard distinctly the crash he made as he fell prostrate and insensible upon the bearskin hearth-rug. The original Hugo Baskerville was even remoter from the scene in time than he was in distance, but he is still as much a living character in the chronicles as the dainty Mary Morstan, who gave me such a charming glimpse of herself, in modern 1888, while she sat and trembled in the chair which Holmes had placed for her. All of them, wherever they were and whatever they did, kept faith in their appointments with Sherlock Holmes— and with us.

There are, of course, many others in the familiar tales beyond the several hundred whose names and quirks and headline biographies I have tried so briefly to record. Some of the great and near-great whose mention has only an incidental relation to the plot have been deliberately omitted from the list—such diverse souls as Petrarch and George Meredith, Hafiz and Horace, Gustave Flaubert, Thoreau, Stradivarius, Paganini and Chopin—but there are, on the other hand, whole battalions of integral characters who come and go throughout the tales under a cloak of anonymity the world can never hope to lift. For this lapse and its resulting lack the good Watson is not in any wise to be blamed: however significant their parts, it is not compulsory for an author to pin *cartes d'identité* on all the supernumerary characters—maids and coachmen; commissionaires, policemen, pages and station-masters; butlers and doctors and gipsies—who scamper through his pages.

We should have liked, perhaps, to have the longer and the richer rolls which franker dealing with these minor nameless would have brought, but it is not for them, after all, that the hackles of our speculation need be raised. It is, rather, for those eminent personages throughout the chronicles whose identity is concealed from us for reasons of diplomacy and state, or because of mere perversity; and for those other less sacred lights whose secrets of the baptismal font could, in all conscience and without fear of national scandal, have been fully and openly disclosed.

The most elusively élite of those who go unidentified in the tales is, beyond doubt, the owner of "one of the highest, noblest, most exalted names in England," who basely pawned the Beryl Coronet. Could this, by any chance, have been the roistering prince who was later, in the sober days of his mother's death, to ascend the very throne of England? Whoever he was, there is no question that Holmes, in common with Alexander Holder, was deeply impressed by the gravity of the situation presented, and the extraordinary energies he threw into the task may well have been inspired by the imminence of royalty itself. We know, in any event, that the House of Wettin held the master in acknowledged esteem, for the "certain gracious lady" who presented him with an emerald tie-pin for the part he played in recovering the Bruce-Partington submarine plans could surely have been none other than the sainted Victoria in regal person.

Scarcely lower in Burke's than these, we may assume, was the Illustrious Client who intervened by proxy to save Violet de Merville from a horrid mating, and the stately lady with delicately curved nose, marked eyebrows, straight mouth and strong little chin, who went so far in her noble enthusiasms as to murder the obnoxious Charles Augustus Milverton. There is, too, the tantalizing reference in *The Hound of the Baskervilles* to "one of the most revered names in England" which was being besmirched by a blackmailer, with the further implication that only Holmes could stop the disastrous scandal impending. Or, to carry the speculations afield, we may pause for a moment to cogitate upon the identity of the nameless foreign potentate who wrote a scorching epistle to the British Foreign Office, the theft of which might well have led to Armageddon, but did instead lead happily to the *Adventure of the Second Stain*.

Of the minor but equally absorbing mysteries there are many. Most amazing of all, perhaps, is the case of the watchman who was murdered by Beddington at Mawson and Williams's (*The Stockbroker's Clerk*), and whose name is incredibly omitted not only from the Watson record but also from the account of the crime as published in the *Evening Standard* and quoted verbatim. Similarly mysterious is the anonymity and apparent inconsequence of the smith, in the *Adventure of the Priory School*, who went complacent and unchallenged about his task while Holmes inspected the smithy where none was more likely than he to have done the actual work on the horses shod with the monstrous hoofs.

For the sake of the picturesque, there is also the captain of the "Gloria Scott," who deserves identification if only because of the fact that he died with his brains smeared over a chart of the Atlantic Ocean; and the huge and rampant mulatto, in the *Adventure of Wisteria Lodge,* who practiced voodoo and frightened constables by peering in at windows.

We cannot complain, I suppose, that no names are given to such purely atmospheric characters as the woman at Margate who put no powder on her nose (*The Adventure of the Second Stain*), or the impecunious young squire to whom Lady Eva Blackwell wrote indiscreet notes (*The Adventure of Charles Augustus Milverton*), or the local blacksmith at Stoke Moran who was hurled over a parapet by the playful Dr. Roylott (*The Adventure of the Speckled Band*). But sometimes the reference is so thickly veiled as to seem designed deliberately to confuse, as in the case of "my old ally the guard" in the *Adventure of the Engineer's Thumb,* and the driver of "the Grosvenor Square furniture van" in the *Adventure of the Noble Bachelor.*

Some of the characters we meet in passing are introduced for no other purpose, of course, than to give Holmes a chance to display his pyrotechnics of deduction; such, for example, as the retired sergeant of marines in *A Study in Scarlet,* and the billiard marker and recently discharged soldier upon whose identification Sherlock and Mycroft played a duet of wits in *The Greek Interpreter.* But on the score of the intimacy or the importance of the parts they played, we could wish to know whether the page boy at Baker Street, who now and again gives a startling air of swank to Mrs. Hudson's lodgings, is the same Billy called by that name in some of the later tales; and we could welcome hearing more of the "three others" besides Professor Moriarty who, we are told in *His Last Bow,* had sworn Holmes's death.

Most intimate of all, in the latter days at least, is the old housekeeper who ministered to the wants of the great master in his declining years upon the Sussex Downs, and who shared the modest estate alone with him and his beloved bees. She it was who was with him when the flame was nearly spent; her knowledge of him must have been a touching one indeed. It is to our sorrow that she lacked the pen of a Watson, and that her story never will be told.

But here, named or nameless, are all the characters in the tales we ever knew. They, too, are growing older—the gaffers are gone with the urgent years; the heroes and the villains in their prime are turning bent and gray; the children are men and women grown. They do not have the immortality in our minds of the master himself or of his rugged Boswell, but they have flitted at least in the shades of a temporary and intermediate purgatory, and I am glad, for my own part, to have been able to call them back for this brief moment, and to pass them in review and parade.

They played their appointed parts in the drama which held the stage in Baker Street, and of them, as of the drama itself, we can say with Sherlock Holmes:

"What is the meaning of it, Watson? What object is served by this circle of misery and violence and fear? It must tend to some end, or else our universe is ruled by chance, which is unthinkable. But what end? There is the great standing perennial problem to which human reason is as far from an answer as ever."

ENVOY

To make the categorical statement that Sherlock Holmes is dead is to assume an onus beyond the strength of any man to bear alone. Proof of so final and absolute a catastrophe is insistently demanded. The burden is one the world at large must share, and evidence, direct or circumstantial, must be produced sufficient before any jury to dispel what lingering doubts and hopes may still persist.

My own argument in support of the verdict that Holmes is dead rests upon the exact record of his age provided in *His Last Bow*, and upon the reference throughout the later tales to his unordered, restless life, his recurrent breakdowns, and his crippling rheumatism—to say nothing of the earlier addiction to drugs which must have sapped so heavily the splendid physical resources he once possessed.

We know beyond a doubt that Holmes was born in the year 1854. The episode of the thwarting of Von Bork's espionage is clearly dated 1914, and we are told, as the chronicle unfolds, that the tall, gaunt Irish-American called Altamont, who came to the spy's study in August of that year, was a man full sixty. Today, as the year 1938 grows old, the Holmes who lurked behind this caricature of Uncle Sam would be more than eighty-four.

He may still live—the mortal may not yet have put on full immortality—but I feel myself that the change from the glorious excitements of Baker Street to the rusting quiet of the Sussex Downs was more than an eager soul like his could bear so long.

A SHERLOCK HOLMES CROSS-WORD

By F. V. MORLEY

LOVERS OF SHERLOCK HOLMES will understand the pleasure
with which we received the following letter. It is good to
know that our old friend Tobias Gregson, late of Scotland
Yard, is still with us. His manner of correspondence has
changed not at all since he wrote the famous letter (Chapter
III of *A Study in Scarlet*) which was the beginning of so many
adventures. He writes from his retirement in Dorset; undoubtedly his love for the full name led him to that county
where so many villages have double nomination.

Here is the letter:—

> *The Laurels, Toller Porcorum, Dorset*
> 10th April 1934

I have noticed the fun which you gentlemen are having with
what you call the Baker Street Irregulars; indeed, the whole affair recalls old times to me. It is not for me to comment on where
your correspondents are amiss; but I should like to ask whether
Mr. Elmer Davis, who is interested in the Moriarty family, is
one of your wealthy book collectors? If so, I know of something that would be to his advantage. I need not say more at
this moment; I shall leave everything *in statu quo* until I hear
from you. I would esteem it a great kindness if you would fa-
vour me with the information.

In the mean time, the name of your club reminded me of an
item I picked up a year or more ago at the Diogenes Club. I
had to go there to see a late chief of mine who, from having seen
too much of the world, had become unsociable enough to be a
member. He knew that I had been a friend of Mr. Mycroft
Holmes, and handed me a scrap of club notepaper which had
been found in the crack between the arm and the seat of Mr.
Mycroft's favourite armchair. It was an unfinished sketch for a

cross-word puzzle; with the heading at the top "No. 221 B," and "Baker Street Irregulars," to explain the design. Certain squares were shaded more heavily than others, to bring the initials S. H. out of the pattern. There is evidence to show that Mr. Mycroft was proud of it, for the sketch, though roughly drawn and as yet unnumbered, was signed "Mycroft Holmes." I conjecture that it was intended as a friendly greeting from Mr. Mycroft to his favourite brother; but that he lacked the energy to post it, and it was lost till my late chief happened to find it and give it to me.

In my retirement, I regularly read the agony columns and do the daily cross-words in the *Times and Telegraph;* childish pastimes, I admit, but if one is energetic and has some knowledge of the classics, one must do something. So I derived pleasure from fitting my own clues to Mr. Mycroft Holmes's cross-word, and send it to you as an intelligence-test (such as we used to have at the Yard) for your "Irregulars." All the clues are as simple as A. B. C. to any student of Mr. Sherlock Holmes's cases. It is not intended to be a real puzzler; I should expect a man of say Lestrade's ability to do it all in half an hour.

Yours faithfully,

TOBIAS GREGSON.

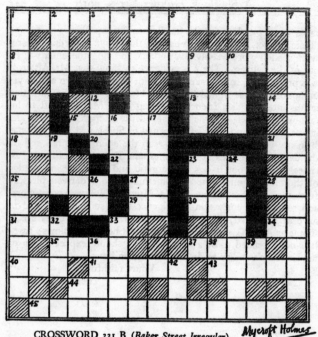

CROSSWORD 221 B *(Baker Street Irregular)*   *Mycroft Holmes*

ACROSS

1. A treatise on this, written at the age of twenty-one, had a European vogue and earned its author a professorship. (2 words, 8, 7)

8. It was of course to see these that Holmes enquired the way from Saxe-Coburg Square to the Strand (2 words, 10, 5)

11. How the pips were set (2)

13. Not an Eley's No. 2 (which is an excellent argument with a gentleman who can twist steel pokers into knots) but the weapon in the tragedy of Birlstone (3)

14. What was done on the opposite wall in bullet-pocks by the patriotic Holmes (2)

15. What Watson recognized when he put his hand on Bartholomew Sholto's leg (5)

18. Where Watson met young Stamford, who introduced him to Sherlock Holmes (3)

20. A kind of pet, over which Dr. Grimesby Roylott hurled the local blacksmith (4)

21. Holmes should have said this before being so sure of catching the murderers of John Openshaw (2)

246

22. The kind of Pedro whence came the tiger (3)
23. Though he knew the methods, Watson sometimes found it difficult to do this (3)
25. Patron saint of old Mr. Farquhar's affliction and perhaps of Abe Slaney's men (5)
27. Perhaps a measure of Holmes's chemicals (2)
28. In short, Watson (2)
29. X X (2)
30. Curious that he did nothing in the nighttime (1)
31. This would obviously not describe the empty house opposite 221b Baker Street (3)
34. It seems likely that Watson's elder brother suffered from this disease (2)
35. Though you might have taken this at Lodge 29, Chicago, nevertheless, you had to pass a test as well at Lodge 341, Vermissa (4)
37. The *Star* of Savannah (4)
40. Mrs. Barclay's reproach (in The Crooked Man, of course) suggests the parable of this (3)
41. Scrawled in blood-red letters across the bare plaster at No. 3, Lauriston Gardens (5)
43. Holmes found this, because he was looking for it in the mud (5)
44. Suggests Jonathan Small's leg (3)
45. The brother who left Watson no choice but to relate The Final Problem (2 words, 5, 8)

DOWN

1. A country district in the west of England where "Cooee" was a common signal (2 words, 8, 6)
2. Charles Augustus Milverton dealt with no niggard hand; therefore this would not describe him (4)
3. The kind of practice indulged by Mr. Williamson, the solitary cyclist's unfrocked clergyman—"there was a man of that name in orders, whose career has been a singularly dark one." (3)

4. There is comparatively as much sense in Hafiz. Indeed, it's a case of identity. (3 words, 2, 2, 6)
5. Caused the rift in the beryl coronet (3)
6. Many of Holmes's opponents had cause to (3)
7. Begins: 'Whose was it?' 'His who is gone.' 'Who shall have it?' 'He who will come.' (2 words, 8, 6)
9. of four (4)
10. The number of Napoleons plus the number of Randall gang (4)
12. One of the five sent 'S.H. for J.O.' (3)
16. To save the dying detective trouble, Mr. Culverton Smith was kind enough to give the signal by turning this up (3)
17. The blundering constable who failed to gain his sergeant's stripes in the Lauriston Gardens Mystery (5)
19. There was a giant one of Sumatra; yet it was unwritten (3)
23. How Watson felt after the Final Problem (3)
24. He was epollicate (8)
26. Initials of the second most dangerous man in London (2)
32. Though Miss Mary Sutherland's boots were not unlike, they were really odd ones; the one having this slightly decorated, and the other plain (3)
33. You may forgive the plural form of these tobaccos, since Holmes smoked so much of them (5)
36. Behind this Black Jack of Ballarat waited and smoked an Indian cigar, of the variety which are rolled in Rotterdam (4)
38 and 39. The best I can make of these is the Latin for the sufferers of the epidemic which pleased Holmes so extremely that he said 'A long shot, Watson, a very long shot,' and pinched the Doctor's arm (4)
42. One of the two in the cardboard box (3)
44. Initials of the street in which Mycroft lodged (2)

ACKNOWLEDGMENTS

GRATEFUL ACKNOWLEDGMENT for permission to reprint certain of the articles in this volume is made as follows: to the *Saturday Review of Literature* for "Was Sherlock Holmes an American?" "Dr. Watson's Secret," "The Other Boarder," and "A Sherlock Holmes Crossword"; and to *The New Yorker* for "Sherlock Holmes in Pictures." Mr. Smith's "Appointment in Baker Street" first appeared in an edition of one hundred copies, privately printed; and "The Unique Hamlet" also was first privately printed for a limited audience. The *clou* of the collection, "The Field Bazaar," by Arthur Conan Doyle, is believed to be a discovery of considerable importance, for it is an authentic footnote to the original group of tales signed with that celebrated name. It first appeared in *The Student*, an Edinburgh University student journal, in November 1896, and was not reprinted until 1934, when Mr. A. G. Macdonell had one hundred copies printed for distribution at the state dinner of the Baker Street Irregulars in December of that year. The other papers appear here for the first time in print.

Mr. Howard Haycraft, editor of *The Boys' Sherlock Holmes* (Harper, 1936), has kindly contributed the illustration of the Doyle house and the map of Baker Street. Grateful acknowledgment for the use of illustrations is made also as follows: to Harper & Brothers, for the drawings by Sidney Paget and W. H. Hyde, illustrating, respectively, *The Adventures of Sherlock Holmes* (1892) and *The Memoirs of Sherlock Holmes* (1894); to Doubleday, Doran & Co., for the depictions of A. I. Keller and C. R. Macauley, illustrating, respectively, *The Valley of Fear* (1914) and *The Return of Sherlock Holmes* (1905); to the J. B. Lippincott Co. for the early illustration by George Hutchinson, from *A Study in Scarlet* (1891); and to Mr. Frederic Dorr Steele for his *Collier's Weekly* illustration of "The Empty House."